The Muses at Work

THE MUSES
AT WORK

Arts, Crafts, and Professions
in Ancient Greece and Rome

edited by Carl Roebuck

THE MIT PRESS
Cambridge, Massachusetts
and London, England

Designed by Dwight E. Agner. Set in Intertype Waverly and printed and bound in the United States of America by The Maple Press Company.

SBN 262 18034 0 (hardcover)

Library of Congress catalog card number: 72-87305

Acknowledgments

Most of the material used from Greek and Roman writers in this book has been translated or paraphrased by the contributors themselves, but that from published translations is acknowledged here: Anonymous, Greek Drinking Song and Epitaph in ed. Edna M. Hooker, *History of Music in Sound* (pamphlet, n.d.); Aeschylus, *The Libation Bearers*, Richmond Lattimore, *The Complete Greek Tragedy*, ed. D. Greene and R. Lattimore (The University of Chicago Press, 1959); Aeschylus, Fragment, *The Oxford Book of Greek Verse in Translation*, ed. T. F. Higham and C. M. Bowra (Oxford, 1950); Aesop, *Fables*, Lloyd W. Daly, *Aesop Without Morals* (New York, 1961); Archilochus, Richmond Lattimore, *Greek Lyrics* (The University of Chicago Press, 1955); Aristophanes, *Frogs*, R. Webb, *The Complete Plays of Aristophanes*, ed. M. Hadas (New York, 1962), Bantam book; Aristophanes, *Thesmophoriazusae*, B. Rogers, *The Complete Plays of Aristophanes*, ed. M. Hadas (New York, 1962), Bantam book; Dio Cassius, *Roman History*, E. Cary, Loeb Classical Library (Harvard University Press, Cambridge, Mass., 1961); Euripides, *The Bacchae*, P. Vellacott (Baltimore, 1954), Penguin book; Herodotus, Aubrey De Sélincourt, *Herodotus, The Histories* (Edinburgh, 1963); Lucilius, Humbert Wolfe, *The Oxford Book of Greek Verse in Translation* (Oxford, 1950); Plato, *Laws*, B. Jowett, *The Dialogues of Plato* (Random House, New York, 1937); Sappho, Richmond Lattimore, *Greek Lyrics* (The University of Chicago Press, 1955); Tacitus, *Annals*, J. Jackson, Loeb Classical Library (Harvard University Press, Cambridge, Mass., 1951); Theocritus, Jack Lindsay, *The Oxford Book of Greek Verse in Translation*, ed. T. F. Higham and C. M. Bowra (Oxford, 1950); Tyrtaeus, C. M. Bowra, *The Oxford Book of Greek Verse in Translation*, ed. T. F. Higham and C. M. Bowra (Oxford, 1950); Vitruvius, *De Architectura*, F. Granger, Loeb Classical Library (Harvard University Press, Cambridge, Mass., 1962). R. S. Cotterill, *The Old South* (Arthur H. Clark Co., Glendale, Cal., 1939). Gene Logsdon, "A Thousand Farmers Call Us Neighbors," *Farm Journal*, Vol. 92, No. 7 (1968).

Preface

This small book began as a series of public lectures given by members of the Archaeological Society of Chicago, one of the local societies of the Archaeological Institute of America. Our purpose was to explain in general terms, using the specific information of classical archaeology, how the Greeks constructed their masterpieces of architecture, how the trade by sea, so important to their economy, developed, and the place music and the theater held in classical Greek life. The enthusiasm of the lecturers was communicated to their audience and suggested the possibility of enlarging the scope of the lectures and of publishing them. Obviously Greek building should be complemented by Roman building, architecture by sculpture in bronze and stone and by the craft of pottery making. Sea trade had to be supplemented by an account of the ships and the sailors who carried the articles of trade and both of these by a description of the most basic activity of all in ancient life, farming. Colleagues were found to undertake papers on these subjects.

Bread alone, of course, did not satisfy the ancient Greeks and Romans, and we might have enlarged the accounts of intellectual activities beyond music and the theater to literature, education, and the sciences. But we wished to show how classical archaeology can help to explain ancient technology, how it can be used to work out an historical process and to illuminate some characteristic activity. In some cases, as in pottery making, the vases themselves, combined with a knowledge of modern chemistry and ceramics, are all important; then, too, while there are many representations of ships in ancient art, information about their construction comes from the wrecks discovered by underwater archaeology. In other cases, archaeology can flesh a bare and fragmentary skeleton of knowledge from the literary tradition: the lines of early Greek trade may be made out by studying the distribution of pottery and the coins found in merchants' hoards. Agriculture was so fundamental that its practice was not only a familiar literary theme but the subject of a technical literature. Yet here, too, archaeology has helped by providing an ancient vineyard excavated near Pompeii. Each writer, in his own way and by using selected material, expresses the intrinsic interest of his subject.

We are conscious, of course, of the debts of Greek and Roman craftsmen to their predecessors and contemporaries in the Near East. In many of the papers there is acknowledgment of this, and we regret there was room for no more. In some of the papers the writer has focused entirely on Greece, when that seemed most significant, in some, exclusively on Rome, while some writers have comprehensively treated both. The text and illustrations are designed to be of general interest, the notes to provide the possibility of further exploration to both the general reader and to colleagues.

Carl Roebuck

Northwestern University
March, 1969

Contents

The Muses at Work

In the biography of Pericles written by Plutarch we are told in one place that rival politicians protested that he spent too much money on public buildings; whereupon Pericles put it to them, "Charge it to me, then, and I will make the dedicatory inscription my own, not yours" (chap. 14). To that the people responded that he should keep on spending as much of the public money as he thought best! In another place (chap. 13), Plutarch says that Pheidias was in charge of everything, although the buildings had great architects and artisans: Callicrates and Ictinus built the Parthenon, and Coroebus began to build the Telesterion at Eleusis and "set the columns and epistyles," and Callicrates did the work on the Long Walls, and others did other things. And in still a third place, Plutarch observes that

the craftsmen who did the labor and made the things were carpenters, molders, smiths, stoneworkers, gilders, ivory carvers, painters, embroiderers [inlayers?], turners; and the people who brought the materials were merchants and sailors and pilots by sea, and on land cartwrights and cattlemen and drivers and ropemakers and flaxworkers and leatherworkers and road makers and quarrymen and miners [chap. 12].

This last observation is offered in evidence of the fact that the money spent on the buildings was widely dispersed throughout the community, giving work and livelihood to many individuals, but it also, taken with the others, shows us that Plutarch, as we ourselves, realized that one can speak of the "builder" of a building in several different senses, at several different levels or modes of the idea "to build."

It would indeed be interesting to know the facts of Pericles' own role as builder of the great monuments of his administration: the various motivations he had, in their relative weight; the degree to which he personally conceived and suggested and brought to reality his own ideas of design; the processes by which he "got the program through" the Council and Assembly of the Athenian People. But this level of the process is not our real concern, and in any case what went on in Pericles' mind must always elude any means of investigation available to us. Nor is the process by which it might be said that "the Athenians" built the buildings our primary concern, though, in spite of our first quotation from Plutarch, it must be admitted that they had a more practical role even than paying the bill. And yet it is both interesting and useful for our main purpose to consider that process in some detail, because it is from it that we get most of our information about the role of the actual craftsmen and architects—the immediate builders.

Authorizing The legislative and administrative processes by which a building *the* program was carried through, of course, would vary from time *Building* to time and from place to place, according to the particular governmental structure of the community or cult concerned. Even in Athens at any one period there was a considerable variety in the degree of relationship between the "city" and the various cults. For our purposes it will not be necessary to elucidate this, but it will be helpful to try to clarify the general situation by describing it in a theoretical way.

The initiation of a major public building enterprise in Athens would lie ultimately, of course, with an individual—Pericles?— but officially with the Council or Assembly of the People, which would pass a decree that a building be constructed. With this decision would go provisions for assigning the responsibility for planning and building the structure to some commission, and perhaps some general provision for financing it. The commission would proceed, with an architect, to develop the general concept of the building, and to make up specifications for it. This proposal, including the specifications, would be referred to the Assembly for approval—and let us assume the Assembly voted its approval. The architect, with the commission, would then proceed to break down the general specifications into subspecifications for various jobs, and these would be offered to contractors in the appropriate trades. The architect and the commission would then come to agreement with the several contractors on the respective jobs— agreements which would include not only the work to be done and the price to be paid but other conditions, such as the time of delivery or completion, the margin of quality, penalties for failure to conform, and so forth; the contractor would provide a bondsman or guarantor for his performance, and the contract would be signed.

From this point the work would proceed on the various jobs until they were finished. Meanwhile, however, the commission would have been keeping detailed accounts of its handling of the money entrusted to it for the completion of the work. This might have been handled in any of several ways. Either the commission would pay out to the contractor the agreed sums according to an agreed calendar, or it might under other conditions have paid all the bills as they came in, day by day or month by month. In the former case, there would be a document amounting to a receipt signed by the contractor for the sums paid him, or conversely a kind of receipt by the commission for the work done. In either case, the accounts of the commission would include all the payments, for whatever purpose.

Finally, on completion of the work, a document of dedication might be composed, or, if some individual had contributed notably to the work in any of several ways, there might be a special decree passed by the Assembly, recording its appreciation and the honor due him.

Throughout the entire process, everyone involved was responsible to the People of Athens for the proper performance of his assignment. This meant that all the records were public documents.[1] They would be kept on paper, or wooden tablets, and submitted to the Council which examined them and then reported to the Assembly. Finally they would be filed in the archives. Beyond this, if there were any special importance attaching to them, they might be inscribed on stone *stelae*, or slabs, and the stelae erected in some public place. Lacking newspapers or other such media for publication, the Athenians in particular cherished the tradition of publication on stone. The purpose of all this was to give every citizen easy access to the accounts and other records of the operation, and either reassure him that things had been done properly, or, if he should suspect malfeasance, give him grounds for initiating some public action against the suspected official. Not every one of the hypothetical documents we have indicated would be so published, and sometimes there was a kind of conflation—as when a "contract offered" would be converted into a "contract assigned" by the addition of the names of the contractor, and even amended as a receipt when the work was done. But whatever disparity in the actual details of publication from situation to situation, the number of such inscribed documents must have amounted to a very considerable volume, and many of them are preserved even now, albeit most of these in quite fragmentary condition. From these inscriptions we learn a great deal about the more detailed processes of construction in the Greek world.

It will illustrate this to quote a decree passed about 450 B.C., or a little later, having to do with the affairs of the cult of Athena Nike, whose temple stands on the bastion just outside the Propylaea of the Acropolis in Athens. Part of the formal parliamentary prescript is missing, but the preserved section begins:

Glaukos moved: that there be appointed a priestess for Athena Nike from among all the Athenian women, to serve for life; and to provide the sanctuary with doors as Callicrates may specify [*syngrapsai*]; that the tax commissioners let out a contract in the month of Leontis; that the priestess get 50 drachmas and the bones and skin of the public offerings; to build a temple and stone altar as Callicrates may specify. Hestiaios moved: that 3 be chosen from the Council; that these men when they have drawn up the specification [*syngrapsai*] with Callicrates exhibit them to the Council. . . .[2]

The rest of the decree is missing, but another decree, dated about 400 B.C., much mutilated and heavily restored, reads in part:

. . . that the People vote with regard to the doorway whether it ought to be made of bronze or of ivory, or of gold; . . . that anyone who wishes [may] make a drawing [*grapsai*] and exhibit it, not less than a cubit . . . , to the overseers. Let the Council not accept it unless judgment be passed about it first by those of the Athenians who wish . . . . Let the treasurer of the Goddess pay the money. . . .[3]

It is not our immediate purpose to examine all the problems raised by these documents, but they do have some points of pertinence, in general and in particular. The first is an example of a decree in which a building program is initiated as only one of several other only slightly related arrangements. It illustrates how in the preliminary stages some of the responsibility might be assigned to an existing authority—the tax commissioners—and some to a special board appointed for the purpose. The two together illustrate how the designated agents were required to report progress at various stages for renewed discussion, and they reflect the kind of disagreement which might arise during this process.

The Work of the Architect Most particularly, these documents introduce us to the actual work of the architect, to his role in the construction of a building.[4] The architect (with the commissioners) is instructed to "make specifications." The verb used is *syngrapsai*, from which there is also a noun in wide use, *syngraphe*. The meaning of the noun must be essentially something like a "written composition": it is used to designate extensive prose compositions such as histories, or "writings" in general; perhaps it has the idea of putting together, in writing, a series of data. In any case it is common in the language of the ancient building industry and seems to have been used for what appear to us as the "specifications" for a building, a detailed description of how the building is to be put together, or as a "contract," a detailed description of what a contractor is to do, and for the other terms of the agreement.

We shall have more to say about the specifications the architect is to produce, but first it is worth calling attention to the second decree in which (avoiding the issue of the restored passages) someone is to "draw" something apparently having to do with the door or gate of the sanctuary. The verb here is *grapsai*, which would commonly be rendered "write," but the word also has a perfectly respectable currency in the sense of "draw," and in this case it seems clear that that which is drawn (by inference, a drawing) has dimension—presumably it is to be "not less than a cubit [long or wide]," which would be more understandable in terms of a drawing than of a piece of writing. From this and other evidence we may believe that drawings were made in the process of designing a building, but it may also be noted that this drawing was not of the whole building, but of a detail—a door.

Vitruvius, four centuries later than Pericles, makes it clear (*De Architectura* I. ii. 2), that the architect of his day did indeed make drawings—plans, elevations, perspectives—of buildings on which he might be working. And, of course, it is entirely possible that the architect of Pericles' day might have made drawings. But a moment's reflection will raise some questions about this, which, taken into account with the absence or ambiguity of direct evidence for the existence of drawings in the Periclean Age, might cause one to wonder whether drawings were of any real significance at that time. Most Greek buildings—temples and stoas—were essentially so simple and so standardized in plan and elevation that the utility of a drawing might be questioned; whereas their differences in detail were so slight and subtle—the slight variations in proportions, the "refinements of curvature"—that one wonders how it would be possible to express them in a drawing so as to be effective for preliminary appraisal or for the instruction of the contractors. The subtleties of a column, for example, are hardly measurable or even visible on any extant modern drawing, however painstaking. For this and other reasons, while admitting that the architect must have made some drawings of some details in the Periclean Age, one is inclined to suspect that on the whole his procedure in designing a building was basically independent of such a device. He may well have made generalized, fairly rough sketches and even models for various purposes, and close, more accurate and refined studies of these kinds for some details, but we must make the effort to realize that probably he did not work primarily in this way, like the modern architect, in developing his conception as a necessary preliminary to arranging for the actual construction.

Rather, we may more fairly assume, following the studies of Bundgaard,[4] that he worked much more directly with his material, like a sculptor or potter, or like the carpenters who worked in the towns and on the farms of America in generations before our own. He was, as his name indicates, not so much a designer as a "master builder" who worked directly with his material in terms of concepts that were almost instinctive, and certainly deeply seated in experience and habit. Of course there was preliminary work to be done; we have seen that the architect was charged with presenting specifications, a *syngraphe* for approval before construction began. We may now consider the procedures involved in this, basing our discussion on a famous example—the specifications for a naval arsenal to be erected in the Peiraeus about 347 B.C.

Omitting the specifications for the interior of the building, the document reads in part as follows:

Gods. Specifications [*syngraphai*] for the stone arsenal for hanging equipment, of Euthydemos the son of Demetrius of Melite and of Philo, son of Exekestides of Eleusis. To build the arsenal for the equipment to be hung up, at Zeia, beginning from the gateway of the market place as you come from the rear of the ship sheds [which have] a common roof, length, 4 *plethra* [400 feet], width, 55 feet, with the walls. Cutting down the place to a depth of 3 feet from the highest point, cleaning to solid rock, he [the contractor] will prepare a bedding and make it even along the top, true according to the level. . . . He will make the bedding 4 feet in thickness, setting the stones alternating crosswise and lengthwise. He will build the walls of the arsenal . . . of Akte stone, setting a leveling course for the walls of stones, width 3 feet, thickness 3 half-feet, length 4 feet, and at the corners 4 feet and 3 palms long. On the leveling course he will set the orthostates at the middle of the leveling course, length 4 feet, thickness 5 half-feet and 1 finger, height 3 feet; those on the corners, length of the measure of the triglyphs. . . . He will make the height of the walls from the leveling course 27 feet including the triglyph under the cornice . . . and he will set on the walls the cornices and he will build gables and he will set cornices on the gables [about half the inscription has to do with details of the interior arrangements] and when he builds the walls of the arsenal he will leave an interval between the joints of the blocks wherever the architect directs. All of this he will work out according to the specifications and according to the measures and the model which the architect may explain. . . .[5]

Several things strike one about this document, in what is specified and even more in what is not specified. We are told, for example, that the building is to measure 400 by 55 feet in ground plan, and we are told the height of the walls, but not of the whole building, nor of the gables. We are told the precise dimensions of most of the blocks of stone for the walls, but not those of the corner blocks; the dimension of the corner blocks is indicated in proportional terms—not as "whatever may be necessary to fill out the total length of the foundations," but rather as "according to the measure of the triglyphs." But we are not told the dimensions of the triglyphs. And, finally for our purposes here, measurements are all given in dimensions of even feet or standard fractions thereof.

Trying, then, to infer from the data given what the architect must have done in formulating his "design" for the building, we may assume that he examined the site available and decided, for the length, on the nearest round number of feet that the site could accommodate. The width he determined, in this case, by selecting a round number that would approximate the space available, the requirements of the function for the particular type of building, the practicalities of roofing with available timbers— and one other factor. This was a derivative of a prior decision— that the building should have a Doric frieze of triglyphs and metopes. Such a decision would set the proportion between the triglyph and the metope according to the prevailing taste and would fix the "module." Of the latter we have a full account in Vitruvius, albeit, as we have said, of four centuries' later date, but there is no reason to doubt that it was not accepted in earlier times. In essence, the principle is that a work of art, a building, is designed not in terms of an external standard of measurement, such as feet and inches, but in terms of an internal one—some arbitrary unit derived from the building itself, so that the structure will be so many units long and wide and high, without regard to the mathematical length of the unit. In a Doric building, the working unit was the width of the triglyph, but this was

derived by subdividing, according to accepted formulas, the width
of the building into a number of such units determined by the
kind of building. However, for practical purposes, the unit must
have been capable of being expressed in terms of standard measurement—feet and inches—so that the stoneworkers could apply
it reasonably. It would be unreasonable, for example, to suggest
such a unit as 3 feet, 7.136 inches in English measure! Rather,
one would adapt the design to a unit of 3 feet, 8 inches, or 3
feet, 6 inches, and if absolutely necessary expand or contract
one or two elements in the composition by a small fraction to
adapt to an over-all discrepancy. Thus we may suppose that
Euthydemos and Philo, having ascertained from the available
space an approximate site for the arsenal, calculated the approximate disposition of triglyphs across the narrow end, reduced this
to a rational arithmetical figure for the width of each triglyph—or
module—and adjusted this with a second calculation of the width
and length, so that the width and length would be commensurable
in terms of a module that was a reasonably working arithmetical
factor.

The arsenal, of course, is not quite a fair example. If we think
rather of a temple, where it would seem that proportions of length
to width were more strictly determined by convention, or taste,
it would seem, from the evidence of preserved remains, that in
the earlier phases of Greek architecture the prevailing taste was
for temples that were conspicuously longer in proportion to their
width than in the later phases. In the Periclean period, it would
seem that the prevailing taste favored buildings approximately
twice as long as their breadth. With this taste we may suppose
that the architects of the period agreed, although we may also
imagine that many architects had ideas of their own, either in
terms of theoretical design or developed to adjust to specific conditions for a particular building. We do not really know, adequately,
the practical conditions faced by the architects of the Parthenon,
but we can probably assume that the architects were in general
accord with the popular preference for a structure approximately
twice as long as wide, and they were given a site with some
limitations for both length and breadth. We can, perhaps, assume
that they staked out the area available for the building, made
a preliminary calculation of the number of modules for the
façade, adjusted this so that the module would constitute a basically measurable unit, and recalculated the width and length in

terms of the module. Actually, as Bundgaard points out, it would not even be necessary to "calculate" the module: in a temple with six columns across the front, the normal number of modules would be twenty-four. After marking by eye a suitable width for the building, a cord might be stretched from corner to corner, and this divided manually into twenty-four segments by gathering it up in twenty-four loops or coils, so that the length, whatever the measurement, would be divided into twenty-four equal parts. One of these could then be measured and the nearest rational measurement taken as the module.

At this point the architects might have turned the whole project over to the contractors, who would have realized that the height of the column, for example, should be, in terms of accepted standards, so many modules. But the architects might have intervened once more and said, in effect, "We think that it would look better if it were a little longer in proportion to that 'normal,' or a little higher—or lower—than usual"; or, "When you make the adjustment for the corner triglyph, do it this way rather than that." And they may have even stipulated some specific detailed variant measurements for certain elements accordingly.

In any case there is ample evidence that the architect did not abandon the project when he had finished writing up the specifications. The contracts are full of provisions that as the work proceeds the contractor shall do things "as the architect directs." It is clear that the architect was in attendance during the work on the building, available for making decisions at any and every point. Many of these would have to do with the acceptability of workmanship on the part of the contractor, many would have to do rather more with the "art" of architecture.

Laying out the Building Basic to the construction, and often to the art, would be the alignment and leveling of various elements of the building. For this both architect and contractor had available such instruments as cords, squares, plumb bobs, and, indeed, levels. Apparently the more common form of the level was a contrivance in the shape of the letter "A," with the two legs precisely equal in length and the halfway point marked on the crossbar. A plumb bob suspended from the apex of the "A" would fall, if the frame were placed vertically on a level surface, on this halfway mark. This instrument seems to have been called a "walker" (*diabetes*), presumably because of its "legs." It could easily be made large enough to be placed on objects separated by as much as fifteen feet or so; if larger surfaces had to be leveled, it could be used together with a sighting device.

Another kind of leveling instrument is described by Vitruvius in his book on architecture (VIII. v). It consisted of a long wooden beam with a deep groove in the top. When the groove was filled with water, the beam would show whether the surface on which it rested was level, because if one end was lower than the other, the water would spill out at that end of the groove. Vitruvius' instrument is mounted in a frame of legs whose design is not entirely clear from his description, so that it, too, might have been used as a level for sighting over long distances in surveying, although it does seem cumbersome for such use. Nevertheless, there is some reason to believe that the Greeks also had such an instrument. In the accounts for the building of the Erechtheum, dated 409/8 B.C., occurs the item:

For sawing the timber for the "gutters," to Rhaidios resident in Kollytos, 1 drachma, 2 obols. To craftsmen by the day, to the one making up the "gutter" and setting it up, 9 days, to Philokles' slave, Kroisos, 9 drachmas.[6]

The word rendered "gutter" is the Greek *ochetos*, which ordinarily means a water conduit of some sort, but here, in spite of some scholarly differences, most likely refers to a version of the instrument described by Vitruvius.

In establishing a foundation, the desideratum would presumably be to have a true horizontal level, which could be effected by the instruments mentioned previously. In structures where horizontal curves were wanted, as in the floor and along the steps of the Parthenon, the levels would also be useful in determining a truly horizontal sight line from which the curve of the actual masonry could be measured. One might suppose that the high point in the middle, the low points at each end, and perhaps three or four intervening points could be established by direct measurement from this sight line. Vitruvius describes, not too clearly, a method of achieving horizontal curvatures by means of *scamilli impares*—"stools, or steps, unequal to each other" (III. iv. 5). One can imagine a set of blocks of graduated height (Figure 1). If they were put in a line with the smallest in the middle, the tops of the blocks would form a curve higher at each end than in the center. But if the surface on which they rested were trimmed so that it was lower at the ends than in the middle, the tops of the blocks would lie at a horizontal level. The character of the curve would be controlled by the range in the heights of the blocks, and the distances by which adjoining pairs were separated from one another. But for any of these operations, if effected in any of the ways suggested, a drawing or model would have been unnecessary and indeed inadequate. The work could have been done either under the direct supervision of the architect as he deployed his strings and levels and *scamilli* himself or by the contractor with a relatively brief written or verbal instruction.

The vertical curvatures which constitute the more numerous and subtle refinements of a fine Greek building would have been even more difficult to conceive in the abstract, but Bundgaard has suggested how they might be accomplished almost mechanically and yet organically by the use of finely seasoned wooden rods, which could be made to curve dynamically, if placed vertically, by determinable pressure at the top, with perhaps measured ties to measured points on a rigid vertical bar. Once "set," such an arrangement would constitute a template for delicate and complex curves that could be applied at will to any number of points. The inclination of a column, which, if it was to have entasis and stand on a foundation with multiple horizontal curvatures, would require an ineffably abstruse calculation of arithmetic or geometry, could have been determined simply and easily by making all the drums for the column with their horizontal surfaces truly horizontal and at right angles to the vertical axis of the drum; then, before setting the drums in place, the lower surface of the bottom drum would have been trimmed so that the drum was an inch or other measurable quantity less thick on the periphery toward the interior of the building than on that toward the exterior. This would have been a quantity that could be defined clearly in directions to the contractor, reviewed by the architect as the work went on, and adjusted if necessary during the cutting of entasis and fluting.

Thus it seems indeed plausible that what we would consider the real function of the architect himself—the general and detailed conception of the form—would have been shared more fully and intimately than now with the contractor; the architect would formulate the general schema of the building, in terms that could be easily intelligible to the contractor, and they would work together in the actual fabrication of the structure, facing various details of construction and design as they arose. But even so, for many elements of the job, the more generalized specifications had to be broken down and reduced to smaller jobs for individual contract, and the architect had to work all this out.

Quarrying and Handling the Blocks To illustrate this subject we may quote a few items from a set of contracts offered at Eleusis about 355 B.C. The document begins with a prescript containing the names of the commissioners and the architects, and some of the jobs offered for contract are the following:

> To cut stones from Aegina, length 5 feet, width 3 feet, thickness 2½ feet, and to hew them out true on all sides, with work surface, and to transport them to Eleusis to the sanctuary sound and unbroken; number, 24. . . . To work 24 triglyphs of the soft Aeginetan stone, height 5 feet, width 3 feet, doing the same work as on the ones already worked in the sanctuary, and to lift them so as to lie in their proper places; to fit the triglyphs tight on all sides and to clamp and dowel and pour lead around; number of triglyphs, 24. To cut Pentelic stones for the metopes, height 5 feet, width 5 feet less 1 palm, thickness 3 palms, and hew them out true on all sides with work surface according to the description the architect gives and to give them over for setting up sound, white, unblemished; number, 15. To transport stones from Pentele to Eleusis, length 5 feet, width 5 feet less 1 palm, thickness 3 palms, and to put them down in the sanctuary sound and unbroken; number, 15. To work 15 metopes of Pentelic marble, height . . . [and so on, as for the triglyphs].[7]

It will be seen that the contracts are not entirely uniform: that quarrying material for triglyphs includes delivery at the sanctuary, whereas in the case of the metopes there is one contract for quarrying, another for transportation to the sanctuary. And for each category there is a special contract for hoisting into place and setting the blocks. The contracts offered do give a suggestion of how large a job might be undertaken by an individual contractor, though it might be wrong to generalize too freely from this particular document. It has to do with the completion of an unfinished job, or for an enlargement of a structure already standing—there are already on the site triglyphs to be matched by the new ones. It is possible that, if a wholly new structure were being erected, all the metopes might be quarried by one contractor, all the triglyphs by another. In this case the triglyphs came from Aegina, by boat, and the contractors would be quite different from those undertaking the quarrying of the metopes of Pentele and their transport to Eleusis by land.

For the transportation itself we get a vivid picture from a set of accounts published for Eleusis some time after 328 B.C. These accounts cover a wide variety of activity during a certain month, but there is one fairly extensive series of items of which the following are illustrative examples:

[this month] we began to bring in a column drum from [a contractor, name missing]; it was brought in 3 days; 31 teams transported it; payment for each team per day, 4 drachmas, ½ obol; for each team for 3 days, 12 drachmas, 1½ obols, according to a decree of the People which Lycurgus moved; this makes for [all] the teams, 376 drachmas, 4½ obols [figures actually missing in the text as preserved]. . . . We began to bring another drum from Euktemon; 33 teams transported it; it was brought in 3 days; payment for the teams, 392 drachmas. . . . We began to bring another drum from (. . .); 27 teams transported it on the first day; on the second day were added 3; it was brought in 3 days; payment for the teams, 360 drachmas, 3 obols. We began to bring 2 drums at one time on a double rig on the tenth of the month; 40 teams transported them on the first day, on the second were added 5; they were brought in 2½ days, payment to the teams 438 drachmas, 5¾ obols.[8]

In all, twenty-three drums were transported in this month.

We may suppose that the starting point was a quarry on Pentele perhaps fifteen or twenty miles from Eleusis. The first part of the trip would be downhill from the quarry and across the Attic plain, which may explain why in some instances a smaller number of teams was used on the first day; on the second day the pass between Athens and Eleusis would have to be traversed. The teams were presumably oxen, and the road from the quarry to Eleusis must have presented an impressive spectacle during this month. We shall consider in more detail later what the drachma in these accounts represents in terms of real value, or modern costs. The latter is particularly elusive, especially in a time of "creeping inflation," but a crude approximation would give for this period a figure of about $10.00. On this basis, the transport of a single column drum would represent about $3,750. This certainly seems costly, but it will quickly be realized that transport may have represented a larger proportion of the cost of a building in antiquity than today. However, it would require an expert in construction accounting to analyze such a problem.

In any case, it is clear that the panorama we have just reviewed represents only one kind of problem of transport. Another emerges from the accounts of the supervisors of the building of the great temple of Apollo Didymaios near Miletus during the Hellenistic period, about two hundred years later than the previous document. Here, at one point, we can make out from a much-mutilated section an item:

for road making from the quarry at Marathe to Ionia City, and for transportation from the quarry of 8 drums, 780⅜ [cubic?] feet at . . . a foot; . . . drachmas; and for putting 8 drums into 2 freight

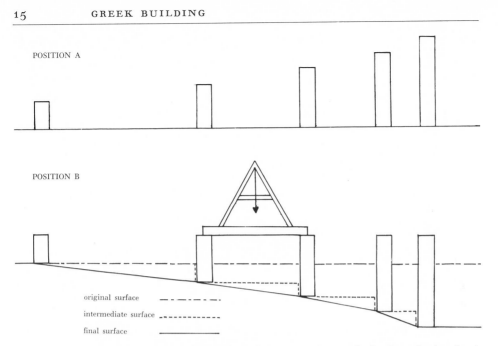

POSITION A

POSITION B

original surface   — — — — —
intermediate surface - - - - - - - - - - -
final surface   ——————————

1   *Scamilli Impares.* Schematic indication of method of producing horizontal curvatures in foundations by the use of *scamilli impares.*
Courtesy, Robert L. Scranton.

2

Contrivance for
transporting block
of stone. A. K.
Orlandos, *Ta Ylika
Domis ton
Archaion Hellinon*
(Athens, 1955–
1960), Part II,
Fig. 37.

boats, 120 drachmas; and for lifting the 8 drums aforementioned out of the freight boats and transportation along the mole up to Panormos, and of 19 drums from Panormos to the sanctuary, as calculated by the computers, 4,459 drachmas, 3 obols, 4 "coppers."

The inscription from Miletus just quoted continues immediately to record:

And for the working of 19 drums, 2,009 drachmas, 3 obols; and for the transportation of the two-legged machine for the raising of the drums and the erection of the third column, 200 drachmas, and for the setting of the drums, the same column, 724 drachmas, 3 obols.[9]

Here we are introduced to the subject of moving stone vertically, rather than horizontally, but before going into this we might observe that simply to bring the hoisting machinery to the site cost almost 28 percent as much as to raise the column itself—an indication, on the one hand, of the proportionally high cost of overland transportation, and, on the other, of the economic advantage of advanced machinery! It might take sixty oxen to move a column drum along the road, but to hoist it into place with a machine could be accomplished by a few men at relatively low cost.

With regard, then, to machinery, the inscriptions give us little information about the equipment for hauling, and, actually, relatively little more about the machinery for hoisting. We know, chiefly from literary sources, in allusive rather than explicit passages, that various ingenious devices for moving heavy weights along the road were employed: for example, fastening the block to solid wheels so that it could be carried by them as though, so to speak, it were their axle (Figure 2). But a conservative view might prefer the hypothesis that they were loaded onto sledges or "stone boats" and hauled along in a more forthright fashion, with rollers as needed (Figure 3). When it came to hoisting, we find numerous references in the inscriptions to pulleys and pulley blocks, both simple and complex, though it is difficult to visualize from the technical nomenclature the particular form of the more complex combinations. There are also numerous references to two- (Figure 4), three-, and four-legged machines, such as the one just cited. Although on the face of the matter these are fairly obvious, there is no way to determine what devices the more complex machines might have employed to multiply the force exerted—for example, whether the classical Greeks ever used any such arrangement as the "squirrel cage" drum for accumulating force on a winding device such as is illustrated in

3   Bringing block down out of quarry on sled. Orlandos, *Archaion
           Hellinon*, Fig. 33.

the Roman relief of the Haterii. But the modern Western mind must make the effort to realize that the advantage of modern machinery is chiefly in time. Given time, and the simplest of machines, the lever, adequate scaffolding, and the relatively simple pulley blocks and timbered hoists that can easily be envisaged from the terminology of the inscriptions, there need be no mystery about the question of how the Greeks hoisted heavy blocks of stone into place on their largest buildings.

Setting the Blocks On the other hand, one important aspect of lifting blocks of stone is apparently never mentioned in the inscriptions: that is, how the blocks were secured to the ropes of the hoisting device. This, however, is amply demonstrated among the actual blocks surviving from the buildings.[10] There were several ways of accomplishing this (Figures 5 and 6). One was simply to throw loops of rope around the block and gather them in a hook at the end of the rope of the hoisting device. This was simple enough in some ways, and though there was some danger of the loops slipping, or rather of the block sliding out from the loop, this was fairly easily obviated by leaving chunky protrusions from the face of the block, to be trimmed off after it had been set in place, if desired. The real difficulties of this method did not appear until the block was dropped into position, and it was necessary to get the loop away from around the block. It would be necessary to set the block down on pieces of wood, leaving space through which the ropes could be drawn; then lift the block with crowbars, in order to remove the pieces of wood, and drop the block into final position on the course below. This might be difficult if the block were being set close to others in the same course, end to end, and sometimes grooves would be cut in surfaces of the block that were later to be concealed in the masonry, in which the ropes could rest and from which they could be withdrawn after the block was in place. Another device was to cut a kind of U-shaped tunnel into the top of the block, so that a rope could be passed through this with both ends emerging from the top of the block, to be lashed to the hoisting hook and subsequently drawn by one end out of the tunnel. A further method would be to use iron tongs, gripping the block at each end, and occasionally blocks are found with slots cut into each end to receive the points of the tongs and keep them from slipping. But here, too, there would be problems if the block were to lie close to another. Finally (Figure 6), a hole might be cut into the top of the block

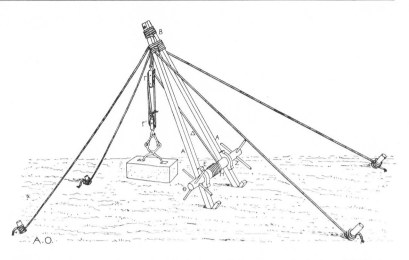

4   "Two-legged" machine for hoisting. Orlandos, *Archaion Hellinon*, Fig. 44.

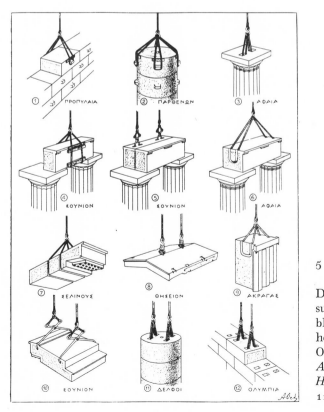

5

Devices for suspending blocks from hoist. Orlandos, *Archaion Hellinon*, Fig. 119.

which was larger at the bottom—toward the interior of the block—than it was at the opening on the surface. Into this would be dropped a "lewis" of iron—a plug of metal larger at the bottom than at the top, with a hook or ring on the top, and with its larger end at the bottom of the hole. This could be pushed into the undercut section of the hole and jammed into position by a plain plug of iron, so that if the lewis was attached to the hoist and lifted, its projecting lower part would be unable to emerge through the small opening in the top of the hole in the stone, and the block of stone would come up with the lewis. When the block was dropped into place, the metal plug would be removed, leaving room to disengage the lewis. This method, too, would allow a block to be set tight against its neighbors, without needing further manipulation. But neither the lewis nor the U-shaped tunnel for a rope would be safe if the stone were soft—it would be likely to crumble or sheer, so that these devices could be used only on good marble or special limestone.

In most situations, however, the conditions permitted the use of crowbars. If there was a question of setting blocks in a foundation or pavement, or in a line of wall, in each course the block at a corner might be set, and then the others set against it from the end; they would be dropped a few inches from the block already in position and pushed against it with crowbars from the other end. To facilitate this process the masons commonly cut grooves or slots in the top of the course below to give purchase to their bars as they pushed, and they might cut slots under the lower edge of the block on which they were working, to improve the purchase if it had to be lifted in order to swing it from side to side, or insert a roller. These cuttings can often be identified on blocks of existing buildings, and give a clue as to the location of particular blocks, since the little grooves could be no more than an inch or two from the end of the block being pushed.

Perhaps the most difficult part of setting the blocks was to ensure a tight joint (Figure 7), and this is reflected in the inscriptions in many places. Commonly the greater part of the joint surface of a block would be fairly roughly cut down, or in, from the true end, so that only the edge which was to be visible from the outside would actually be tight against the neighbor, and perhaps the edge across the top. The actual joint surface, then, would be a band four or five inches wide, running along the

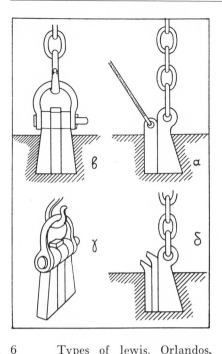

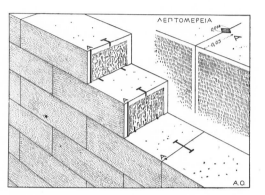

6   Types of lewis. Orlandos, *Archaion Hellinon*, Fig. 128.

8   Setting blocks: anathyrosis, cuttings for clamps and dowels. Orlandos, *Archaion Hellinon*, Fig. 15

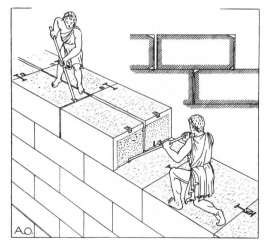

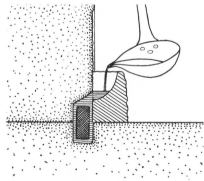

9   Pouring lead on dowel. Orlandos, *Archaion Hellinon*, Fig. 14.

7   Setting blocks on wall. Orlandos, *Archaion Hellinon*, Fig. 70.

vertical edge of the end of the block, and along the top, anathyrosis. This would be finished with great care, cut finely smooth and "true to the *kanon*" (rule, or template), and would have to be inspected by the architect before the block was finally set in position. At this point, and again the inscriptions are replete with references: clamps and dowels would be inserted (Figure 8). The dowels were plugs of metal fitted into a hole on the top of a block and projecting higher than the top of the block, the projecting part fitting into a hole cut into the bottom of the end of a block on the superincumbent course. The clamps were metal bars, fitted into slots cut in the top of two adjoining blocks, crossing the joint line, so that half the bar was resting in the slot on one block, the other half in the slot on the top of its mate. Normally there would be a hook of some sort at each end of the clamp—either thrusting vertically into the top of each block, or in a T-shaped crosscutting at the end. Thus, the clamp would prevent any one block from separating from its neighbor, or shifting to one side, under stress of an earthquake, for example; and the dowel would prevent it from sliding out of position with relation to the block beneath it. The clamps and dowels would be cemented into place with molten lead poured around them (Figure 9).

All that we have said about the setting of blocks (Figure 10) might be expressed in the inscriptions quite briefly, as in a passage already quoted (with regard to the triglyphs at Eleusis), "to lift them so as to lie in their proper places; to fit them tight on all sides and to clamp and dowel and pour lead around." Or we may read it expressed with impressive detail (though not always perfect intelligibility) in a Hellenistic contract from Lebadeia having to do with the pavement of a temple:

He will make anathyrosis [the special joint surface described previously] on the joints according to the stone *kanon* [ruler] . . . he will dress . . . the footing stones with a firm, well-whetted, toothed chisel, and the subleveling course with a pointed chisel . . . and he will show them [to the architect] dressed approvably. Then he will set the paving slabs, working exactly as was written . . . as was shown him . . . and he will use for all the *kanones* [rulers] clean olive oil, and Sinopian red "miltos"; if he does not use Sinopian red "miltos" or clean olive oil, he will be assessed damages by the building supervisors . . . ; and no stone will be closed tight by him before he shows it to the building supervisors that he is using approved Sinopian red "miltos" and clean olive oil. And he will show the work and the setting to the architect, and the joints of all the stones and the bedding surfaces to the subarchitect at the same time

10   Setting blocks in entablature of Stoa of Attalos in Athenian Agora.
Courtesy of the American School of Classical Studies at Athens.

as he rubs them down with green olive oil . . . When he completes the joint, having cleaned it with carbonate of soda and having washed it with clean water, then let him close it tight. The putting in of the dowels and the clamps, and the . . . and the weight of these and all the lead sealing he will show to the building supervisors, the contractor himself being present in person. Let him close nothing tight unless shown to the building supervisors; if he does close any-thing tight [before showing it] he shall take it up again and do it all over from the beginning, and be assessed damages. . . ."[11]

To some of the questions raised in this document—the Sinopian *miltos* and the *kanones*—we may return later, but meanwhile it may be interesting to view the problem of setting stones in a different situation as it appears in some of the inscriptions from Miletus. These are accounts of the administrators of the sanctuary of Apollo Didymaios for work on the walls of the great temple during the Hellenistic period, and were apparently issued on an annual basis. In one year their statement reads, after the prescript:

There were set in the temple 328 [marble blocks], the measure of which was 3,858 solid feet [cubic feet?], set at 4 drachmas a foot; this makes 15,432 drachmas; and 147 [limestone blocks], the mea-sure of which was 1,414 solid feet, set at a drachma a foot, this makes 1,414 drachmas.

Then some other categories of work are given, in similar summary terms (including the setting of 170 other blocks), and then the stones that were set are listed individually:

The [workmen] with Apollonides set, in the thirteenth course, begin-ning from the north, the corner [stone], and on the outside [row of the course] 26 blocks, thickness 1½ feet, of which the first was [provided by a contractor—or donor—whose name is lost from the inscription]: the second, Callicrates'; the third, sacred [i.e., presum-ably quarried by slaves of the sanctuary]; the fourth, . . . ; the fifth, . . . ; the sixth, . . . ; the seventh, Miletus'; the eighth, Megakles'; . . ."[12]

and so forth, listing each of the remainder of the 26 and after that all the other stones set during the year. Assuming, then, that this is an annual account, about 645 stones were set, or about 2 a day—apart, of course, from other kinds of work going on at the same time. (These seem to have been set by the cubic foot; in the Erechtheum, blocks were set by linear measure at so much the "*tetrapos*," four-foot unit.)

Finishing the Blocks It is clear from the phraseology of the inscriptions, as might have been assumed in any case, and as is also clear in the remains of ancient buildings, a block for a particular purpose was dressed to approximate size and shape in the quarry, delivered to the site (Figure 11), trimmed so that the joint and bedding surfaces were true, then set in place. Finally, after the block was in place, the visible faces would be trimmed down to their final surface and finished. In the inscriptions, as we have seen at Eleusis, the contract for quarrying will give dimensions for the quarried block that are identical with those for the finished block, but it is often stipulated, and otherwise may be assumed to have been taken for granted, that the quarry block would have a "work surface"— that is, would not have been cut down to the size actually mentioned, by a standard amount of surplus. For the work of cutting and trimming a large number of tools are named in the inscriptions: hammers, axes, chisels (pointed, flat, toothed), files, rubbers, and so forth. It is not possible to determine the particular form of each of these from the nomenclature, and indeed the various terms, coming from many places and many periods, may include some referring to the same tool under different names (Figure 12; also Figure 6 of chap. 4).

A glimpse of the process of finishing may be had in the inscription from Lebadeia from which we have already quoted, referring still to the making of a pavement, although the specific instruction is far from clear:

Having stretched the flax [line] . . . and having engraved the lines in the presence of the architect, let him remove the work projecting with a point, making the specified width, making everything true, precise; and let him apply *miltos* to the top of all 13 stones lying in place, according to the long *kanon* [ruler] not less than 20 feet [long], thickness 6 fingers, height a half-foot, applying the *miltos* with a smooth smoother, well-whetted.[13]

Disregarding the actual operation being described, which involves a number of problems, it is clear that the process of finishing involved stretched cords, a *kanon*, several kinds of finishing tools, and *miltos*. Of these, the function of the linen cord hardly needs explanation. *Miltos* is a red substance highly important in Greek building, of which the best and most highly valued came from Sinope, or, near at hand, from Keos. Surprisingly enough there is some doubt as to exactly what it was, but it was certainly red, presumably of a chalky texture, and may also have had an abrasive quality. At least we seem to see it sometimes being applied to a surface which was intended to be flat, with a straight-edge, so that projecting surfaces would be colored with the red, and would thus be marked for further reduction; and sometimes it seems to be used in the process of rubbing itself, as though it were a fine polishing abrasive.

In this case it is being used in connection with a *"kanon"* twenty feet long, six fingers wide, and half a foot thick. Greek feet varied slightly in length, but were approximately the same as ours; there were sixteen fingers to a foot. Thus this *kanon* was about six inches by a little less than five inches in cross section, and twenty feet long. It would be, for all practical purposes, a "straightedge"—it could hardly have had any significant "give" or bend to it. In the accounts for the Erechtheum of 409/8 B.C. we note payments, "For chiseling up and working up *kanones,* by the day, for 10 days, to Gerys, 10 drachmas. For gauging a *kanon* by the day, for 2 days, to Mikion, 2 drachmas,"[14]—an indication that the preparation of *kanones* of various kinds for various purposes was a constant necessity.

In the accounts of the Erechtheum for 408/7 B.C. and following, we find a series of items having to do with the finishing of columns. The accounts were kept by the month, and for one month we read:

For stonework. For channeling of the columns toward the east, those opposite the altar. The one toward the altar of Dione, Laossos of Alopeke, 10 drachmas; Philon of Erchia, 10 drachmas; Laossos' (slave) Parmenon, 10 drachmas; Laossos' slave Karion, 10 drachmas; Hikaros, 10 drachmas." Omitting the next column we come to "The [column] coming next, Ameiniades, resident in Coela, 10 drachmas; Aeschines, 10 drachmas; Lysanias, 10 drachmas; Meiniades' Somenes, 10 drachmas; Timokrates, 10 drachmas.[15]

The Cost Here we may pause to observe that throughout the Erechtheum accounts, and in many other documents, we find that normally when wages are specified as being by the day, the wage is one drachma a day. This seems to have been the normal day's wage up to the end of the fifth century in Athens for any kind of work, whether it be the lowliest laborer or the architect himself! Disregarding the social and economic problems raised by this, it seems to have been a fact. On this basis, then, we might suggest that the value of the drachma in this period might be put as the equivalent of $15.00 today—that sum being more, to be sure, than the least paid worker today, and certainly less than the best! But perhaps it might make a rough average or mean for labor,

11 Blocks with work surface as delivered to masons' sheds during reconstruction of Stoa of Attalos. Courtesy of the American School of Classical Studies at Athens.

12 Mason's tools employed on reconstruction of Stoa of Attalos. Courtesy of the American School of Classical Studies at Athens.

skilled and unskilled. Moreover, unless otherwise specified, the number of drachmas paid to an individual might be taken, hypothetically and schematically, as the number of days he worked. On this basis we would calculate that five men worked ten days each on the first column during this month; five other men also worked ten days each on the second column, and so it was for the others, although there are, to be sure, some complications in the accounts for this hypothesis. On the fourth column, seven men were working, receiving seven drachmas, one obol each—but it will be observed that the total paid for each column was fifty drachmas, regardless of the number of men working. So perhaps we should assume that fifty drachmas represents the contract price for the work on a column during the month. During subsequent months other payments are recorded for the same individuals working on the same columns. In the accounts for one month, two payments to each crew are reported, but it might be that one of them was for a previous month in which payments were held over. In all, four sets of payments are recorded among the preserved fragments. Not every column is listed in every set. The fifth column, for example, is missing from the first-preserved month's account. Thus the situation is far from clear. Nevertheless, we can, generally speaking, visualize (Figure 13) groups of five to eight men working on the fluting of the columns of the building through a period of at least three consecutive months at a total cost of 350 drachmas per column (or $5,250?). The columns had already been erected, but as piles of spherical drums. The contractor, no doubt under the eagle eye of the architect, counted out the number of channels to be cut and made a corresponding number of marks at the bottom and at the top, stretched a string from each mark at the top to its mate below, and drew the line—with red *miltos;* he may also have engraved the line lightly with a chisel; then the several workmen proceeded to cut the flutes. There must have been a *kanon* to check the profile of the flutes, and another to check the entasis of the column, if there was to be any. And, finally, there were many hours of rubbing and smoothing.

Another aspect of the situation emerges from the Erechtheum texts just quoted, in the names of individuals at work. We see the name Laossos of Alopeke—Laossos of the "deme" or township called Alopeke. A person whose name is given with a "demotic" may be assumed to be a full Athenian citizen. Then there is Laossos' Karion—Karion was presumably a slave of Laossos.

13   Cutting flutes in columns of Stoa of Attalos. Courtesy of the American
School of Classical Studies at Athens.

Hikaros, with no further designation, may have been a freed-man—not a slave, not a citizen, but one who had been given or who had bought his freedom—or a man descended from such a person, whose only residence was Athens. And there is Ameiniades, *resident* in Coele, which is different from somebody *of* Coele, who would be a citizen. Ameiniades was a "metic," a non-Athenian, presumably free, who chose to live in Athens as a resident alien. All these are working side by side on the same job and receiving the same wage. Whether Laossos later con-fiscated some of Karion's salary would be up to him and his good nature. He may well have taken some to pay for Karion's keep, and as a profit on his investment in him, but he may have allowed Karion to keep some of it to save toward purchase of his freedom or for any other purpose.

No one is explicitly designated as boss, or foreman, or contrac-tor, though the first name in each list might reasonably be taken as one of these. Whether the fluting of each column was let out as a contract, or whether the supervisors of the construction of the Erechtheum dispensed with contracts and themselves made their own arrangements of hiring and purchase cannot really be proved on the basis of their accounts, though it does seem probable that the latter was the fact.

Ceiling, Roof, and Ornament The ceilings and roofs of Greek buildings were usually made of wood, but although there are abundant references to this part of the work in the inscriptions, the problems are too complicated to express simply, or even to understand fully.[16] This does, how-ever, bring us to the subject of carpentry, and it is interesting to observe a few details about this. In the Erechtheum accounts of 409/8 B.C. are recorded wages:

> to sawyers working by the day, to 2 men each receiving a drachma [a day], for 12 days, to Rhaidios, resident in Kollytos and his fellow worker, 24 drachmas. For sawing through timbers, 14 eight-foot poles, 84 cuts at 2 obols the cut, to Rhaidios, resident in Kollytos, 26 drach-mas. To a sawyer for sawing through a timber, length 24 feet, 5 cuts at 1 drachma the cut, to Rhaidios, resident in Kollytos, 5 drachmas.[17]

From these figures it would appear that a sawyer might work either by the day or by the foot (an obol for a four-foot cut); presumably on the average he might make a twenty-four-foot cut in one day. We are not told the size of the timbers involved in the payments indicated earlier, but almost surely they would be substantial timbers, so that in fact Rhaidios was cutting fair-sized planks out of a heavy beam.

Apart from the uses of wood for what we might consider crude or basic carpentry, it also appears in forms that refer rather to cabinet making or joinery, as in the ornamental ceiling-panels of the Erechtheum:

> To Evainetus of Alopeke for making up the "ladder frames" for this panel, and 2 small frames of the boxwood, 30 drachmas. For doweling on the astragal [molding], having received it turned on the lathe, to this ladder frame, 12 drachmas. . . . total cash [paid] 89 drachmas. . . . [name missing] . . . was working on the boxwood frames of this panel, 2 in number, chiseling them up to fit and fastening them, at 6 drachmas each, 12 drachmas. For doweling on the astragal having received it turned on the lathe, 37 drachmas. For fastening "finger nails" [another molding] on the 2 ladder frames and evening them out according to the stone *kanon*, at 10 drachmas each, 20 drachmas. . . . For fastening [gluing?] on the small cymatia [still another molding], 10 in number, and chiseling them to fit, according to the stone rule, at 3 drachmas each, 30 drachmas.[18]

The "ladder frames" are presumably the basic structural part of a panel, the two long sides resting on two neighboring beams and spanning the whole area between the two beams. The square openings in the frame that make it resemble a ladder would then be covered by a series of successively smaller square frames to make a coffer at each of the openings, covered at the top with a solid plaque. The edges of the panel and of the successively smaller elements of the coffer would be ornamented with moldings. The cutting, fitting, and fashioning of the whole fabric would represent joinery and wood carving of the highest degree of refinement. An entire panel would probably be assembled in a workshop and set up as a completed unit on the beams in the temple.

Attached to the plaque closing the coffer at the top there might normally have been an ornament such as a rosette, and there are a number of interesting references to such rosettes in the Erechtheum inscriptions. It is not certain whether all these references are to rosettes for the wooden coffer panels of the interior of the building, or for marble coffer panels on the porches, but the basic conception is the same. In one place we read of payments to

> wax-modelers for making models of the rosettes for the cover pieces, to Neseus, resident in Melite, 8 drachmas. For making another model,

the acanthus, for the cover pieces, Agathenor, resident in Alopeke, 8 drachmas. Total for wax-modelers, 16 drachmas.

And later:

For working 6 rosettes, to Manis, resident in Kollytos, 84 drachmas. For working 11 rosettes, to Stasianax, resident in Kollytos, 154 drachmas. For working 1 rosette, to Aristippos of Kettios, 14 drachmas. . . . For making a model, the acanthus, for the ceiling, which we did not use, to Stasianax, resident in Kollytos, 8 drachmas.[19]

When the stone and wood work were ready, the painters moved in:

For building scaffolding for the encaustic painters inside beneath the ceiling, to Manis, resident in Kollytos, 1 drachma, 3 obols. For carrying paint pots, to Prepon, resident in Agryle, 1 drachma; to Manis, resident in Melite, 1 drachma.[20] To a painter for drawing [*graphein*] on the 14 cover pieces for the ceiling, for the panels over the statue, at 4 drachmas a cover piece . . . 54 drachmas.[21]

Many details of the stonework, too, were painted, "To encaustic painters, painting in encaustic the cymation on the architrave inside, at 5 obols a foot, the contractor Dionysidoros, resident in Melite, the guarantor Herakleides of Oa, 30 drachmas."[22]

Some details were actually covered with gold leaf: "Gold was bought for the rosettes, 166 leaves, a drachma each leaf, from Adonis, dwelling in Melite, 166 drachmas." It is a striking coincidence that the previous two entries were, "Two sheets of paper were bought, on which we wrote copies of the accounts, 2 drachmas, 4 obols. For boards [presumably four tablets for recording accounts] 4 drachmas." Of course the sheets of paper were undoubtedly larger than the individual sheets of gold leaf, but the item does suggest the difference in values that occur under varying conditions. And, a little below, "Two leaves of gold were bought for gilding the eyes of the column, from Adonis, resident in Melite, 2 drachmas."[23]

Finally, although we are too often inclined to regard sculpture as a different art or craft from architecture, it was far from being the case in Greek antiquity, and we find it rewarding to notice a section of the Erechtheum accounts of 408/7 B.C. dealing with the sculptural frieze of the building. Here we must pause to recall that the frieze on this building consisted of a plain band of dark blue-black Eleusinian limestone, against which were fastened figures of white marble, made separately. The figures were small— the frieze itself was barely two feet high. The accounts read:

. . . Phyromachos of Kephisia [made] the youth beside the breast plate, 60 drachmas. Praxias, dwelling in Melite, [made] the horse and the man appearing behind it striking it on the flank, 120 drachmas. Antiphanes of Kerameis [made] the chariot and the youth and the two horses being harnessed, 240 drachmas. Phyromachos of Kephisia [made] the man leading the horse, 60 drachmas. Mynnion, resident in Melite, [made] the horse and the man striking it and the stele, set in addition later, 127 drachmas. Soklos, dwelling in Alopeke, [made] the man holding the bridle, 60 drachmas. Phyromachos of Kephisia [made] the man leaning on the staff, the one beside the altar, 60 drachmas. Iasos of Kollytos [made] the woman on which the child is leaning, 80 drachmas. Total of sculpture, 3,315 drachmas.[24]

A number of points stand out, most conspicuous that the figures were contracted for by the piece, at a standard sixty drachmas each, although there are exceptions: Iasos' woman with the child leaning on her evidently counted for only one and one-third figures; the extra stele by the horse made by Minnion cost only seven drachmas. If we were to apply rigidly our rough standard of a drachma a day for all work done, it would seem that it was allowed that each figure would require approximately two months to make—and the seven drachmas charge for the stele (which would have been merely the simplest rectangular prism of stone) might encourage this conception, though of course we are scarcely entitled to be absolutely sure.

Another point would be that the figures were contracted for individually, and presumably done independently in the workshops of the individual sculptors, and were not actually assembled until they were doweled to the frieze in final position. It is true that Phyromachos made three figures, but they seem to be quite distinct from one another, belonging to groups on which others also worked. It is true that since they were to be doweled separately to the frieze, the problem of physical contacts between one figure and another would have not been the same as if they were being carved directly on continuous slabs. Nevertheless, we obviously have to recognize a factor not represented in the inscriptions—the man, or men, who designed the frieze as a whole determined its iconographic theme and the separate poses of the individual figures. Whether this was the architect or a man commissioned especially to design the frieze can hardly be determined, but even more important is the problem of how he conveyed his conception to Phyromachos and his associates. We have, in short, the same situation as with the architect of the building.

Did the designer of the sculptures make a drawing of the frieze, or a model, or simply a verbal description—a *syngraphe*, which, like the architect, he subdivided into individual jobs to be contracted out? The question, of course, is crucial in our understanding of the process by which "the ancient sculptor" worked, and cannot be solved on the basis of our evidence. Nevertheless, it might be suggested that the document before us could be taken to imply that the individual sculptors, Phyromachos, Praxias, and Antiphanes and the others, worked with considerable autonomy. Like the other stoneworkers they may well simply have been told that there was to be a frieze of certain dimensions with a certain theme, and that they were to make certain figures belonging to certain groups rather generally described, and carried the matter on from there according to their own personal instincts, deeply embedded in experience and habits of working.

There is not space here to exhaust the possibilities of the inscriptions in illuminating other aspects of Greek building—the metal industry, which provided the clamps and dowels, nails and tools; the ceramic industry, which provided the tiles for roofs; the brick industry, which provided sun-dried mud brick for the construction of fortifications and less monumental buildings. Nor is there space to call attention to the inscriptions which give information about other kinds of construction—fortifications, bridges, stoas, drains, even statues. Nor can we discuss here the documents relating to other important and famous buildings, such as the Parthenon itself, or the buildings at Delphi and Epidaurus, where the larger interest of the documents is in the form in which they were kept rather than in the intelligible detail they give about particular structures. This would take us back to the administrative authority as the "builders." But the documents we have noticed do provide, however sketchily, more vividly, in their prosaic and one-sided way, a glimpse into the reality behind the bare statement of Plutarch that

the craftsmen who did the labor and made the things were carpenters, molders, smiths, stoneworkers, gilders, ivory carvers, painters [inlayers?], turners; and the people who brought the materials were merchants and sailors and pilots by sea, and on land cartwrights and cattlemen and drivers and ropemakers and flaxworkers and leatherworkers and road makers and quarrymen and miners.

And, of course, the architect of the Erechtheum, Archilochus of Agryle, and the other architects: Philo of Eleusis, Callicrates, Ictinus, and Pheidias, and Pericles.

Like their contemporaries in other arts and professions, the architects of the early Roman Empire were the products of a very ancient tradition. Consequently, before their achievements can be set in proper perspective, we must have some conception of the evolution through which their art had passed prior to the founding of the Empire in 31 B.C.

Architecture of the Roman Republic The first builders of monumental structures in Rome were the Etruscan chieftains who had dominated the city during the greater part of the sixth century before Christ. Through their extensive projects, they had provided Romans with the skills necessary to erect those impressive public and private structures which reproduced for the Republic the general features of contemporary forms in the Greek world.[1]

Steeped in Etruscan traditions, therefore, early Republican architects designed temples which were in essence rectangular boxes. Frontal orientation, high podiums, and deep porches (few Roman temples were peripteral) characterized these shrines. Yet, such features were only regional variations on a basic Greek plan: a rectangular shrine (*cella*) wholly or partially surrounded by columns.[2] In similar fashion, residences of the Republican nobility, like the House of the Surgeon at Pompeii, were composed of rows of rooms surrounding a central court—a plan long popular in Greece.[3] Among public and private buildings, the basilica stands out as an original form created by Roman builders after the introduction into Italy of the Hellenistic timber truss. Yet even basilicas display a design typical of early Roman buildings: a more or less rectangular plan defined by straight perimetric walls meeting at right angles.[4] Of course, different sorts of structures were partitioned internally into rooms of varying size and use, but most inner chambers were normally square or rectangular. For the first few centuries of Rome's existence, therefore, her architects were content simply to surround and define internal space. Consequently, down to the early part of the second century B.C. they usually designed masonry boxes, or combinations of boxes, protected by tile and timber roofs.

While the gradual introduction of faced concrete during the

third century B.C. eventually produced a complete alteration in these traditional habits of architectural thought, some time elapsed before Roman builders fully appreciated the new material.[5] First they had to perfect it. Initially, it was only an adhesive, a mortar used to join the stone blocks of masonry arches and vaults.[6] Subsequently, its use was extended until it formed whole walls and vaults. From that point forward, only its outer facing changed.

Beginning with the second century B.C., small stones, set into place without any apparent pattern (*opus incertum*), formed the outer skin of concrete walls. One hundred years later, the stones of the facing, usually of yellowish-brown local tufa, had begun to assume a roughly netlike pattern (*opus quasi reticulatum*), which by the beginning of the first century after Christ had become entirely regular (*opus reticulatum*). Toward the latter half of the century, brick (*opus latericium*) came into fashion as a wall facing. At first, it was confined to quoins and bands of several courses separated by large stretches of reticulate. At the end of the century, reticulate had almost vanished, and by the reign of Antoninus Pius (A.D. 138–161), brick alone survived as a facing. In the middle of the third century, brick was partially supplanted by tufa blocks, and wall facings of brick and tufa blocks (*opus mixtum*) continued in use, with some large-scale exceptions, for the limited amount of construction undertaken between the latter part of the third century after Christ and A.D. 476, the traditional date for the end of the Western Roman Empire.[7]

The ubiquitous concrete appeared in every sort of building: temples, theaters, porticoes, amphitheaters, warehouses, mansions, and apartment houses. The carefully drafted stone masonry (*opus saxum* or *opus quadratum*) which the architects of the Empire had inherited from their Republican predecessors was occasionally used. Yet, from the first century after Christ, it was normally confined to wall facings, moldings, and columns. The stonework of the Empire was usually only an adjunct to concrete.[8]

The new building material produced an architectural revolution which gathered force slowly during the last centuries of the Republic. It was no longer necessary to cut and carve recalcitrant stone. Concrete was poured as a liquid and thus assumed any shape for which a wooden form could be built. For the first time, it became practical not only to enclose interior spaces but also to mold them into a variety of complex patterns. But the full implications of the new material were not immediately realized, and, by comparison with their early Imperial descendants, the first concrete structures were relatively simple.

One of the most impressive examples of such early concrete architecture is the Porticus Aemilia, a vast warehouse, dating in its present form from 174 B.C. (Figure 1). The structure consisted of a series of barrel-vaulted chambers which stretched for nearly a quarter of a mile along the banks of the Tiber just southeast of the Aventine Hill. The novelty of the building lay not in the shapes of its rooms, each separated from the next by a row of eight piers, but in its vast size and in the fact that each room reproduced the others.[9]

By the end of the first century B.C., Roman architects were ready to vary the simple themes represented by the Basilica Aemilia. One of the most spectacular triumphs of their art is the Temple of Fortune at Praeneste.[10] Inspired by the elaborate, almost baroque, scenic architecture of the Hellenistic East, its designer created a shrine conceived on a magnificent scale (Figure 2). The principal buildings of the temple marched up the slopes of Monte Glicestro whose rock, quarried into eight successive levels, formed the foundations for numerous ramps and vaulted colonnades. Seen at first glance from the ground, these features must have presented a chaotic impression. A second look, however, would have revealed a tightly ordered structure. The ramps which joined the third and fourth levels led the eye immediately to the center of the architectural composition, a point further emphasized above by the great stairways connecting the fourth, fifth, sixth, and seventh terraces. The structure was entirely symmetrical on either side of the ramps and stairways. Thus on the fourth level, two large hemicycles flanked the central stair; on the fifth, five arches. On the sixth, two identical colonnades faced one another across a great piazza. On the seventh was a small theater, closed above by a semicircular colonnade; on the eighth, surmounting the colonnade, stood a small, open colonnaded shrine which sheltered a statue of the goddess under its dome. That shrine and the cult statue within stood at the center of the composition, and the eye of the viewer was led directly to that point by the majestic sweep of the ascending ramps and stairways.

In the Temple of Fortune, the new concrete architecture found the fullest expression it was to achieve until the Early Empire.[11] No other late Republican structure martialed form and size in quite so impressive a manner. The curves of the hemicycles emphasized the straight, ordered lines of the superimposed colon-

Porticus Aemilia. Remains of the southwest wall, from the Via Florio.
Fototeca Unione, Rome.

1

nades which themselves alternated with arcades. The sheer magnitude of the building's seven terraces with their flanking porticoes created an unforgettable impression. Nowhere else in the Roman world was "Fortune more fortunate" in the manner of her housing.[12]

Architects'
and
Workers'
Guilds

The store of professional knowledge derived from vast projects like the Temple of Fortune was increased and perfected by the architects who worked in and around Rome during the next century. Unlike many of their counterparts in the provinces, who were often no more than advanced military engineers, the designers of buildings in the capital were competent professionals.[13] From the Augustan architect Vitruvius we learn something of the manner in which these men were educated. The true architect will possess a sound knowledge both of theory and practice, and he will be capable of profiting from his technical experience. In addition:

> He should be a man of letters, a skilful draughtsman, a mathematician, familiar with historical studies, a diligent student of philosophy, acquainted with music; not ignorant of medicine, learned in the responses of the jurisconsults, familiar with astronomy and astronomical calculations. . . . Since, therefore, so great a profession as this is adorned by, and abounds in, varied and numerous accomplishments, I can think that only these persons can forthwith justly claim to be architects who from boyhood have mounted by the steps of these studies and, being trained generally in the knowledge of arts and sciences, have reached the temple of architecture at the top.[14]

Until the beginning of the third century after Christ, when Septimius Severus established official professors of architecture whose salaries were paid by the state, such training was usually the result of an arduous apprenticeship.[15]

The vast amount of building done in Rome in the Early Empire suggested that there were a great many architects in the capital, and Vitruvius confirms this impression. Many were apparently not overly scrupulous and "beg and wrangle to obtain commissions." These were probably the same men who were "ignorant not only of architecture, but even of construction . . . falsely called architects in the absence of a genuine training." The best practitioners of the art were, however, thoroughly reliable both in matters relating to their profession and in the expenditure of the large sums of money entrusted to them. Vitruvius suggests that these individuals formed a small, closed circle. They were of "approved descent, well brought up . . . , men with a sense of honor [who] trained only their children and kindred and those apprentices who were worthy."[16] Nero's architects, Severus and Celer, probably came from such circles as did that Decrianus, who provided the technical skill required to move the colossal statute of Nero from its original position on the site of the projected Temple of Venus and Rome to a spot nearer the Flavian Amphitheater.[17]

Not all the architects practicing in Rome were of Roman descent however. In a letter to Pliny the Younger, Trajan notes that many Greek architects had come to the capital (*Epistulae* x. 40). The most famous such artist was the Emperor's own master builder, Apollodorus of Damascus. During the early years of the second century after Christ, Apollodorus' position in Rome was exalted. As the Emperor's architect-in-chief, he is credited with the design of Trajan's Markets and Forum, which included the famous Column, Greek and Latin Libraries, and the celebrated Basilica Ulpia.[18] While Trajan lived, Apollodorus even presumed to patronize princes of the imperial house:

Once when Trajan was consulting him [Apollodorus] on some point about the buildings he had said to Hadrian [the Emperor's nephew and successor], who had interrupted with some remark: "Be off and draw your gourds. You don't understand any of these matters." (It chanced that Hadrian at that time was pluming himself upon some such drawing.)

If Dio Cassius is to be believed, that tactless remark cost the haughty architect his life. For when Hadrian

became emperor . . . he remembered this slight and would not endure the man's freedom of speech. He sent him the plan of the Temple of Venus and Rome by way of showing him that a great work could be accomplished without his aid and asked Apollodorus whether the proposed structure was satisfactory. The architect in his reply stated that, first, in regard to the temple, that it ought to have been built on high ground and that the earth should have been excavated beneath it so that it might have stood more conspicuously on the Sacred Way from its higher position, and it might also have accommodated the machines in its basement so that they could be put together and brought into the theater without anyone being aware before hand. Secondly, in regard to the statues, he said that they had been made too tall for the height of the cella. "For now," he said, "if the goddesses wish to get up and go out, they will be unable to do so." When he wrote this so bluntly to Hadrian, the emperor was both vexed and exceedingly grieved because he had fallen into a mistake that could not be righted, and he restrained neither his anger nor his grief, but slew the man.[19]

Whether or not Hadrian, who prided himself on his architectural expertise, ever carried professional jealousy so far as Dio Cassius suggests, Dio's anecdote at least clearly indicates that Roman architects worked from carefully prepared plans (*diagrammata*) drawn with the aid of a compass (*circinus*) and architect's rule (*euthygrammum*). In order to demonstrate the appearance of the finished structure to his client, the architect also made elaborate drawings. These consisted of elevations (*orthographiae*) and perspective views (*scaenographiae*). The latter were often tinted so as to give the viewer a better idea of the effect to be produced by the completed building.[20] On request, architects could also produce their designs as models of terra cotta or marble (and probably of wood and plaster).[21] By these means, they demonstrated the three-dimensional effects of their structures, clearly indicating the spatial relationships between each new building and an existing or proposed complex.

When the architects had completed their plans, they left their execution to highly skilled laborers organized into guilds. The names of these guilds survive and indicate the degree to which the Roman building industry had been divided into specialized crafts. If older structures were to be removed, that task was accomplished by a demolition gang (*collegium subrutorum*). When the site had been cleared, the carpenters (*tignuarii*) appeared. Initially, they provided forms for the foundations; later, those on which the domes and vaults were poured. Finally, they cut and placed the beams for wood and plaster ceilings (*contignationes*) and roofs. Artists in the decorative crafts were equally regimented: carpenters specializing in interiors (*fabri subaedani*), marble cutters (*marmorarii*), workers in stucco (*tectores*), and mosaicists (*pavimentarii*) all had their own guilds.[22]

Such artisans provided the talents necessary to erect every variety of structure from palaces, libraries, baths, and basilicas to porticoes, markets, and apartment houses. While these buildings differed in design and ornamentation, they were constructed in exactly the same way.[23] On the cleared site, the plan was laid out by means of furrows. The foundation trenches were dug between the lines, and wooden forms were set within the trenches. Each form was composed of a row of posts, joined by boards, facing one another across the trenches. Concrete was then poured between the forms until the walls had reached ground level. From that point until the walls had attained their final elevation, bricks, rather than wood forms, served to hold the concrete until it had cured. The bricks used for this purpose were normally the large *bipedales* (two Roman feet square) diagonally sawn in half and inserted in the wall so that the apex of the triangle thus created faced the inside of the wall. Sockets (putlog holes) left in the walls sustained wooden braces. These held up the scaffolds used by masons erecting the higher sections of the wall, which were begun as soon as those below had hardened enough to bear the additional weight.

When the walls had reached the desired height, wooden forms for the vaults were set in place. Sometimes these forms were supported by wooden members resting on the ground, sometimes by beams set into the walls, often by a combination of the two methods. Long barrel vaults were frequently poured on a single form, which was then decentered and moved along the course of the passage to additional positions when the first section of the vault had cured. Very often the form was strengthened by overlaying it first with a layer of *bipedales* and then with a layer of *sesquipedales* (tiles one and one-half Roman feet square). These tiles aided in supporting the weight of the liquid concrete until it had hardened. More complex vaults and domes differed from barrel vaults only in that they required more involved forms.

Not uncommonly, *contignationes*, plank ceilings, rather than vaults, supported upper floors. Opposed rows of either brick cornices or travertine consoles sustained these *contignationes*. Frequently, both types of supports appear in the same building.[24] Such ceilings were found in every type of structure. In low buildings, they substituted for expensive vaults; in multistoried structures, they lightened the load exerted by the building on its foundations. In the latter case, *contignationes* supported the floor of the mezzanine and then alternated with vaults. Thus, in a five-story building, the floors of the third and fifth stories would have been supported by vaults; the others, by *contignationes*. Trabeated (beamed) buildings usually had sloping timber roofs, externally sheathed with tile, and tiles also furnished many vaulted structures with additional protection.[25]

Highly developed techniques of construction like these made possible the large-scale projects financially supported by the generous patronage of an interested imperial government.[26] Among the emperors, Hadrian alone claimed to be an architect. Yet, his love of building only continued an imperial tradition. To the Caesars, impressive architecture and widespread public works not only provided immediate benefits but also served as visible, three-dimensional symbols of the power of the state.[27]

Early Imperial Building The politically astute Augustus was among the first to employ this important means of propaganda. In his autobiography (*Res Gestae*), he claims both to have enriched Rome with new structures and to have repaired many already standing.[28] Augustus' kinsmen and successors, the Julio-Claudians, continued to build lavishly, and to Nero, last surviving member of the dynasty, construction was nothing less than a passion. No project was too grandiose for the ambition of an emperor, described by Tacitus as constantly "desirous of the incredible" (*Annales* xv. 42). At first, large-scale public works outside the capital excited his interest By taking advantage of the low, waterlogged Pontine Marshes, he intended to link Puteoli to Rome by means of a great canal.[29] A cut through the Isthmus of Corinth would have permitted marine traffic to pass directly from the Corinthian to the Saronic Gulf.[30] These vast projects remained unfulfilled, but fate gave Nero the opportunity to indulge his architectural schemes in Rome itself.

Between the nineteenth and the twenty-fifth of July, A.D. 64, Rome was ravaged by a vast conflagration which engulfed nearly the entire city. According to Tacitus, the fire

took its rise in the part of the Circus touching the Palatine and Caelian Hills; where among the shops packed with inflammable goods [it] broke out, gathered strength in the same moment, and, impelled by the wind, swept the full length of the Circus: for there were neither mansions screened by boundary walls, nor temples surrounded by stone enclosures, nor obstacles of any description, to bar its progress. The flames, which in full career overran the level districts first, then shot up to the heights, and sank again to harry the lower parts, kept ahead of all remedial measures, the mischief travelling fast, and the town being an easy prey owing to the narrow, twisting lanes and formless streets typical of old Rome. . . . [Of the fourteen Regions into which the capital was divided] four remained intact, while three were laid level with the ground: in the other seven nothing survived but a few dilapidated and half-burned relics of houses.
It would not be easy to attempt an estimate of the private dwellings, tenement blocks, and temples which were lost. . . .[31]

Some of Nero's provisions for the disaster were exemplary. Not only did he lower the price of grain, but he also threw open public buildings, and even his own gardens, to the homeless (*An-*

nales xv. 39). By imperial decree, the city was to be rebuilt in an orderly fashion. All boats coming up the Tiber from Ostia to Rome were required to return to the coast laden with debris. Moreover, the structures which replaced those which had been destroyed were to be better planned, more stable, and more sanitary than their predecessors had been. Restricted in height, with handsome arcades, paid for by the Emperor's generosity, they were to line broad avenues driven through the fields of ruins (*Annales* xv. 43). Although many new buildings failed to comply with the new construction code, Nero's measures marked a milestone in urban development.[32]

The Emperor's other actions were less praiseworthy. Himself suspected of arson by the populace, he was forced to satisfy the mob by placating its fury with suitable scapegoats. Consequently, as Tacitus informs us:

Nero substituted as culprits, and punished with the utmost refinements of cruelty, a class of men loathed for their vices, whom the crowd styled Christians. . . . First, then, the confessed members of the sect were arrested; next, on their disclosures, vast numbers were convicted, not so much on the count of arson as for hatred of the human race. And derision accompanied their end: they were covered with wild beasts' skins and torn by dogs; or they were fastened on crosses, and, when daylight failed, were burned to serve as lamps by night [*Annales* xv. 44].

So savage an exhibition alienated even the hardened Roman proletariat, and the Emperor fell still lower in the estimation of his subjects when he turned the recent disaster to his own advantage. A vast section of central Rome was expropriated to serve as the grounds for a great imperial palace. The ruins of the buildings which had occupied the area between the Palatine, Caelian, and Oppian Hills were leveled, and in their place rose a handsome residence.[33] Although the new palace was derisively christened the "Golden House," it was criticized not so much for its sumptuous appointments as for the fact that it unnecessarily filled premium downtown property with the varied buildings of an extensive country villa.[34]

Nero's reign did not long survive the completion of the "Golden House." After his demise in A.D. 68, his ultimate successor, the prudent and earthy Vespasian (A.D. 69–79), reversed Neronic policies, returning to public use the lands on which the Golden House had stood. The depression which held the villa's ornamental lake was drained and used for the foundations of the

Amphitheatrum Flavium, the Colosseum.[35] Only the domestic wing of the palace survived for a few years on the Oppian Hill. Ultimately, it, too, was partially demolished, and the surviving ruins were incorporated in the substructures of the public baths which bore the name of the Emperor Trajan.[36] That monarch, whose reign (A.D. 98–117) was filled with distant battles and foreign campaigns, devoted himself almost equally to fighting and building. In addition to his Baths and his monumental Forum in Rome (p. 41), he provided Ostia with a second harbor and rebuilt some sections of the port.[37] These Trajanic policies were continued on an even greater scale by Hadrian. As we have seen, Hadrian himself was an architect of some skill who built continuously. He embellished Rome with several new buildings—of which one of the most important is the Pantheon—restored others, and put up handsome structures in almost every province.[38] Hadrian's successors, however, failed to continue his lavish architectural programs. In subsequent reigns, the number of new structures gradually decreased to the point where the building industry had become nearly extinct during the troubled years of the third century after Christ. Diocletian, Constantine, and their successors barely managed to restore the ailing building trades to some semblance of health.[39] In a very real sense, then, the reign of Hadrian, embodying and summing up the architectural evolution of the two previous centuries, marks the high point of Imperial building activity. In order to understand early Imperial architecture, therefore, we must examine closely both the designs and techniques of construction manifest in Hadrianic buildings.

Nowhere else in central Italy are these features so clearly illustrated as in Ostia and in Hadrian's Villa near Tivoli, two sites representing opposite but complementary ends of the architectural spectrum. Ostia was no more than a utilitarian port intended to receive and store Rome's food supply, while at the same time providing ample accommodations for the busy tradesmen who saw to its collection and transportation. Yet, as a town, the port represents a remarkable achievement: a model community embodying the best of the sound, simple, austerely attractive urban architecture so characteristic of Rome in the second century after Christ. Hadrian's Villa, on the other hand, was the Emperor's own country residence, a great palace displaying every subtlety of which Roman architectural science was capable. By inspecting both sites, then, we can achieve a well-rounded picture of the architectural achievement of the Age of Hadrian.

Apartments In the time of Hadrian, Ostia was already several centuries old,
at Ostia yet, in the last few decades, the ancient city had been undergoing
a remarkable transformation. The construction of the new
Trajanic harbor facilities had transformed it into a boom town.
Once and for all it had replaced its chief rival, Puteoli, as the
capital's principal port, becoming almost solely responsible for
handling the enormous volume of goods consumed by imperial
Rome. The necessity of storing these goods before they were
shipped up the Tiber to Rome required the construction of new
warehouses, and the expansion of the port facilities created a
rapidly growing population which urgently demanded new housing. Since Ostia was so vital to the life of the capital, its problems
necessitated the immediate attention of the imperial administration.

With the resources of the entire Empire at its disposal, the
government accomplished the rebuilding of Ostia with remarkable
dispatch. Within a few years, whole sections of the older city
were leveled and rebuilt so that most of the existing ruins date
from the reign of Hadrian.[40] Such extensive urban renewal
changed the entire complexion of the city. Gone were the spacious
mansions which had characterized the port on the accession of
Trajan.[41] In their place stretched row after row of multistoried
apartment houses, warehouses, and offices. These structures, fashioned of brick-faced concrete, were distinguished by great size
and regular design. Often they were put up not as individual
units but as parts of a larger design which included whole sections
of the city.

The Garden House Complex (Region III, block ix, buildings
1–26) constitutes one of the most impressive such quarters (Figure
3). The architect for the project had at his disposal a vast tract
of more than 15,000 square meters in the previously undeveloped
northwest quarter of the city. The site was bounded to the south
by an existing block of flats which flanked the city's main street,
the Decumanus Maximus. To the northeast ran another important
road, the Cardo degli Aurighi. This was the area which was to
be laid out as shops, workshops, and residences intended for upper-
and lower-middle-class inhabitants.

The completed design for the project is at once handsome and
practical: a continuous series of buildings surrounding an inner
court (approximately 80 $\times$ 95 meters). In the center of the court
are two identical rectangular buildings and, flanking it on two
sides, six attractive fountains (three to the east and three to the

west), which provided residents with a continuous supply of fresh drinking water. To the west, through a triple arch, lies the main entrance to the court. From a small open square immediately in front of this gate, the façade of the building must have presented an appearance not unlike that of a Roman fortress or palace: a long expanse of wall broken only by a gate flanked by two towers. In the Garden Houses, the two buildings which project out on either side of the entrance, the Insula del Graffito (III, ix, 21) and the Domus dei Dioscuri (III, ix, 1), take the place of the military towers.[42]

Most of the buildings around the court are residential, although the type of accommodations enjoyed by the different inhabitants varied enormously. In the northeast corner of the court was a handsome private mansion, the Insula delle Muse (III, ix, 22), for the owner of the complex (?), consisting of a single row of rooms arranged around an inner court. The number of rooms in the building—eight on the ground floor and at least thirteen on the second—and the quality of their handsome decorations suggest a tenant of considerable wealth.[43] The other buildings bordering the court were less elaborate, and many contained standardized two-story apartments arranged on the ground floor about an inner corridor running along the façade. At either end of the corridor are two more important chambers emphasized by height (two stories) and decorations. Opposite a row of regularly spaced windows, smaller, one-story rooms open off the hall. With the omission of the two large end chambers[44] the second story, reached from a stair in the vestibule, duplicates the first. There were at least six such buildings around the court, and the two central houses followed the same plan. In all these structures—each four stories high—the third and fourth floors were probably occupied by apartments which reproduced those of the first two stories.[45] The other buildings bordering the court were also four stories in height, but shops or factories take up the ground floors. The entire complex is screened from the Cardo degli Aurighi by a long, narrow commercial structure only one shop wide.[46]

Although the number and size of the buildings included among the Garden Houses give the group the appearance of complexity, the elements which compose its plan are in reality extremely simple. Virtually all rooms are either square or rectangular without domes or apses. Most are lighted by single windows, double

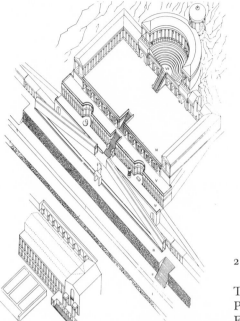

2

Temple of Fortuna at
Praeneste. Restored view.
Fototeca Unione, Rome.

3   Garden Houses in Ostia. Plan. Fototeca Unione, Rome.

windows (*bifore*), or triple windows (*trifore*).[47] The two-story end rooms of the more elaborate flats are illuminated by two *trifore*, one set above the other. Ceilings are equally simple. In the central buildings—and undoubtedly most of the structures around the court—barrel vaults rising to the level of the third floor support the two upper stories. The floors of the second and fourth stories were sustained by *contignationes*.[48] The vanished roofs were probably of wood externally protected by tiles.[49]

Like most buildings in imperial Ostia, the Garden Houses are of concrete faced with brick (in the walls) or tiles (in the vaults). Save for wood, the only other material of importance in the complex is travertine which regularly appears in thresholds, imposts of arches, external stairways, and certain architectural ornaments. Roman engineers used travertine for these purposes because they seem to have considered it stronger than brick and thus suited to places subject either to structural stress (imposts) or heavy wear (thresholds and stairs).

The external decoration of the Garden Houses is also comparatively simple. The regular courses of brick, which today constitute the most pleasing feature of the facades, were, in antiquity, concealed by a heavy layer of stucco, some of which may still be seen near the north entrance to III, ix, 20.[50] This stucco may have been painted in pastel shades, but the only other external decoration came from simple brick moldings and the graceful pilasters which flanked the more important entrances. The bases and shafts of these pilasters were of brick; the capitals, of travertine. Like the walls to which they were attached, the pilasters may have been covered with stucco, a material which may also have served to disguise the rough texture of the capitals, giving them greater delicacy of outline and finish.[51]

The interior decoration of the houses was equally simple. Many of the small one- and two-room apartments were extremely plain: their floors were covered by brick laid in a herringbone pattern (*opus spiccatum*); their walls, concealed by a coat of plain, white stucco. The large two-story flats were finished with greater elegance. Black and white mosaics, laid in intricate geometric designs, serve as pavements. Walls display mythological and floral motifs set against backgrounds of red and yellow panels, decorations sometimes echoed in the painted designs of the ceilings. All such ornamentation, although found only in the best Garden Houses, is relatively inexpensive. Like the architecture of the entire complex, it is the product of a middle class which, while its tastes were comparatively refined, did not have the funds to indulge in extravagant luxuries.

The Villa Far different was the character of the enormous suburban palace
of Hadrian which Hadrian erected for himself twenty-eight kilometers from Rome on the slopes of the Alban Hills near the ancient town of Tibur (the modern Tivoli). Where Ostian buildings are uniform, simple in conception and execution, Hadrian's Villa is complex, novel in design and construction. It was Hadrian's wish to create for himself a palace which would reproduce the features of many of the buildings he had seen on his extensive travels. In order to fulfill that conception, he designed a group of buildings, both fanciful and elegant, which utilized the most advanced architectural conceptions of his day.[52]

In their general arrangement, these structures reproduced the usual plan of the aristocratic suburban villa: a series of halls and pavilions linked by colonnades and arcades and set in parks and gardens.[53] What distinguished Hadrian's residence from its predecessors was its vast size and the profusion and complexity of its components. The existing palace (Figure 4), surrounding the nucleus of an older, late Republican villa, represents three distinct phases of construction: A.D. 118 to 125, A.D. 125 to 133, and A.D. 133 to 138. At the conclusion of the final period, which terminated with the death of the emperor, the estate had assumed its final form.[54] It had come to occupy an enormous site, a ridge over one kilometer long and eight hundred meters wide, delimited to the north and south by shallow valleys: on the north, the Fossa dell'Acqua Ferrate (christened by Hadrian the "Vale of Tempe" after the famous pass in northeast Greece); on the south, the Fossa di Riscoli. Between these two depressions, adhering to a north-south axis, lie the four great sections of the Villa.

Located to the north and bounded by the Vale of Tempe on the northeast (see Figure 4), the first of these, generally called the "Imperial Palace" (A), apparently served the court as a winter residence. Within this group stand Latin and Greek Libraries (numbers 1 and 2), a Guest House (number 3), a *triclinium* or dining room (number 4), large and small peristyles (numbers 5 and 6), and a handsome complex consisting of several large and small domed pavilions set around a large open court, the so-called Piazza d'Oro (number 7).

The second section of the estate (B) included the *Poikile*, a vast peristyle (232 × 97 meters), named for the famous Portico of the Frescoes in the Market Place in Athens. There are also a Library (number 8), a circular portico (number 9)—the Maritime Theater, which probably served Hadrian as a study and retreat—an exedra (number 10), a large *nymphaeum* (number 11), and a remarkable structure whose chief feature was a fish pond enclosed by a sunken cryptoporticus (number 12). No less than three sets of baths (numbers 13, 14, and 15) distinguish the third section of the villa (C), which also possesses an enormous reflecting pool (number 16), terminated by a spectacular semidomed *nymphaeum* (number 17) which housed a shrine of Serapis. The latter group, Hadrian's "Canopus," took its name from the wealthy and luxurious suburb of Egyptian Alexandria.[55] The last group (D) extends along the south side of the estate and is bounded by the Fossa di Riscoli. Here were the Academy (number 18), summer residence of the Emperor, and a multistoried belvedere (number 19), the Roccabruna, which perhaps copied the Tower of Timon near the Academy in Athens. During the eighteenth century, the Academy produced a rich harvest of elaborate colored mosaics and statues of rare marbles.

The size and complexity of the entire Villa preclude any detailed descriptions of its different structures. Nonetheless, some notion of its magnificence may be gained from closer inspection of the buildings which compose the Piazza d'Oro, even in its decay one of the most sumptuous of the palace's many reception halls.[56] The complex is entered through an octagonal vestibule roofed by a segmental vault whose north half remains in position. The north entrance of the vestibule is mirrored by a south door which opens onto a quadruple portico surrounding a forecourt. Six large niches are set into the walls of the vestibule. The two to the east and west, pierced by ample windows (of which that to the east survives virtually intact), are square; the others are semicircular. Additional light was supplied by an opening (*oculus*) in the center of the dome, and the decoration of the room was completed by columns in each of the eight corners.

A continuous row of blind arches, flanked by engaged brick half-columns, originally stuccoed so as to give the appearance of fine marble, ran along the walls of the portico. These blind arches mirrored true arches which opened into the great court to the south. A central row of Corinthian columns, their shafts alternately of cipollino and eastern granite, helped support the portico's timber and plaster ceiling, which was probably elabo-

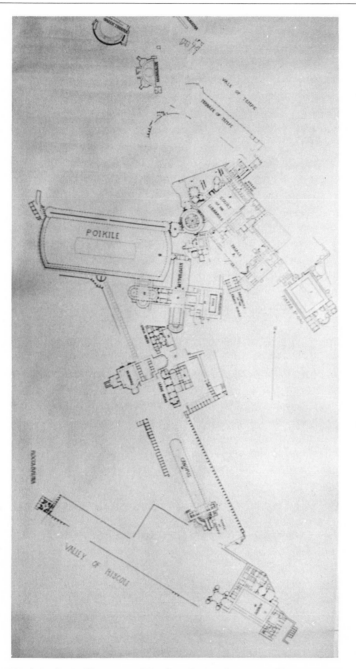

4   Hadrian's Villa near Tivoli. General Plan. Edmund Bacon, *The Design of Cities* (New York, 1967), pp. 76–77.

rately coffered. The entire portico must have had at least one, and perhaps two, additional stories.

The south side of the court is closed by the remains of a rectangular building, the Piazza d'Oro, the last and most sumptuous structure of the group (Figure 5). Its plan is extremely complex. On either side of a central hall is a suite of five lesser rooms arranged around a small court screened by eight columns, two to a side. The north and south sides of the courts are straight, while those to the east and west are convex. The center of the curves faced the rectangular basin which occupied the center of each court. Extensive restorations have been undertaken recently in the east court. There, capitals and entablatures, fashioned from a concrete which contains fragments of the ancient marbles, have been replaced in their former positions, thus giving the casual visitor an excellent idea of the original appearance of the area.

In general form, the great hall is a rectangle opening to the south on a large apse into which are set the alternately square and round niches of an elaborate fountain (*nymphaeum*). The segmental dome of the chamber, probably pierced by an *oculus*, was partially buttressed by eight half-domes (Figures 6 and 7). These were masked by the eight central arches which, from the interior, alone appeared to sustain the main dome. The disposition of these inner arches is that of a Greek cross whose sides are composed of eight equal curved segments which are (seen from the center of the room) alternately concave (to the north, south, east, and west) and convex. Between each of the arches were two columns which aided in carrying an entablature which followed and emphasized the cruciform plan of the arches. The extrados of the arches were left open above the entablature so as to reveal the eight half-domes.

The sumptuous decorations of the chamber, some part of which were discovered in the excavations of the eighteenth century, consisted of elaborate polychrome designs executed in costly marble veneers, wall paintings, and colored stuccos. The magnificent effect produced by the plan of the room and its ornaments must have been enhanced by the continual playing of water. The elaborate *nymphaeum* set into the south apse had no less than five jets which, issuing at the feet of the statues in each niche, fell into marble basins. In addition, there were four smaller, still partially extant, fountains placed in each of the four corners of the room. The decor was completed by a colossal statue stand-

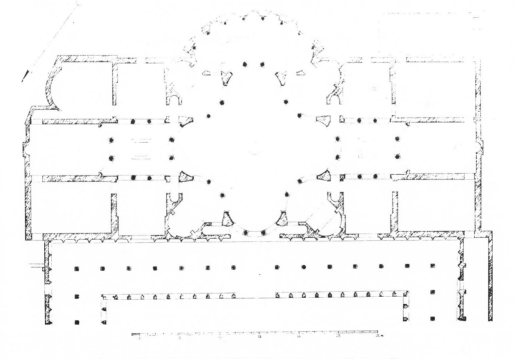

5   Piazza d'Oro. Hadrian's Villa. Plan. Fototeca Unione, Rome.

ing on a centrally located base (which has now entirely disappeared) directly under the *oculus*.

Although it is one of the most ambitious sections of Hadrian's Villa, the Piazza d'Oro only summarizes within a comparatively small space the architectural and ornamental devices freely used throughout the rest of the estate. Its remarkable design and decoration clearly represent the most advanced building techniques known to the Romans in Hadrian's day, and not a few of the features described may have been the Emperor's own innovations.[57] Consequently, regardless of its true architect, the Villa as a whole points the direction in which most later imperial architecture was to evolve.[58]

In Ostia, straight lines predominate, and the designers have emphasized great numbers of plain, unadorned spaces which served as either dwellings or storerooms. In Hadrian's palace everything is intended to dazzle and delight. To those ends, the straight lines and right angles characterizing utilitarian Ostia have been largely abandoned in favor of continuously curving surfaces. Almost every building in the Piazza d'Oro—and elsewhere within the villa—enclosed and shaped inner space by an orderly variety of complex architectural forms. Niches, apses, vaults, domes, and half-domes constantly surrounded and delighted the visitor. The impression given by the façades was essentially unimportant, merely an "untidy complex of domes and gables," as one modern critic has written of such buildings.[59] What did matter was the psychological effect created by the interiors, swirling surfaces which, chaotic at first glance, on closer inspection resolved themselves into orderly, harmonious, geometric designs whose features balanced, mirrored, and repeated one another.

The ultimate effect which the architects of Hadrian's Villa hoped to create was only partially achieved through the use of domed and vaulted structures. The complexities of such buildings could become confusing or overwhelming if the structures were not placed in suitable settings. Thus each vaulted or domed building was set off by conventional colonnades which, by simple verticals, provided a pleasing contrast to the intricacies of the vaulted style. At the same time, gardens enhanced the different pavilions. Each garden represented a "natural setting" but in a contrived fashion which smacked more of the stage than the open countryside.[60] Both gardens and interiors were enhanced by water shows which, throughout the Villa, contributed to a general impression

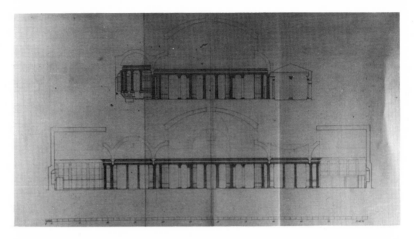

6   Piazza d'Oro. Hadrian's Villa. Restored Section. E. Hansen, "La Piazza d'Oro e la sua cupola," *Analecta romana*, Instituti Danici, I *Supplementum* (Copenhagen, 1960), pp. 64–65.

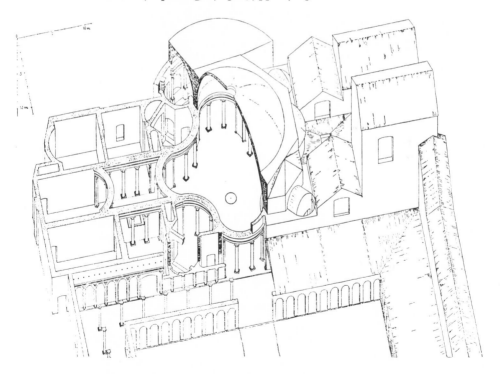

7   Piazza d'Oro. Hadrian's Villa. Isometric Restoration. Fototeca Unione, Rome.

of leisurely magnificence. That impression was achieved in two ways. First, flowing water produced a cooling effect. Numerous fountains and *nymphaea* acted within the shadowed pavilions as a kind of air conditioning system. Second, rising jets and ever-filled channels added life and movement to the elaborate yet motionless decorations of the various buildings.[61] And these ornaments themselves amplified the effect begun by vaults, domes, and constantly splashing fountains. Most surfaces shone with highly polished, varicolored marbles or flashing mosaics laid in involved geometric designs or pleasing pastoral scenes, motifs which were continued in the airy tracery of white or colored stuccos.[62]

Finally, the position of the buildings relative to one another was all important. By the skillful use of architectural forms, the visitor's glance was led from one imposing pavilion to another: here by well-placed colonnade or arcade; there by a group of statuary, a jet of water, or an artfully contrived bit of greenery. By an alternation of enclosed and open spaces, a delightful variation in lighting was achieved. A number of vistas could often be obtained from a single building. On one side there might extend an open garden, brilliantly lit by the burning sun; on the other, a cool *nymphaeum*, inviting the thirsty visitor to repose in the shade of its statuary, refreshing himself with its constantly replenished streams. On a third side might open a court or a long colonnade. Such continual surprises and endless variations could not fail to astound and charm even the most jaded sophisticate.

Palaces so elaborate and complex at first might seem to have little in common with the utilitarian structures of Ostia. Yet, as we have seen, both groups of buildings were constructed by the same methods. Only design and finish distinguish one site from the other. In Ostia, except for the more important public structures, the Capitolium, the Forum Baths, the "Basilica," the Baths of Neptune, most structures are relatively drab. Where mosaic floors appear, they are, with notable exceptions, either plain or composed of black and white *tesserae* laid in straightforward geometric or, more rarely, figured designs.[63] Colored mosaics are not common on the site, and marble veneers and architectural ornaments are normally confined either to public buildings or to the rare private mansions.[64] Wall paintings, usually frescoes, sometimes create pleasing effects, but they seldom rise above the level of fourth-rate provincial mediocrity. With minor exceptions, stuccoes, colored and plain, seem to have been absent from most Ostian buildings.[65] Even external architectural ornament, while pleasant in over-all impression, was mass-produced, manufactured in advance and then set into various structures in the appropriate places. In short, the legions of specialized (and expensive) crafts-men, the marble cutters, sculptors, mosaicists, stuccoworkers, and the like—the men who made Hadrian's palace one of the marvels of its day—were never called in for most of the houses in Ostia. But their absence in dwellings at once so unpretentious and so unabashedly middle-class is hardly surprising.

Thus both Hadrian's Villa and Ostia sum up and epitomize the salient characteristics of early Imperial Roman architecture. By its large-scale organization of the members of the various building trades into well-disciplined guilds, the art had the means to construct rapidly and well. By the early part of the second century, therefore, it had proved itself equal to almost any task, whether building an entire new city or erecting a splendid para-dise for an imperial dilettante. And even while it created sumptu-ous settings for the rich and powerful, its over-all effects were highly beneficial to the urban masses. It provided them with cheap, soundly constructed, attractive housing as well as magnificent public structures, the fora, baths, colonnades, porti-coes, amphitheaters, circuses, and theaters with which each suc-cessive emperor adorned Rome and the cities of the provinces. Prior to the advent of the industrial revolution, almost no archi-tectural technology did so much so well for so many.

Bronze To clear the decks for our discussion of metalwork in Greece, Etruria, and the Roman Empire, let us dispose once and for all of a misleading term, "Bronze Age." The Bronze Age was *not* the classical age of Greece and Rome, and it is *not* the subject of this paper. It is a correct term for designating a much earlier period in human history, and it came into use as follows. The first modern anthropologists, in agreement with certain ancients, like Lucretius the scientific poet, realized that iron appeared late in history and divided the era of civilized man into a Stone Age (Palaeolithic and Neolithic, Old and New Stone), a Bronze Age, and an Iron Age. This classification is quite satisfactory for the Old World of Europe and the Near and Middle East, though not for the New World, which developed differently. The first period was that during which all tools were of stone and ended about 3000 B.C.; the second knew the use of all metals except iron and lasted until about 1000 B.C.; the third began around 1000 B.C.; and we are still in it! Recently there has been some hatchet work on the Bronze Age, lopping off time from both ends, and, in particular, tests have shown that some metal objects previously supposed to be bronze were copper, not bronze; in fact, bronze may not have been used exclusively until nearly 1400 B.C., toward the end of the "Bronze Age." Since habits change slowly and since iron, when it finally became known, proved unsuitable for certain purposes and was, at best, ugly, expensive, difficult to work, and subject to rapid deterioration, bronze continued to be in very extensive use throughout the remainder of antiquity. In fact, one might warn the beginning amateur archaeologist that if and when he finds himself in a museum room loaded with small bronzes, with safety pins and chains draped on strings from floor to ceiling and with statuettes stacked in repellent military formation he is in the Iron Age division! Similarly, if he discovers, as happened recently with this writer, a book dealing with the Greek Bronze Age on the shelf next to literature on Greek bronzes—well, the librarian must have been sleepy! After this much negative advice by way of introduction, let us approach and study the bronze industry of Greece, Italy, and the Roman Empire during the first millennium and a half of the Iron Age (roughly 1000 B.C. to A.D. 500).

Bronze is an alloy of copper and tin. Without tin, copper cannot be worked easily by either hammering or casting, and therefore metalwork of the beginning of the so-called "Bronze Age" was poorly executed and rare. Brass is an alloy of copper and zinc with more or less tin. The ancients did not distinguish verbally between copper, bronze, and brass, a single word having to serve for all three in both Greek and Latin, and, truth to tell, archaeologists are not too careful about the distinction. Zinc is the uncertain factor. From all antiquity there are only several examples of metallic zinc preserved, a fact that is evidence that the ancients knew little about zinc, but not evidence against their having made use of it as found in natural alloys. Greek bronzes contain only traces of zinc, and their normal color is dark red, penny color. Surprisingly, bronze vessels of the eighth century B.C. from Gordion in Asia Minor, a site lengendary to the classical Greeks, have been found to contain a high percentage of zinc. Their color is bright yellow. Just possibly, the story the Greeks loved to tell of Midas, King of Phrygia and resident of Gordion—that he had a golden touch and changed everything to gold, eventually to his own undoing—sprang from the fact that for him and his courtiers, goldlike vessels were produced from copper! Of course this is mere conjecture, but what is certain is that Greek bronzes did not contain much zinc and that bronzes, supposedly Greek but with high zinc content, are automatically suspect. Another fixed point is the beginning of the Roman Empire, the age of Augustus, about the time of Christ, when the Romans regularly began to add zinc to their copper *coinage*, turning their coins yellow. The pieces are correctly to be designated brass. Between and around these two fixed points—the bronze vessels of early Gordion and the Roman coinage—is a sea of misinformation on the subject of zinc content, in which the collector and the student swim, each at his peril. Further, much genuine late Greek and Roman sculpture, as well as the contemporary implements, are yellow, yet their color does not necessarily indicate zinc; in fact, it probably does not, for lead content is a good substitute. Until many more analyses are made and the results tabulated and compared, it will continue to be dangerous to pontificate about the composition of bronzes, other than coins.

An additional problem is posed, and a little zest added, from the study of the word *aurichalcum* used in Latin technical literature. As it stands, the term is Latin for "gold bronze," but it seems to come from an older Greek word, *orichalcum*, which means "mountain gold." The latter was fabulous, mythological in its implications. In its latest usage, the term meant brass, the brass of the coinage, but otherwise its meaning remains difficult, and we dare not pretend to interpret.

Where did the ancients get their copper and tin, not to mention their zinc and lead? Greece is notoriously poor in metals (least so in silver), though copper mines which were worked in antiquity have been recognized at various places in the Peloponnese and on certain Cycladic islands, and there is a tradition for them in Attica, in Euboea, and in Thrace; but tin there is not. Italy is much richer, with mines around Populonia and directly opposite on the island of Elba, producing, altogether, iron, copper, and tin. South Italy is poorly endowed, especially Campania, which nevertheless had a metal industry, but north Italy was hardly capable of supplying both peninsulas. Cyprus was a potential source of copper, as her very name implies. It was Sinai that had supplied the Egyptians, but there is no evidence of the continued use of the mines there through the classical period. Spanish mines were rich and became important, but only after Italy closed hers down during the first century B.C. The main source of tin was Britain, even in very early times. The account of the tin trade across and around Europe would make wonderful reading, if it only could be written—tales of perilous voyages in small boats (see pp. 212–213) before the piratical and inimical Carthaginians closed the Straits of Gibralter completely, and of hazardous land traffic on sledges across forest-clad Europe, all for the tin that *had* to be supplied to classical lands. In addition to Greece and Cyprus, there are zinc deposits at Gressenich near Aachen in Germany, and this may have been a primary Roman source, whereas there is no zinc in the Campanian part of South Italy, despite Pliny's specific mention of it there. Lead is a common impurity and appears everywhere. Gold and silver included in the bronze alloy have never been found by analysis of classical bronze but were talked about in the literature.

Mining during classical times ranged from mere grubbing in banks to fairly good systems of shafts connected by level galleries. Even in early times some mines were systematically exploited by levels, but in no case is there evidence of real understanding of geological principles. At best, an ancient mine had connecting shafts, drainage channels and wheels for removing water, a windlass to raise the ore, and iron tools for cutting it. At worst, it was a maze, constructed by methods which the provincials had inherited from their primitive forebears.

Techniques Having located and mined ores of copper, tin, lead, and zinc
of Working in sufficient quantity, how did the ancient craftsman go about producing a spear, a statue, or a vase? On the whole question of technique, the smelting, alloying, and the shaping of the final product, we modern archaeologists are guessing in the dark. True scientific distinctions were unknown to the metalworker; he lacked the basic knowledge about elements and compounds, that backbone of high school chemistry. Therefore, even if there were a record of what ores he mixed, the chemical composition of the product would not be revealed. Also, any practical knowledge which a master gained he must, lacking the protection of patents, guard zealously and transmit to the son who would succeed him or, lacking a son, take it into his grave. Further, the ancient mind did not consider details of craftsmanship a fitting subject for books. The single exception, the elder Pliny, in his *Natural History*, while appreciating that technical knowledge could be organized into a scientific pattern, yet was stymied at every step by businessmen who refused information of value to themselves, or, one suspects, deliberately misled him with false statements, as does every good cook. The modern scholar must depend upon his own observations. Excavational discoveries of smelting and mining equipment and of tools help, but they are rare. Chemical analysis helps more but is usually impractical, being destructive of works of art. The newer analyses, spectrographic and the like, have barely been tried. A modern artist's opinon of how he would make an ancient object is not necessarily how his Greek predecessor did make it. And, if it is remarked that all study of lost arts is similarly impeded, it may be rejoined that few crafts are as complicated as metalworking and few demand such vast scientific knowledge. Greek and Italic metalworkers continue to arouse our admiration and curiosity.

Much as we would like to know how classical bronzes were made, we are at least as desirous, and with almost as little satisfaction, to learn why and how the objects have changed since ancient times—not to mention how they looked when they first appeared on public display. This raises the whole question of *patina* and *patination*. Every surface of bronze or brass acquires a crust, rough or smooth, thick or thin, blue or green or another color, a crust which does not come off with water or such ordinary solvents as loosen mud. This crust is called a *patina*. Most copper compounds are green or blue, and so the normal patina is a varied surface of green and blue crystals, sometimes as coarse as granu-lated sugar, sometimes very smooth and revealed as crystalline only with the help of a powerful microscope. An additional com-mon formation is red cuprite. The mixture of colors and surface textures delights the student, the bungler who tries to reduce the patination to something more agreeable to his own taste, the scientific crystallographer, and the faker who can create a pretty good imitation on a modern object. Bronzes from Pompeii and Herculaneum, long buried in the volcanic ash of Vesuvius, have notoriously beautiful patinas, and equally notorious imitators (including some honest imitators who at the turn of the last cen-tury made and sold widely honest reproductions which today are passed off as antiques).

After long argument it has been fairly well established that though the color of ancient bronzes varied, usually they were kept bright. There are records of job contracts for cleaning the bronzes in sanctuaries. Moreover, the fairly general use of inlay at certain periods, not to mention the sparser niello and enamel, would be inexplicable for bronzes that were to be left patinated; also, gilding would prevent corrosion. Authors comment upon the peculiar color of bronze already old. Undoubtedly the ancient practice was to make objects of bright metal and normally to keep them bright but, if and when an antique happened to have acquired through age a perfectly beautiful patina, to leave that undisturbed out of respect for age and beauty. Conceivably, later Roman craftsmen accelerated the formation of patina in imitation of the antique Greek; thus "Corinthian" bronze as described by Pausanias (ii. 3.3) might be artificially patinated bronze, imitat-ing the antiques excavated at Corinth during its rebuilding under Julius Caesar. But the term as used by Pliny, Cicero, and Strabo must mean something quite different.[1]

It is a far cry from natural patina to the black lacquer which now covers a few fine ancient bronzes. In the course of a discus-sion of patinas, the learned Pliny remarked upon the surely rare and sporadic application of bitumen to bronze (*N.H.* xxxiv. 15 and xxxv. 182). We are not quite sure what he meant. But sculptors of the Renaissance who read and believed every ancient written document and saw very few works of art, leaped to the bait, convinced themselves that ancient bronzes were always artificially patinated black, and applied a black coating to their own creations, as has remained customary almost down to our own time. Further, following the excavation of ancient bronzes these scholars undertook to replace the black which, they knew, should have been present but inexplicably never was! Some very important eighteenth-century collections of small classical bronzes were given a black coating which they still keep. The great collection in France's Bibliothèque Nationale includes the group excavated by a farmer at Chalon-sur-Saône in 1764 and immediately bought by Caylus, who exultantly proclaimed that they were found in the lacquered state! But since real archaeologists began excavating, not one single example coated with this heavy black lacquer has been known to emerge from the ground. Some scholars still believe in a sort of blackening in ancient times, but the evidence grows weaker every day.

But this much we can venture about techniques: two were basic, hammering and casting, and it is hard to imagine anyone wanting to use metal without being aware of both possibilities. On the whole, hammering was preferred in early times and casting later, a trend not unconnected with the fact that, since hammering produced thin wares, it was economical of material though costly of labor, while casting was easy but produced thick wares, and so was wasteful of material. For large statues the choice between the two techniques was easy. They had to be cast. There were experiments with hammering when Greek art was just beginning and the concept of large statues was revolutionary; preserved are three thin and, of course, hollow, hammered bronze figures from Dreros, Crete, dating from the seventh century B.C., of which one is half as tall as a human being. These are comparable to the child figure in the group of Pepi and his son, made in Egypt about two thousand years earlier. Evidence of casting large statues in Greece goes back only to some damaged casting pits of the latter part of the sixth century B.C.; the figures stood upright on their feet, hollow around a sandy core, in molds which obviously duplicated the modeling of wax.[2] These statues, then, were made by the *cire perdue* (lost wax) process, which, interrupted at the end of antiquity and rediscovered during the Renaissance, has continued down to our own day (see pp. 72–76). However, scholars have deduced that some early casting utilized sand molds with extensive piecing and have suggested that the originals behind the sand molds were of wood. Favoring this solution is the fact that assembling a bronze statue from pieces is illustrated on a vase scene from Athens (early fifth century B.C.). Sand casting returned in the later period, it seems. That there was more than one process is a likely supposition, but, clearly, through most of Greek times *cire perdue* casting predominated, for its results can be recognized in thin-walled sculpture with the interior surface following the exterior very exactly. With equal certainty one may say that there were other methods before and after the artistic peak. On statues so made, seams frequently appear; it is not easy to tell on a finished bronze surface, faintly revealing a seam, whether two bronze parts were joined or merely two parts of a model, in which case the seam of the model was copied! X-ray is a help in locating and interpreting the joints, as well as in locating the iron pieces which separated the mold from the core. Additional limited evidence of piecing comes from the finished but unattached locks of bronze hair which have been excavated and from such extraordinary literary bits as Horace's expression of pity for the frustrated artisan who could make only metal fingernails and curls but never a statue! (*De Arte Poetica* 32ff.)

Whether or not a statue was extensively pieced, a certain amount of surface finishing was necessary. Tooling is rarely obvious on the plain surfaces but is always recognizable in hair and eyebrows; the ancient sculptor always drew fine hairs, though never enough hairs, in contrast to certain other sculptors who let a puffy bulk stand for the total hair mass. Eyes were made frequently of glass or stone of realistic colors; to see a statue like the Charioteer at Delphi staring at you from colored eyes can be a terrifying experience; statues which have lost their eyes must be accepted with tolerance, as well as those whose eyeballs were left blank, devoid of color differentiation. Lips might be inlaid in pure copper, redder than the bronze fabric. Inlaying, plating, and gilding will be mentioned as we pursue the history of sculpture, and other decorative techniques when we discuss vases and ornaments.

Monumental Now, as for the large bronzes themselves, one matter that has
Sculpture not been appreciated is their very great quantity. Despite much commonly expressed opinion to the contrary, a tremendous proportion of all ancient statuary was bronze. The idea that in ancient days one always walked through a veritable sea of blazing white marble, the statuary as ubiquitous and glittering as the temples and colonnaded streets that formed its background, found justi-

fiable credence during the Italian Renaissance, but today it can be proved that the picture was erroneous, except perhaps for limited periods in a few places. Generally speaking, the important sculpture was bronze.

The old view of the preponderance of marble sculpture arose from sporadic early excavations of small but sculpturally well-stocked areas, such as Hadrian's Villa at Tivoli near Rome (see pp. 51–57), the Baths of Caracalla Hercules Farnese and the Dirce group), and the Palace of Titus (Laocoön) within the city, all of mid-imperial date. Small wonder if Michelangelo lovingly fondled the mutilated marble Torso Belvedere—not the same Greek sculptor's complete bronze boxer which was not discovered until 1885! Artists studied what was available, while critics down through Lessing and Winckelmann admired what was to be seen, such as the Apollo Belvedere and the Laocoön. And how little bronze sculpture there was for them to excavate, since, valuable as marble had been for burning to produce lime, its value was as nothing compared to that of bronze in the metal-poor and destructive age before the Renaissance!

The proportion began to change with the discovery and excavation of a rich villa outside Herculaneum in the 1750's. In this palatial home were statues and busts, singly and in sets, portraits, deities, philosophers—in fact, the greatest bronze haul ever made, now displayed in the Naples National Museum. Here, for the first time, one could see things as they appeared in early imperial Roman times. But before this fact could soak into human consciousness, Greek architectural sculpture, found *in situ*, refocused attention on marbles. Early nineteenth-century discoveries included the sculptures of the Parthenon, the temple at Aegina, and the Mausoleum at Halicarnassus, while later nineteenth-century excavations uncovered the high-relief slabs of the Altar of Zeus at Pergamon (Biblical "Satan's seat"). No wonder sculpture was supposed to be marble! Yet, it should be remembered that these mighty blocks were not on the street level with the ancient passers-by, not down among the bronzes, as they are in museums, but stood high up on buildings until those buildings crumbled with the civilization they typified. To repeat, what was among the people and what was considered sculpture was bronze.

The pendulum began to swing again when modern excavation started: at Delphi, where the French began in 1892 to be rewarded with the Charioteer and other bronzes, and at Dodona and Olympia from the 1870's, which yielded incredible Greek bronze statuettes. The excavation of Greek sanctuaries, all originally rich in bronzes, has continued down to our own day, though with diminishing returns. The twentieth century owes its greatest gain in bronzes to chance discoveries from the sea. Cape Artemisium, on the northern tip of Euboea, in 1928 yielded bronzes from a foundered bronze cargo. This harvest surpassed that from the wreck off Mahdia in Africa, discovered in 1907, and that from little Antikythera, an island between Crete and the Greek mainland, in 1900. Today, with underwater archaeology still in its infancy and growing by leaps and bounds, one expects great discoveries, but the first bronze statues are yet to be rescued from the sea by underwater excavators who live in hopes of a discovery at a depth which they can negotiate. The greatest recent find on land was the accidental discovery of a sanctuary in Peiraeus, the port of Athens, in 1959. Thanks to these discoveries, we know: sculpture was bronze.

One might begin a list of bronze sculpture in antiquity with all those colossal bronzes of which only a dim memory remains. The Athena Promachos by Pheidias stood on the Athenian Acropolis and could be seen far out at sea: estimated height, thirty feet. It wound up in Constantinople, where it stood until A.D. 1203—its span of life almost seventeen hundred years! Slightly later there was the Colossos of Rhodes, 105 feet tall, standing beside the harbor, not astride it, for fifty-six years before collapsing. A statue, variously first Nero, then the sun-god, then Commodus, 110 or 120 feet tall, was moved about in a small area not far from the (later) Colosseum to which it gave its name; the statue lasted at least three hundred years, being last mentioned in the records in A.D. 354. In comparison with these three, our Statue of Liberty has a chance for a good record: it is slightly over 151 feet and has stood since 1884. One has grounds for hope of its continued survival especially since, like Athena, Dame Liberty has the benefit of a good broad skirt for base and balance!

It was not always appreciated and emphasized that bronze was preferred by the great-name Greek sculptors. But in 1935 A. J. B. Wace assembled evidence, chiefly literary, showing that each Greek sculptor had a favorite, if not a sole, medium and that bronze was preferred by many great sculptors including Polykleitos (fifth century B.C.), the master of athletic creations. Wace concluded that bronze was the generally favored medium from the late sixth century B.C. until the mid-fourth, that is, through all the age which we are wont to consider "classical" style. A chief source for Wace's work was Pliny, who carefully separated his sculptors by their preferred media. Whatever we may have said against Pliny as a scientist, he did know his history of art and managed to incorporate histories compiled by Greek authors, though he made little effort to bring the story down to his own time (he died in the eruption of Vesuvius in A.D. 79 when the villa of bronzes at Herculaneum was buried). Subsequent discoveries have corroborated Wace's work. Included in the recent Peiraeus find was an archaic "Apollo" of bronze, raising from one to two the complete bronze statues preserved from the sixth century B.C. (but both the Peiraeus and the other, found in the sea at Piombino during the nineteenth century, have been accused of being later copies—just to show how little we really know of the subject!).

Now the bronze creations of these most famous sculptors included the majority of the cult images for great temples, the Hephaisteion at Athens, for instance. We have always looked up at the lovely marble frieze, still in place, even back in the days when the building was wrongly called the Theseion. Excavations have recovered the marble figures of its pediments and some marble acroteria that graced the corners of its peaked roof. Excavations have also revealed not, alas, the bronze cult statutes of Athena and Hephaistos by Alkamenes, documented both by tradition and epigraphic evidence and by the actual marked pedestals —no, not even a scrap of the statues—but tantalizing fragments of the baked clay molds and the pit where the casting took place, located not far from the temple.

Another matter over which issue might be taken with our predecessors in order to extend the boundaries of bronze dominance even beyond Wace's limits is the copies. The point process of copying in marble was known and used by the first century B.C. (see pp. 112–114), but that is a far cry from saying that it was already practiced on a mammoth scale. The bronze Diadoumenos by Polykleitos was copied in marble for use in a house in Delos which survived until the first century B.C; but from Pompeii and Herculaneum together, vibrating with life for more than a century after Delos succumbed to fate, there has emerged but a single marble copy of Polykleitos' Doryphoros to balance the many bronze copies from the villa and many more found in the two cities. To mention a few copies in bronze from these two towns: there are bronze copies of the head of the Doryphoros, of Herakles, of the Amazon by Polykleitos, a complete seated Hermes, so wonderful that it used to be called an original by Lysippos, the wrestler group, its sculptor unknown but surely one of the great creations of antiquity, and maidens and athletes of early fifth century date—all life-size, of course. Now the destruction of Herculaneum and Pompeii in A.D. 79 is very close to the date, A.D. 64, of Nero's great fire in Rome (see, pp. 44–45) and the consequent rebuilding and redecorating of the capital. One may at least suggest that marble copying by the point process received a boost after the fire but had previously been less usual than copying in bronze. It happens that the author with the most to say about copying is Pausanias, who lived in the second century after Christ, long after Nero's fall and Rome's rebuilding.

Bronze, too, was a favorite medium for honorific statues which tended to be equestrian or chariot groups, royal perquisites on the whole.[3] Before 500 B.C. a bronze chariot group was erected near the entrance to the Athenian Acropolis to celebrate the victory of the Athenians over the Chalcidians of Euboea. It has always been assumed that the group was life-size, but it may have been tiny, for detached horses and parts of only small chariot groups of bronze have been found from earlier times. The first life-size group is that found at Delphi, from which the charioteer is preserved (about 480 B.C.). The first actual-size equestrian statue of gilded bronze that the Romans remembered was dedicated in Rome in 191 B.C., but the number rapidly increased thereafter. A most spectacular bronze group of the Julio-Claudian imperial family was discovered in East Italy in 1946, and there was no lack of such pieces at Pompeii and Herculaneum during the next generations. The only equestrian honorary statue to stand through the Middle Ages was the Marcus Aurelius now on the Capitoline, spared in the belief that it was Constantine, a Christian ruler. One huge class of monuments should be noted, for it offers a contrast to what I have said about architectural sculpture being marble and elevated far above the crowds: the Roman triumphal marble arch was regularly crowned by a chariot group of bronze. The four horses of St. Mark's, Venice, are the only extant likely candidates for such position of honor. Some recently discovered great bronzes of the third century, not equestrian, are the Septimius Severus in Cyprus and many beautiful imperial statues from Asia Minor. From the Constantinian and later eras there are a few great bronzes, more names of lost ones; the best example on view is the colossal statue at Barletta in South Italy, originally erected elsewhere. The founding of Constantinople offered a rich field for bronze sculpture, and only a part of it was filched from older cities. There, Theodosius appeared in bronze at least once, and Justinian on horseback kept him company. Symmachus was in bronze in both capitals, and Theodosius honored his father with bronze statuary in Canossa and Stobi, perhaps also in Rome and Antioch. The last great imperial monument to be erected in the city of Rome was the column of Phocas, A.D. 608. The tourist who sees it interrupting the vista of temples and basilicas in the Forum usually neglects to read the inscription which announces the gilded bronze statue that once crowned the column. Charlemagne stole a great statue from Ravenna for Aachen, and it may have been stolen and moved previously. Private persons continued to have bronze statues down to the end, as the inscriptions tell.

And these inscriptions lead us to a new subject: golden statuary. Just when the empire is at its poorest, statues are erected all over the world which are shining with pure gold, or so the inscriptions say! But it is unthinkable for these statues to have been made of gold, by nature too soft for huge statues; besides, not a scrap of a gold statue has survived. We must suppose that these last Roman statues were plated or gilded bronzes, as certain very similar dedicatory inscriptions admit. Some need not even have been gilded, for the yellow fabric previously mentioned might be taken for gold if well shined. Remember, the distinction between gold and brass remained unclear, and alchemy was a respected science at a much more recent date!

But even before thin gilding with mercury attachment was possible and before yellow bronze was ever used in statuary, there were, if we believe the records, gold statues. But let's not believe them! The statues were bronze with gold plates—thick gold plates. An example, dating from the fifth century B.C., is a head of Nike found in the Agora of Athens.[4] Numerous inscriptions refer to Nike statues like this, always golden, though the preserved head is bronze; however, along the hair line was cut a deep groove, with similar grooves running vertically up the sides of the neck, and in the grooves folded sheet gold is secured, fragments of an original over-all gold plating. Apparently the same thing was happening in the fourth century B.C. when Lysippos was at work. He made a statue of Alexander the Great as a boy which, according the Pliny (N.H. xxxiv. 63), Nero had gilded centuries later, though the gold was removed, leaving the cuttings into which the gold had been fastened. Ridiculous! In the light of the Nike which we have just considered, there is no doubt that the Alexander was a bronze originally covered with gold plates, stolen, as were those of Nike's head, leaving similar cuttings. Pliny and his contemporaries turned out another good Nero story! Indeed, wherever in ancient literature gold statuary is recorded, we might better read bronze, either gold plated or gilded, or else brass, shined. As for the gold parts of the chryselephantine colossi like the Athena Parthenos, the Zeus at Olympia, and the rest—well, there is no evidence that the gold was applied over bronze, but neither is there any evidence to the contrary, and not one scrap of a solid gold piece of drapery has ever been discovered.

So let us picture the ancient world throughout most of its history as a world of bronze statuary, placed amid and before white marble buildings of which the decoration was sculptured marble with color and metal trimmings. By the second century after Christ the bronzes were fewer in proportion to the marbles which were being turned out by high-speed versatile copyists using a splendid mechanical process (see, pp. 112–114).

Statuettes The world of the bronze statuettes was something quite different.[5] Common at all periods, they were artistic pathfinders. Experimenting with small bronzes, Greek sculptors broke the shackles that had bound the art of modeling in all previous civilizations and produced human beings that seemed to live and breathe. Proof of this statement lies in the observable fact that in torsion and multifaciality Greek bronze statuettes sometimes precede monumental sculpture by nearly two centuries (shown by Neugebauer).[6]

There were some experimental techniques for statuette production. A few, very primitive, animal figures were made by folding sheet metal. Some others, animals and men, suggest construction by hammering rods together, though others, with almost identical form, are cast and merely reproduce rod construction of a model. But surely the great majority were cast by *cire perdue*, even from very early times (theoretically a *cire perdue* casting can derive from wax, wood, or bronze, the latter two translated into wax). The molds were fired clay; not one is preserved. Statuettes of men and bulls and horses were cast head down, as is apparent from the crude hands on even fine statuettes due to the difficulty of making molten metal run *up* in a mold, and tangs on the feet of men and animals, witnessing the casting gates; the same

1

Statuette of Harpocrates from Egypt. Probably Early Imperial Roman. Courtesy, Walters Art Gallery, Baltimore.

2   Statuette of Harpocrates, showing sand core. Courtesy, Walters Art Gallery, Baltimore.

tangs occur on Egyptian bronzes. Up to five or six inches tall, statuettes were cast solid, but larger ones required a core, sandy material, not always removed. Women's figures in floor-length dresses were more frequently hollow than nude male figures of equal scale.

For making a bronze by *cire perdue*, a model must be formed of wax (if large, of a sandy baked core covered with wax). The real sculptural work is done in the wax. The wax model is then covered with clay and baked so that the clay solidifies and the wax runs out through holes, two holes being in the feet; then molten bronze is poured into the mold through the hole under one foot and replaces the lost wax (if a core was used, it has to be supported by iron pegs between core and mold). The sequence is: model, mold, bronze statuette. For every statuette a wax model must be destroyed, so it follows that duplication will be rare, but such duplication was practiced commonly at certain times and in certain places, notably in Egypt in Roman times. The sculptor had merely to make and save an extra mold of the original model or even of the finished statuette; the sequence then became model or bronze, mold, wax model, mold, bronze statuette. This is the way modern sculptors work, and in Egypt there had long been such demands for deities of bronze that manufacturers had learned to use molds for half-arms, half-legs, torsos, and heads; Greeks and Romans, or Egyptians working for the Roman trade, picked up the tricks of duplication. An interesting group of four figures made in Egypt and belonging to the Louvre consists of Dionysos leading his festive troop. There remain, beside the leader, a satyr, with flutes and two maenads who are exactly alike in head and costume but turn their heads in opposite directions. Obviously, the sculptor made two bodies and two heads in molds and combined the parts at will; one would like to see the rest of the entourage, which may have been large. Even if there were ten maenads, his technique would have been adequate, and he could vary the attributes.

A curious partial technique which I cannot pretend to understand is indicated for the Horus-Cupid (Harpocrates) in Figures 1 and 2. I make no claim to interpret the evidence but call your attention to the fact that a sandy core remains within, visible through breaks in the right shoulder and in the thighs. The legs are divided above the knees by cross sections of bronze upon which the core rests (similar cross sections occur at neck and lower arm of Figure 3). As a guess, I suggest that the various

3

Statuette of Woman. Etruscan,
5th–4th century B.C. Courtesy,
Walters Art Gallery, Baltimore.

4   Detail of No. 3, showing
hooks for mounting. Cour-
tesy, Walters Art Gallery,
Baltimore.

parts were shaped individually of sandy core and each completely coated with wax, then stuck together and encased in a mold, from which the wax was melted out as usual and replaced by bronze which imitated even the end coverings of the severed limbs. The left arm was cast separately, solid, and doweled to the stub at the shoulder: one sees the hole for the pin that secured the dowel. Perhaps! The deceased artist may be laughing at me right now, at me and my attempts to ferret out his trade secrets!

Broken out of its mold, the cast statuette needed some trimming and finishing and, in some cases, embellishment. Silver plating and silver inlay, chiefly for eyes, were common. An unusual case was the small bronze bust of Augustus, with his birthplace, Thurii, added in iron letters, which Suetonius gave to his own reigning sovereign, Hadrian (Suetonius *Augustus* II. vii. 1). If there were gates in addition to those under the feet, the resultant bronze projections must have been removed. The surface might be polished and chiseled. It has been noticed that bronzes from Italy more frequently show wide, flat planes, made with a chisel, than do these from Greece. Bubbles in the bronze could be repaired by hammering. However, some of the finest of all statuettes have been left with their bubbles uncorrected and with their surfaces just a little spongy-looking.

The question most frequently asked about the bronze statuettes and their truly amazing profusion is: what were they used for? The related question is: how were they set up? Probability is against their having all been purely ornamental, just "works of art." The preponderance of sacred subjects is against pure uselessness and in favor of the bronzes' having been "votive," that is, dedicated to a god, in a sanctuary or elsewhere.

Now the little protuberances I have mentioned as forming on the feet of statuettes, due to the intake and the exhaust of the flowing molten bronze, provided the perfect means of attachment to a base, and so they were used regularly in early times. There are cases dating from the sixth century B.C. where the two bars, trimmed to rectangular form and each perforated, were set through a bronze base and secured, each by a crosspin below. This is a perfect Egyptian mechanism. In other cases, the rods were set in lead and presumably attached to a pedestal. An Etruscan figure with the rods cut to form hooks for better holding in lead is illustrated in Figures 3 and 4, another, with feet still attached to the lead mass, in Figure 5. A few tall pedestals for such mounting exist, several from early Athens; a fragmentary

5

Statuette of youth,
showing attachments
for feet. Courtesy,
British Museum,
London.

example from Italy is shown in Figures 6 and 7. Does it surprise
you that tiny bronzes stood alone on pedestals as votive images
dedicated to the gods? How pretty they must have been! In fair-
ness one must admit that not very many such dedications are
documented. For the unlovely figurines, mass-produced and mass-
dedicated, less elegant mounting is indicated. In some cases many
bronzes, each with a pointed rod cast below each foot, were set
into holes in a plank or log of wood or in a large stone base.
And really cheap dedications need not have been mounted at
all; it was enough to throw them into a pit.

After the fifth century B.C. it appears that fewer and fewer
statuettes were mounted in the simple and obvious way, by the
bars under their feet. By Roman times statuettes were most frequently attached to cheap little bronze bases by a poor solder
which always fails before modern excavation; one cannot help
wondering how strong it was in the first place. And remounting
was frequent; marks on bases prove as much. Not unrelated to
the Greek and Etruscan dedication of votive bronzes in sanctuaries
was the Roman custom of erecting a *lararium*, an altar of the
family gods. Tiny figures of gods, Olympians and lesser lights,
stood in the small housefront-shaped niche that served as a shrine.
It is likely that shrines by the wayside had a similar selection
of divine subjects, though protecting them must have been difficult! When a group has been excavated with its shrine, it has
been noticed that there is no stylistic agreement of the various
statuettes, for the dedicator purchased members of the group at
his convenience. But there were definite rules about selection,
size, and placing. A favored group was two *lares* dancing and
holding two ritual vessels (*patera, rhyton, situla*) and a single
man wearing a toga. He is a *genius*, the personification of spirit,
of the owner of the house, and he is always smaller than the
lares (but when the *genius* of the emperor substituted for the
ruler he was semidivine, hence bigger). If any major gods were
added—Jupiter, Juno, Fortuna, Mercury—they were bigger than
all the others or mounted on blocks to appear higher. Statuettes
from a *lararium*, part of a large group, found long ago near Para-
mythia in the northern part of the Greek peninsula, fooled generations of scholars into dating them in the fourth and the third
century B.C., the acme of Greek art; it waited for Neugebauer
in our time to recognize them as Roman works of the second
century after Christ (even the *lar* is included!).

6   Limestone pedestal, shaped like a fragmentary capital. Ca. 500–480 B.C. Courtesy, Museum of Fine Arts, Boston, H. L. Pierce Fund.

7   Top of No. 6. Inscribed (in Greek): "Polulos dedicated it; Eupidas made it." Courtesy, Museum of Fine Arts, Boston, H. L. Pierce Fund.

But nothing like the total of statuettes can be accounted for on these religious grounds, to be used as votive dedications and in the *lararium*. All kinds of local customs must be responsible for them. A special case is that of Aphrodite statuettes in Syria in Roman times; they were placed unmounted, each under the head of a Syrian woman in her grave, with intent which, though religious in a sense, was not that of the votives or the shrine figures. A fair proportion of "works of art" seems likely in later periods, when earlier statuettes were being collected; Horace remarks upon having outgrown the urge to collect Etruscan statuettes, which had mastered him (*Epist.* II. 2. 180ff.). At Pompeii there were bronze and sculpture shops and probably bronze statuettes were their chief stock in trade. Finally, a warning: the number of anthropomorphic bronzes that were really decorative pieces and have been *trimmed to make statuettes for the modern collector* is considerable.

Vessels So far, as we talked about statuary, we could assume that the reader knew what we were talking about and knew where to go to see examples of the subject matter. But who is aware of that huge ancient bronze industry that produced bronze implements? It was thriving throughout antiquity, employed thousands of workers, and left us most beautiful treasures. In the *Iliad*, Priam brought treasure including gold vessels and tripods to ransom Hektor's body; but the vase painters of the sixth century B.C. illustrated the scene with vessels that look very like the preserved bronzes of the Iron Age! The biggest Greek vase in the world, measuring four feet in each direction and looking even bigger, is a bronze krater for mixing wine; it was manufactured during the sixth century B.C. and transported to Vix in Burgundy, there to be hidden in a tomb and be rediscovered in our own day. Beautiful hydrias (see pp. 83–86) of bronze bore water from the spring to the home, and a selection of hydrias, along with an amphora or two, were filled with honey and dedicated to Hera in a subterranean chamber at Paestum in South Italy, while other hydrias received the ashes of the dead, as sometimes happened to a great bowl (*lebes*) which could also serve in the world of the living to honor a god or a victor or just for cooking. Bronze vessels were prizes earned in athletic festivals and were inscribed as such. Certain special forms of pail, called *situlas*, some beautifully decorated and others incredibly bizarre, seem to have existed purely for ritual purposes; and maybe some long-nosed little bronze jugs did the same. Bronze foot tubs of great beauty existed in Greek times; Horace, the Roman poet, speaks (*Satires* II. iii. 21) of the collector who hunted for Sisyphos' foot tub, doubtless meaning a bronze piece from Corinth where Sisyphos had lived. From the ashes of Boscoreale, a suburb of Pompeii, came two full-length bronze bathtubs. Metalware in addition to sculpture was stolen from Sicily by the greedy Verres, if we can believe the opposing lawyer Cicero, who incidentally worked up some snobbery-in-reverse and pretended that he knew little about such artistic matters! Youths scraped their oily bodies with bronze strigils, girls dipped perfume from tall thin bottles with bronze applicators having fancy handles, and for a thousand years women gazed at themselves in polished bronze mirrors without any feeling of deprivation or any longing for mercury mirrors to be invented. Bronze lampstands, with a resemblance to our awful floor lamps, supported the inadequate oil lamps, four or five to a stand, that offered miserable illumination to otherwise festive banquets.

We know very little about the industrial organization which produced this mass of metal objects.[7] It is uncertain whether sculptors made bronze vessels or considered themselves too lofty. Only in Roman times did manufacturers of vases sign their works, and then primarily on some miserable cheap pans which the Germans call casseroles. In early Greece, when local styles flourished, the figural details of implements followed the styles of the statues, but this is not proof that one man ever worked at both jobs. Concerning one specialty there are statements by Roman authors: the great sculptors Myron, Pheidias, and Polykleitos are supposed to have been famous for their repoussé work, a technique of vast importance for vessels of gold, silver, and bronze. Repoussé is a technique of raising relief by hammering freehand on sheet metal backed temporarily with pitch. It developed to great heights during the fifth century B.C., the age of the sculptors mentioned, and in the following century reached an apogee in the covers of certain types of Greek mirrors. The height of the relief and the thinness of fabric delight us as much as the beautiful three-dimensional pictorial effects of these feminine trifles. Repoussé was one of the decorative techniques for hammered bronze. Another was matrix relief, a rival in early times. The matrix was a kind of mold of stone or baked clay into which sheet metal was forced by blows from the back. A mass product is the natural result. From sets of a few matrices, craftsmen of very early times produced bronze straps with multiple mythological scenes for carrying the heavy Greek shield on the warrior's arm. Matrices also impressed simple borders and geometric patterns on thin metalwork. And there was cast low relief in the heavier ware, and skin casting, which so closely resembles repoussé that it fools us frequently, as, of course, its perpetrator intended it should. The polishing we have mentioned for mirror surfaces may have been executed with the help of a lathe. Lathe turning, too, was used to cut concentric circles. There was engraving, some of the finest in history, and we shall return to its use later. In late times thin metal was punched for decoration, while at the same time heavy vessels grew huge cast beads on their edges. Related to punching was "chip carving," giving a result rather like cuneiform writing. Enamel, that is, colored glass run onto a metal background, a technique which had been reserved to jewelers, in later Roman times blossomed into enameled bronze vessels (but the thread does not run direct from them to Medieval enamels, so far as we can tell). These techniques which we have listed are some of the methods of embellishing bronzeware in addition to plating, gilding, and inlaying, the decorative techniques which they share with sculpture.

Now for the bronze vases! As has been said, hammered metal was economical and cast wasteful, but a more important distinction is that of strength. Most vessels before the Roman age were made by combined techniques: their bodies were of thin hammered bronze, the handles and bases and perhaps some other parts of heavy cast bronze. The joining was sometimes achieved by rivets, but more frequently by solder, which does not hold—but had the advantage of not perforating the vase! This method of construction is important for the connoisseur to grasp, for it is the cause of our extraordinary museum displays of numerous perfectly preserved handles with not a vase in sight! The bodies long ago distintegrated. Just the result of time, and neither the artist nor the original owner cared in the slightest.

Though sculpture was rarely duplicated, vases were standardized if not quite duplicated. The casting technique of the handles lent itself to repetition: molds for the wax model of a youth who arched his back to form a handle, vertical or horizontal; molds to stamp relief designs on the flat parts of the wax models for separate little vase feet; molds for the wax models of the heads of lions, griffins, or women to peer over the edge of a vase—with these molds it was possible to standardize the decoration, each element typical of a certain shape at a specific moment. Find a handle detached (see Figure 11), and you can assign it not only to a date but to a shape of vessel.

But the time came when it was cheaper to cast all of the vase than to hammer out the plain parts. Cheaper, too, to cast it in parts and put them together on the assembly line. Little bronze long-nosed jugs, like that in Figure 8, were cast in four parts: base, body, neck, and handle. Actually these little jugs come apart even more frequently than the older Greek and Etruscan types, and every museum possesses some disconnected but complete parts. This assembly process for making good wares cheaply did for the Romans what the Industrial Revolution did for modern Europeans and Americans. That the result was not too cheap, using the word in its derogatory sense, is apparent from the truly beautiful decoration on certain handles, as Figure 9. Mass produce the parts, put them together by assembly process, but spend all day inlaying the back of one handle with silver details (eyes, etc.) and edging it with tiny silver beads!

A question perennially and not altogether profitably debated is the relationship of vase shapes in bronze and pottery. Because metal vases were more expensive than pottery, it is sometimes assumed that whenever the same form occurs in both materials, the pottery must be a poor man's imitation of the metal. Further, the black glaze of Greek pottery, especially when not relieved with painted scenes, is thought to imitate silver. Nobody has been foolish enough to suggest that green vitreous glaze outside and yellow within, as it occurs on Roman cups of Cicero's time, was imitation of dirty and clean bronze, so let me not start here on such a false scent! Is it not true that today has fashions of form, that silverware, glass, coarse pottery, and china follow a common course so that one can readily distinguish the wares of the 1920's, 1930's, 1940's, and 1950's? Further, warning should be broadcast against calling something a "metallic shape" just because it has sharp angles which today's heavy pressure machinery would so easily achieve on metalware. Remember that in antiquity the lighter tools would not master angular shapes as easily. But there can be no doubt that pottery sometimes imitates details and decorative elements from metal, and perhaps by mechanical means of copying. If a pottery hydria has lumps where rivets would

8   Jug, cast in four parts. Roman, 1st century after Christ. Courtesy,
Walters Art Gallery, Baltimore.

9   Handle ornamentation on No. 8. Courtesy, Walters Art Gallery,
Baltimore.

unite the hammered body and the cast handle of a bronze hydria, it obviously is a case of imitation. And black-glazed plates from Italy of the fourth century B.C. have elaborate relief scenes that were produced by molds taken from contemporary or even antique silverware or bronzeware with repoussé. But in general, while commending the imaginative metal craftsman, we would do well not to belittle the potter for perennial imitation (Figures 10, 11, 12).

There is a development and change of each form, both in pottery and in bronze, over the years and the centuries; it is easy to tell a fourth-century hydria from one made in the sixth. But there is a curious phenomenon of reoccurrence more apparent in metal than in pottery. In some cases it is possible that the same form changed yet endured for centuries (see Figures 10, 11, 12), but sometimes it seems more probable that one was revived. A taste for archaeology was a Roman characteristic, and it would not be surprising if, in addition to collecting ancient vessels, the Roman collectors, even persons of very moderate means, had tableware made in ancient patterns. A possible example is the jug with trefoil mouth and short, almost spherical body. We illustrate two pieces (Figures 13 and 14), one Greek, dated in the fifth century B.C., and one Roman, not earlier than the first century after Christ. The Greek example is relatively rare (Figure 13), the Roman, standard (Figure 14). The similarity is startling, and it is small wonder that the common Roman type was in the past classified as Greek. This problem of archaism or continuity in vase shapes needs to be investigated; at the moment one but suggests it.

A final word about some extraordinary bronze vases, of a type that will demand study in the years immediately to come: the covered *cistae* that were the exclusive product of Praeneste (modern Palestrina), a small town east of Rome, artistically affiliated with the Etruscans but speaking Latin, and knowing a great artistic bloom in the fifth, fourth, and third centuries B.C. The peculiar vase is a covered cylindrical can, a foot or more tall and up to a foot in diameter, whose sides and cover are decorated with most beautiful engraved drawings of complicated scenes, usually mythological, less frequently historical or genre. The engraved lines (as on mirrors, cf. Figure 15) are always deep with straight sides and flat bottom, never scratched with a point. The drawing, always perfectly composed, meets around the side of the cylinder. Once this gorgeous artistic work was

10

Pottery pitcher. Greek black-figure, ca. 520 B.C. Courtesy, Walters Art Gallery, Baltimore.

11   Bronze pitcher. Etruscan, 500–450 B.C. Courtesy, Museum of Fine Arts, Boston, Perkins Collection; purchased of E. P. Warren.

12   Silver pitcher. Roman. 2nd century after Christ (?). Courtesy, Walters Art Gallery, Baltimore.

completed, dangling chains were attached by little discs and pins, disrupting and concealing parts of the drawing; a bizarre handle, such as a group of two soldiers carrying a dead comrade, was stuck on as cover handle, again without consideration of the artistic work already achieved. Finally, a lady of Praeneste stuffed the can with all her cosmetic equipment, her rags soiled with rouge, spatulas and applicators, perfume bottles and mirrors, and ultimately took the whole thing into her grave!

Now her Praenestine mirrors were hand mirrors with a reflecting surface, not round but pear-shaped; the back would be decorated with engraved scenes. Meanwhile, all the towns of Etruria, just north of Praeneste, made their mirrors with circular reflecting surface and the same long handle. A typical example is Figure 15, where we see a marriage with the bride crowned by a winged deity, all in the presence of Hercules. It looks like the Greek myth of Dionysos and Ariadne, but the names are different, except for Hercules (Ercle). The mirror was engraved in one Etruscan town about 300 B.C. by an artist whose name is unknown but whom we call "The Master of the Tall Figures," because of peculiarities of drawing on this and some other mirrors *which can be attributed to his hand.* Now, to return to the subject of Praeneste and the *cistae;* it is the study of the work of engraving about which we may expect to hear in the next few years. We want to learn about Praenestine artists as we have about the Etruscan "Master of the Tall Figures."

Furniture   Another very important branch of the bronze industry was furniture production. Assyria and Urartu (Armenia) had heavy bronze furniture as early as the eighth century B.C., but in Mediterranean lands in early times, as in colonial America, the wood supply was sufficient to render all-metal furniture unnecessary. As time went on, more and more metal was used, but even so it tended to be a subsidiary material. I know of no early Greek bronze chair or bed, though a few remain from Etruria, always richer in metal supply. Couches of the Hellenistic Greek and the Roman period were regularly of wood with raised bolsters at the head, sometimes, apparently, at the foot also. They were for banquets. The wood bolster ends each had metal frames and two ornaments—on the lower part, a circular medallion, perhaps ornamented with a human head, and a top projecting member

13

Bronze pitcher. Greek. 5th
century B.C. Courtesy,
Museum of Fine Arts,
Boston, Perkins Collection;
purchased of E. P.
Warren.

14

Bronze pitcher. Roman.
1st century after Christ.
Courtesy, The Danish
National Museum,
Copenhagen.

for which the usual and eminently suitable subject was an animal's head on a long neck. The heads may be those of ducks, panthers, lions, horses, and dogs (Figure 16), but the commonest is the mule's head. Juvenal, the Roman satirist, railed (*Satires* XI. 97) against loungers on couches with *coronati caput aselli* (the head of a garlanded ass) for ornament. The couches which had these ornamented bolsters were usually equipped with bronze legs and with bronze facing for parts of their horizontal members—actually, the two quarters nearest the ends, because the center of the couch was invariably concealed by the draping bedclothes, and hence was mere wood. This fact is responsible for the erroneous reconstruction in the past of many bronze "thrones" with arms. In fact, what existed in every case was the bronze legs, revetments, and two terminal bolsters with bronze trim of a wood-and-bronze couch of which the central all-wood part had rotted away.

The only piece of furniture that was regularly bronze and bronze alone throughout the centuries was the tripod, or three-legged table. Bronze tripods have been found on the island of Ithaca, the home of Odysseus, dating from the eighth century B.C., when the Odyssey was young! Tripods (some were iron) supporting bronze cauldrons decorated with huge protruding griffin heads were dedications at Olympia and other sanctuaries as early as the seventh and sixth centuries B.C. There are all-bronze tables and tripods from the debris of Pompeii and Herculaneum, including folding tripods. Such folding tripods, adjustable as to height and width and capable of carrying trays of various sizes at appropriate heights, continued to be made and used throughout Roman history. A common type in later times, chiefly the third century after Christ, had two straight legs and a third leg interrupted in its shaft at half-height, with a bow at this point forming a handle to transport the tripod when it was collapsed (Figures 17 and 18). Such objects were produced after a standard design. We illustrate the broken handle-parts of two tripods; they have identical form and the same decoration: panther's head on spotted neck, acanthus leaves, and a relief of a *kantharos*, a two-handled cup; they were found separately. There are many such found at various places, chiefly in northern Europe. The design was standardized; that exactly similar objects were produced at various points is possible, but they may all emanate from one factory.

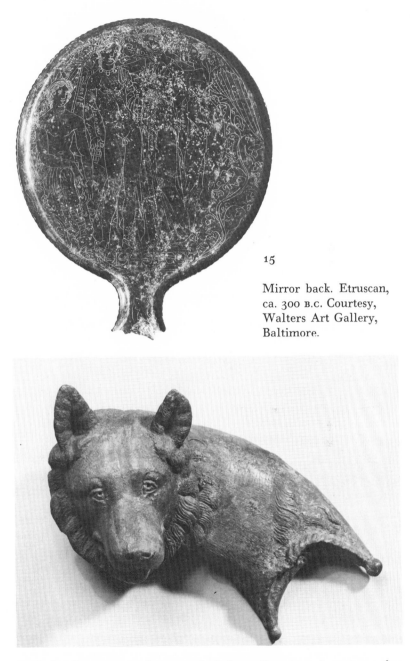

15

Mirror back. Etruscan,
ca. 300 B.C. Courtesy,
Walters Art Gallery,
Baltimore.

16   Dog's head ornament from couch bolster. Roman, 1st century after
Christ. Courtesy, Walters Art Gallery, Baltimore.

One general and uncomplimentary observation may be made on metal furniture construction. The forms are attractive, the decoration is tasteful, its execution masterly, even the imagination is praiseworthy, but the mechanics, to judge by our standards, are extremely bad. Our old pieces cannot be expected to work; but clearly, even when new, such furniture would have been troublesome. The couch with its bolsters terminating in garlanded asses' heads is beautifully conceived, but through the centuries of its manufacture it never once occurred to a furniture maker to use a lengthwise brace! Cross braces, indeed, but nothing to stop the legs from spreading beyond the ends. And their folding tripods, with the beautiful and practical handles, must have been very shaky. Trained as we are to admire Roman roads and bridges, we naturally think of the Romans as great engineers, and so they were. It just never occurred to them to apply engineering principles to the little jobs on the small objects that were being manufactured in the shops.

Arms and Armor One last big subject is arms and armor. Our period is the Iron Age, that is, the period when iron was available in some quantity. Even in Homer there are references to iron weapons, though also to bronze. Bronze daggers and javelins and spear points are preserved from the early part of the new age, especially from Italy, but they do not long continue in use even there. Instead, iron for offensive weapons took over, and for archaeology this was a tragedy—since iron does not last, and very few weapons therefore exist from all the remainder of antiquity! But with defensive armor it was otherwise. Shields of bronze over wood are preserved at least in fragments, and helmets of several types, greaves, and ankle, thigh, and arm guards have survived from all periods in Greece. In general, the designs are good and functional. There are rare and beautifully decorated examples of helmets, with borders, even pictures, incised or embossed on them. On the whole, though, the helmets—and they are by far the most frequently excavated pieces of armor—tend to be simple and standardized. Just as today—military equipment is G.I. Some distinctions may have been made in the crests, but they are never preserved. Tradition of individual emblems on shields is mere tradition: there are few examples to prove it. And one could scratch his name on his helmet for personal identification, and regularly did so when, after battle or armor race, he dedicated his helmet in gratitude to one of the great deities by nailing it to the wall

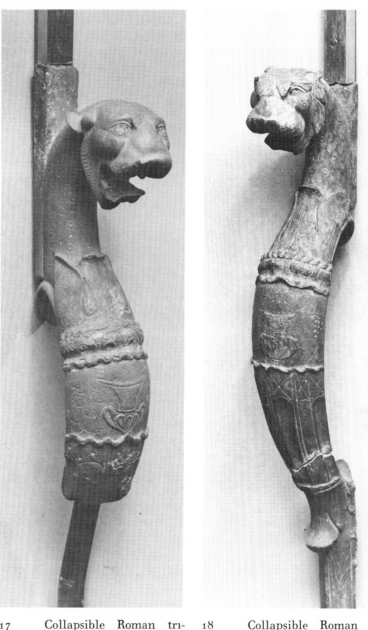

17   Collapsible Roman tri-   18   Collapsible Roman tri-
      pod table leg. Courtesy,   pod table leg. Courtesy,
      Walters Art   Gallery,   Walters Art   Gallery,
      Baltimore.   Baltimore.

by a hole at the back of the neck. Although leather could be used for protection of the main body area, the Greeks frequently used bronze, shaped in exact duplication of the torso, breast, nipples, navel, and all; below the body-shaped cuirass hung tabs of leather or of metal to protect the lower parts without impeding movement. The type endured and is to be seen most frequently copied on marble statuary of Roman times, almost always on statues of the emperor. Body, bronze, marble—the sequence causes some difficulty for the spectator; Lady Hester Stanhope in the early nineteenth century came upon such a marble statue in Palestine, and nobody knew what to make of it! Another confusion is that according to literature the emperor wore a gold cuirass—a statement to be questioned and amended; as with other items so described, were not the cuirasses of gilded bronze or just polished yellow bronze?

Generally speaking, however, bronze armor was not used by the time of the Roman conquering armies, and therefore our museum displays are unbalanced. The Roman legionary's helmet was iron, and how few exist! Handbooks and children's books illustrate them, and helmets appear in modern movies wherever Roman soldiers are needed—but the artists must take their cue from the marble reliefs depicting the army at work. That there was some life, however, in the tradition of bronze armor is evident not only from the imperial cuirasses which we have mentioned. Gladiators, too, sometimes wore it—handsome gladiatorial armor is preserved. There is also bronze "parade armor," particularly helmets, most amazingly bizarre and theatrical, each with a complete face (visor) and an extraordinary and fantastic hair arrangement. These sets of "parade armor" are commonest in the provinces in the third century after Christ. One explanatory theory is that the Roman army posts used to stage, instead of a review or parade, a sort of mock battle or a battle from a mythological tale, and that the helmets helped distinguish from the good guys the bad (and usually barbarian) guys who were the enemy. The true explanation remains in doubt, though the artistic quality and technical perfection of some of this "parade armor" is notable.

This chapter has been a mere review of the creations of the Greek, Etruscan, and Roman bronzeworkers. It has attempted to explain what they made and how important it was quantitatively and how high in quality. Statues, statuettes, vases, mirrors, furniture, and armor have been the categories. I have omitted many commonplace items like common hardware—hinges, locks, keys—and such rarer items as sparkling roofs of buildings. Occasionally I have made attempts to explain the technical processes involved and in a few cases to suggest the organization of the craft. But on the whole, I must leave many problems about their manufacture unanswered.

Interest in ancient sculpture is not a recent phenomenon, as the many Renaissance replicas and imitations well attest. Much more recent, however, is our interest in ancient technology, sharpened not simply by the natural curiosity of knowing how something was made but also by the realization that our aesthetic enjoyment can be heightened by such knowledge. Indeed technique often conditions style, and, though tradition and individual genius are mostly responsible for the appearance of a work of art, medium and mode of manufacture often play an almost equally important role. The perfect balance is attained when both technique and artistic conception are taken into account as interplaying and independent factors, but, since much has already been written on the aesthetic value of ancient sculpture, we can here concentrate on its purely technical aspect.

Origin In Greek sculpture the problem of technique is strictly connected with the problem of origin.[1] Unlike the artistic development of other civilizations, Greek sculpture in stone began almost *ex abrupto*, in nearly perfected technical form, just as the Greek goddess Athena had sprung fully grown and armed from the head of Zeus. Attempts have been made to derive the sculptural production of the late seventh/early sixth century B.C. from local traditions of terra-cotta modeling and wood carving, but while these speculations are justifiable on a purely stylistic basis, they become less plausible once the difference in techniques is taken into account. The soft consistency of clay as contrasted with the hardness of limestone or marble needs little comment; but even wood carving, at first seemingly related to stone cutting, proves to be quite different when we consider the problem of supply: the difficulty of cutting down a tree and shaping its trunk is minimal compared to the difficulty of quarrying stone. Finally, despite the many learned arguments brought forth to prove the dependence of marble statues on terra cotta, bronze, or even ivory statuettes, the variation in dimensions, from small to life-size, implies a corresponding variation in approach as well as technique. The many details so easily blurred or abbreviated in a statuette could not be overlooked in natural proportions, and

1   Unfinished statuettes of King Mycerinus. Egypt. IV Dynasty, ca. 2500 B.C. Courtesy, Museum of Fine Arts, Boston, MFA Expedition.

2   Male torso from Naxos, Greece. Archaic Period. C. Blümel, *Griechische Bildhauer an der Arbeit* (Leipzig, 1927), Pl. V.

3   Side View of No. 2. Blümel, *Griechische Bildhauer an der Arbeit*, Pl. VI.

the earliest extant Greek stone statues are far from being magnified translations of smaller prototypes.

The conclusion seems inescapable: if the Greeks dared quarry large blocks and fashion them into clearly articulated, technically sound human representations, without obvious experimenting and fumbling, they must have learned their technique elsewhere, from another country where stone carving was a long-established tradition. This technical necessity seems to me so compelling as to render idle speculation whether the early Greek *kouroi* (naked youths) or *korai* (draped girls) resemble Egyptian statuary. Technique and style may be interconnected, but learning a technique does not necessarily imply accepting a style, and the Greeks could have learned Egyptian methods without necessarily also adopting their repertoire. If stylistic similarities do not appear as pronounced to some scholars as to others, nonetheless technical affinities can be objectively pointed out: the use of the same tools, the four-sided approach to a block, the finishing of a statue through the removal of successive layers, as if unveiling the body underneath its stone wrappings (Figures 1–3).

The use of a specific canon, based on Egyptian methods and measurements, is perhaps more debatable.[2] Though Egyptian blocks with superimposed grid lines have been found, as well as representations of statuary within such grids, no comparable example exists among extant Greek sculpture. The horse from Sparta (Figure 4), the one well-known instance of carving along outlines, does not prove or disprove the practice because it is not a human form (therefore the canon was not applicable) and because it is of small dimensions and therefore easy enough to attack from one side only, along a given contour. Whether the archaic Greek sculptor adopted Egyptian proportions, and for how long, has, however, little bearing on where he learned his technique. It is here assumed that this happened either directly in Egypt, in some of the Greek trading posts or mercenary colonies established there, or perhaps even in Greek territory, probably in the marble-bearing Cyclades, the so-called "stepping stones" for sailors between Greece and the African coast. That the Greeks were justly proud of their newly learned skill is shown by one of the early *kouroi*, set up in Delos by the Naxian Euthykartides, who emphatically inscribed the base as both the maker and the dedicator of the statue.[3] It is thus shown that the sculptor can supply his own demand, and that therefore the production of stone sculpture is not determined exclusively by the sudden open-

4   Statuette of horse and rider from Sparta, Greece. Archaic period. C. Blümel, *Greek Sculptors at Work* (London, 1955), Fig. 9.

ing of a market or the advent of favorable conditions but also and most important by the acquisition of sculpting ability. It is also interesting to note that the beginning of monumental sculpture in Greece coincides with the beginning of monumental stone architecture not so much because a stone temple demanded a stone cult statue but because the same technique and the same tools could be used for both architecture and sculpture. In a way, every Greek stonemason was a sculptor, and the skill involved in the fluting of a column was as great as that required for the making of a statue; the difference between the two artisans—the mason and the sculptor—was a difference of conception rather than of competence, and any stone cutter of antiquity must have achieved a very high level of technical proficiency.

Greek Technique— Archaic Period (Ca. 625– 480 B.C.) The making of a Greek statue began in the quarry.[4] Naxos and Paros, among the Cyclades, were the most frequently used sources of stone: their white marble is coarse-grained and sugary in appearance, relatively easy to carve when freshly cut. Toward the end of the archaic period Athens started exploiting its domestic quarries on Mount Penteli on a large scale; Pentelic marble is finer in texture than the island marble and contains iron, which rusts when exposed to prolonged weathering (hence the famous honey color of the Parthenon), but it has a brilliant whiteness when just carved (notice for instance the newly reconstructed Stoa of Attalos in the Athenian Agora). Marble from the island of Thasos is characterized by shiny specks in its texture, Hymettian marble (from Mount Hymettos near Athens) by its bluish tinge. Other important quarries existed elsewhere in the Greek world, the most historically famous being perhaps the *Latomie* of Syracuse, where the Athenian prisoners were put to work after the disastrous expedition against Sicily during the Peloponnesian War (415–413 B.C.).

We do not know for sure whether the sculptor traveled to the source of stone or whether his specifications were carried out by the quarriers, but certainly each block was outlined for cutting with the basic shape of the statue-to-be in mind, so that a minimum of waste would result. In some cases even triangular blocks have been postulated, and, to go back to architectural example, there is evidence that column drums were often quarried along circular outlines. To separate the block from the rock the masons usually cut shallow grooves along predetermined contours, using either a metal saw (in limestone or poros, soft limestone, quarries) or pick hammer, punch or point, and mallet. They then deepened these grooves, either with chisels or by drilling a series of holes at short intervals and then breaking the intervening stone "bridges." The final detachment of the block from the hillside was accomplished with wedges, sometimes of metal but more often of wood wetted to promote swelling[5] (Figure 5).

Since even the early archaic statues were often of colossal proportions, the blocks involved were extremely heavy, and transportation from the quarry to the harbor and then to the sculptor's workshop was among the most difficult and expensive items involved in the making of a monument. It is therefore understandable that some preliminary shaping and elimination of superfluous stone would have taken place in the quarry itself, as indicated by some unfinished pieces abandoned there in antiquity, possibly because of the discovery of some flaw in the block. This preliminary work, usually carried out with the point, punch, and mallet, was probably more extensive during the archaic period when statues traditionally adhered to types and the *kouros* was standardized in a fixed position with arms straight along the flanks and left leg forward. The *kore* (female type) afforded the individual sculptor more choice in the rendering of the costume, and therefore proportionately less stone could be removed by the quarriers.[6] Though it has been suggested that this practice was dropped ca. 500 B.C., the presence in the quarry of some roughly shaped Roman examples would seem to indicate that the preliminary carving was never entirely discontinued, or at least that in some cases, when the size in particular might have made it advisable, the sculptor indeed traveled to the source and did some initial work there.[7] In Roman times we also know of sarcophagi being roughly carved in the quarries prior to shipment to Rome or other parts of the Roman Empire, but by the late second century after Christ the production of sarcophagi had become so standardized that such practice is not surprising and cannot readily be compared with that of more creative periods of ancient art.

In the sculptor's workshop the most important phase in the making of a statue began. If the block had not been already shaped in the quarry, the artist probably drew an outline of the figure he intended to make on all four sides of his stone, thus flattening a potentially three-dimensional composition on a two-dimensional plane.[8] He then attacked his block at right angles, along the predetermined outlines, but taking care to progress at the same rate of speed on all sides, so that at no point during his work would the front of the statue be more advanced than the back or the sides. Again, this process can be likened to the fluting of a column, where first the protective mantle around the circular drum was removed by faceting, and then each facet was deepened into a flute, but in different stages. Thus the last layer, that which formed the last protection before the final surface was reached, could be removed by the most skilled master, while the preliminary phase could be carried out by a minor apprentice.

This graduated approach had a twofold purpose: first, it prevented the sculptor from seriously miscutting his block, since a mistake in the upper layers would be much easier to correct than a mistake at the final depth; second, it allowed him to follow coherently, from front to back and vice versa, all the various details of his figure, be it the extension of a muscle or the course of a fold. Greek sculpture is indeed eminently logical, even if not always true to nature, and discrepancies between front and back very seldom occur (in contrast to the practice in Roman copies) because of this "unveiling" approach. Even in pedimental statues, where the back was not to be seen, it differed from the front only in the degree of finish, not of carving, and not because of religious scruples, as sometimes suggested ("The god could see it, even if the human eye could not"), but because of the sculptor's need to keep track of his composition at all stages.

The tools (Figure 6) used to accomplish this "revealing" of the inner statue from within the block were basically the same as those in use today. It is generally believed that ancient Greek tools were made of bronze, which would have made imperative a constant sharpening of cutting edges and points. But literary references and actual finds attest that iron was well known and used in the archaic period, and therefore there is no reason to assume that the ancient stone cutters did not use it for their tools simply because none have survived.[9] Of these tools we have already mentioned the saw, the pick hammer, the punch, the point, the mallet, the drill, and the chisel. This last instrument occurred in a variety of sizes and forms: with a broad blade over three centimeters wide (drove), with the cutting edge straight (flat chisel), or curved (bull-nosed or curved chisel), or dented (claw or toothed chisel). This last form seems to have been a definite Greek invention of ca. 560–550 B.C., used both for statuary and for architecture, and spread abroad by traveling Greek workmen, for instance to Persia.[10] Conversely, the drove, inherited from the Egyptians, was not used in the classical period, perhaps

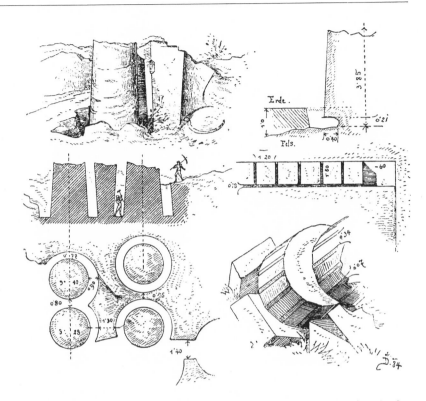

5 Quarrying of columns at Selinus, Sicily. J. Dürm, *Handbuch der Architektur: Die Baukunst der Griechen.* 3rd ed. (Leipzig, 1910), p. 94, Fig. 62.

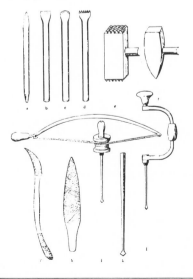

6

Sculptors' tools: *a*, punch; *b*, flat chisel; *c*, curved chisel; *d*, claw chisel; *e*, boucharde; *f*, trimming hammer; *g, h*, rasps; *i*, bow drill; *k*, drill; *l*, auger. Blümel, *Greek Sculptors*, p. 28, Fig. 17.

because it was replaced by the claw and flat chisels, which were easier to handle.

Other chronological hints can be obtained from the drill. To judge by the traces on available monuments, the simple type. which bored a vertical hole, was the only form of the instrument in use until the introduction of the running drill between 370 and 350 B.C. The basic difference between the two consisted in the fact that the newer variety could bore a channel along a horizontal surface, if held at the proper angle; previously, grooves were carved by drilling a series of holes at short intervals and then by eliminating the interconnecting "membranes" of stone, as described previously for the quarrying process. Despite the obvious advantages afforded by the running drill, and the fact that a similar tool is used by Greek and Italian masons today, some scholars deny that it ever existed in antiquity, a position partly supported by the observation that the older manner of cutting channels, with the simple drill, was never entirely discontinued[11] (Figure 7).

Equally controversial is the flat chisel, not in its occurrence, but in the manner of its use. Some scholars contend that the Greeks carved their statues mainly by means of the point or punch, held at right angles to the block, which "stunned" or "bruised" the marble by breaking the crystalline formation under the surface.[12] The Romans, the same scholars hold, carved their statues with a flat chisel which simply "peeled" but did not stun the marble: hence the difference between the velvety surface of a Greek original and the shiny appearance of a Roman copy. The most recent discussion of the subject denies any basic difference in technique between Greeks and Romans but emphasizes simply the extreme accuracy with which the Greeks used the flat chisel on specific areas, to carve rather than to smooth the shapes they wanted.[13] It is, however, true that in Roman times the traces of the flat chisel are more readily discerned in places where the Greek sculptor would have carefully eliminated them, and in some extreme cases, such as Palmyrene sculpture in soft limestone (Figure 8), the chisel was used to create textural effects reminiscent of wood carving. It is perhaps correct to state that the Greeks used their tools primarily for utilitarian reasons, trying to eliminate all traces of tooling from the completed work, while the sculptors of Roman times exploited certain technical processes for aesthetic and coloristic purposes. It is also pertinent to repeat

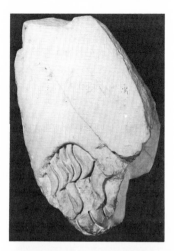

7

Unfinished head, showing locks carved with drill. Hellenistic period. Private collection. Photo, P. Cleaver.

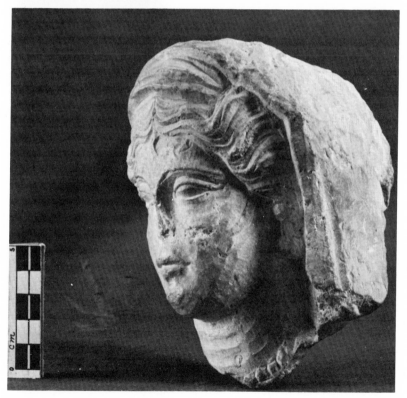

8   Palmyrene head from Carthage, showing marks of flat chisel. Roman period. Courtesy, Bryn Mawr College, Ella Riegel Museum. Photo, K. Dimler.

here Adam's statement that the Greek sculptor "used the most convenient tool in the most convenient way for any job."[14]

When a Greek statue had been entirely "revealed" from its enveloping block, and the surface had been smoothed over with natural abrasives or metal rasps, a great deal of detailed work still remained to be done. Since economy was the strict rule in carving, any projecting part which might have caused considerable waste of stone was usually added separately. For instance, in archaic *korai* whose arms are bent and hands outstretched with an offering, the forearm was usually carved from a separate piece of marble and inserted into an appropriate socket at the elbow, where it was secured in position by one or more of several means: glue, marble cement, marble tenons, or metal dowels. The same "piecing" system was at times followed for elaborate folds, helmet crests, and other accessories, and, as early as the sixth century B.C., for separately carved heads, attached by means of a marble tenon into a corresponding socket between the shoulders.[15] Many accessories were added in bronze or lead: not only objects that in nature would also have been of metal (such as pins, earrings, necklaces, mantle clasps, weapons, helmets, and other pieces of armor) (Figure 9) but even curls or eyelashes. In the latter case the entire eye was often, though by no means always, made of a vitreous paste or some other contrasting material and inserted separately in the empty orbital cavity: a technique "borrowed" from bronze casting, where the hollow heads could easily be supplied with eyes introduced from within.

If the eyes of a statue were carved of the same marble as the head, the required effect was obtained by painting pupil and iris. This was only one of the many touches of color applied to the finished piece: the lips were also painted red, the hair was tinted, and the many garments were differentiated by color more effectively than by carved patterns. We do not know to what extent the fleshy parts of a statue were also painted over, but presumably there was some attempt to distinguish between the whiter complexion of a woman and the ruddier skin of a man, as traditional in monumental and vase painting, while Negroid figures were made of a darker tone.[16] Some distinction should also be made between the process of painting and that of *ganosis,* as applied to statuary. According to ancient authors, wax was spread over the tinted parts of a naked marble figure, not only to preserve the color but also to give a certain polish and shine to the surface. Accordingly, we may surmise that

9   *Kouros* from Ilissos, Greece, showing inserted arm and holes for attachment of metal clasps on breast. 6th century B.C. National Museum, Athens, Greece. Photo, German Archaeological Institute, Athens.

though the structure of the marble itself played little part in Greek sculpture (and hence little attention was given to the natural color or veining of certain stones), the high polish later attained by the Romans was perhaps partly supplied in earlier times by this process of *ganosis*.[17] Our own taste, formed over generations of unpainted sculpture, finds it difficult to appreciate the gaudy appearance of certain classical reconstructions. The ancient marbles themselves have seldom preserved extensive traces of their original coloring; when this survives, it is usually so faded as to suggest that pastel tones only were originally used. Poros sculptures, however, because of the highly absorbent nature of the medium, have retained sufficient paint to indicate that lively hues were prevalently employed, partly because they were considered truer to nature, partly because Greek monuments were mostly displayed outdoors. The vivid light of the Mediterranean sun renders the untinted whiteness of freshly cut marble almost blinding to the naked eye.

The advantages of painting are particularly noticeable in the case of relief, where the neutral background was at first colored a solid red and, from ca. 530 B.C. onward, predominantly blue. This process allowed the individual figures to stand out more clearly against the contrasting "backdrop"; this same emphasis on contours and shapes, voids and masses, characterized a great deal of Greek artistic production, from architecture to sculpture, to painting and mosaics, until at least the Hellenistic period.

The Use of Models— Severe and High Classical Periods (480–400 B.C.)   Toward the end of the sixth century B.C., an increased skill in bronze casting rendered stone statuary practically obsolete. The demand was for athletic monuments in lively poses, almost impossible in the more brittle medium of marble, while cult statues, because of their nature, were made akrolithic[18] (so as to be colossal with little expense) or in gold and ivory when expense was of no concern. Indeed Pliny, or his ancient sources, list no sculptors in marble for the first half of the fifth century B.C., while many bronze masters are mentioned for the same period.[19]

But marble carving was still indispensable for the adornment of architecture, and the great temple of Zeus at Olympia was erected during the crucial span from 470 to 456 B.C.[20] The many statues which filled its pediments, and the metopal reliefs, are remarkable not only for their new style but also for their new textural appearance, which suggests a different technical process.

While an archaic treasury or other small structure involved a sculptural program limited enough to be carried out by a few masters, the colossal enterprises of the following periods imposed the necessity of a master mind with many carvers under his orders. In view of the large dimensions involved, the necessity for advanced planning, the coherence of the decorative program, the intricacy of the composition, it is only logical to postulate that some preliminary models were required, and while for the metopes they could have been simple drawings or sketches, for the more complex pedimental figures they must have been three-dimensional, presumably in wax or clay. Of these two media the latter is perhaps the more probable, since bronze casting, which was the popular form of sculpture at the time, required the use of clay for the making of the "prototype" and of the mold. Indeed the drapery of the Olympia figures looks so different from the crisp rendering of the archaic period that only one term seems to describe it graphically enough: doughy. The manner in which cloth is made to adhere to the bodies, to collapse when it touches the ground, to arrange itself in wide, flat ridges with channels that bulge at the edges, as if a stick had been drawn through a plastic medium, suggests inevitably the existence of clay prototypes.

Though many scholars would admit the necessity for models of a sort at this early date, few would agree on whether and how the dimensions of the trial piece could be magnified and transferred into stone. The intentional breaking of the law of frontality in the sculpture of the severe style of this period implies that the grid system could no longer be followed, and the new three-dimensional appearance of statuary in the fifth century is incompatible with the previous four-sided approach; we, therefore, can no longer think in terms of outlines drawn on the surface of the quarry block. It is possible that a rudimentary pointing system had already been invented as early as 470 B.C., by which specific prominent areas were selected in the model and transferred first to the uncarved block to serve as main reference points. From them other measurements could be taken by means of calipers and plumb lines. Obviously the model was not worked out in all details, and a certain degree of freedom and inventiveness could be exercised by the individual master who executed the piece; but the general proportions and the relationship of the figure to the surrounding elements could easily be worked out in this fashion. In the Olympia sculptures, several instances of an uncarved area in the center of the forehead may suggest that one of the initial "points" was located there.[21]

An interesting example of a slightly different method is provided by a female head in the Rhode Island School of Design Museum[22] (Figure 10). Usually considered an original of ca. 420 B.C., this piece probably belonged to a pedimental or other protected setting, for it once carried metal jewelry. But while some holes in the marble can be explained in terms of bronze attachments, three of them are too shallow for actual insertions and are in positions incompatible with standard adornments: one appears over the hair on the axis of the forehead, while the other two are located in front of the ears, just below the strands covering the temples. These unexplainable holes could be the remains of a rudimentary pointing system by which the head was copied from the original model. The technique used in modern times can leave traces of two kinds: either small holes in the center of mounds, or, as in this case, fairly large holes as centers of depressions.[23] These measuring points would help the master in determining the depth of carving required in any given area to imitate the prototype; sunk first at the necessary level, they would be automatically eliminated by removing the surrounding stone to achieve the final finish. They are still visible in the Providence head probably because the monument was not meant for close inspection, and the greater relief of the right half of the asymmetrical face would account for the deeper hole over that temple.

It is impossible to tell whether the difference in method between the Olympia sculptures and the Providence head, approximately forty years younger, depends purely on chronology. It is, however, certain that classical sculpture, from the early fifth century B.C. onward, looks remarkably different from that of the archaic period. Though other factors contributed to this change, unquestionably a technical factor, such as the introduction of plastic models postulated before, must also have intervened. The doughy quality of early fifth-century drapery tends to disappear with the passing of time, but changes in appearance should now be attributed to style, not to technique. From the point of view of sheer workmanship and technical ability, it could perhaps be maintained that the sixth century had already achieved a peak never to be surpassed in later periods, and all further experimentation lay in the direction of balance, three-dimensionality, and naturalism: fields in which bronze statuary could contribute more effective solutions than could marble carving.

Technique and Style— Praxiteles (Fourth Century B.C.) It is all the more remarkable that in a period of famous metal workers such as the fourth century B.C. a master carver like Praxiteles could emerge; but he is known to have also worked in bronze, and his main achievement in marble consists perhaps in his skillful inclusion of technical necessities into the composition. Since marble statues tend to break at the weakest points, which in a human figure are the wrists and the ankles, they need to be reinforced and supported in such areas, and toward the end of the archaic phase this was traditionally done by leaving small portions of the original block uncarved between the various limbs. These unseemly struts had, however, no parallel in nature, and the answer to the problem was ultimately found in the use of metal, for it did not require such strengthening devices. Praxiteles boldly introduced tree trunks and other supports alongside his major figures, but as part of the subject matter: his Apollo Sauroktonos leans against a tree in order to kill the lizard, the Knidian Aphrodite holds her drapery over the vessel which contains the water for her bath. The nonprofessional viewer senses no contradiction in these extraneous elements, and indeed he would miss them should they be removed from the composition; yet they owe their existence primarily to structural necessity.

Admittedly Praxiteles was also interested in experimentation with off-balance poses, and the argument becomes somewhat circular: his statues lean to justify the support, yet the support allows them to lean. But since the famous Knidian Aphrodite is the most traditionally balanced of all Praxitelean compositions and yet the support is still needed and cleverly dissimulated within the general scheme, it is perhaps legitimate to assume that technical requirements have here a slight predominance over stylistic inclinations.

From this moment onward it is admittedly most difficult to distinguish between technique and style. For instance, the same Praxiteles is famous for his *sfumato* technique, which blurred the outlines of facial features and lent the statue a shimmering appearance, as if viewed through a thin curtain of smoke. This effect was probably obtained by rubbing over the carved details, and it is therefore a technique, but it was obviously prompted by artistic taste. Similarly, the master emphasized the contrast between the smooth skin of the face and the rougher texture of the hair: a coloristic contrast rendered through technical means but for aesthetic purposes. The Hellenistic period excelled in these practices, and a few could here be mentioned as borderline cases between technique and style: the practice of drilling a furrow between hair and cheek to emphasize the separation and different texture of the two; the general rendering of hair strands by means of channels of shadow; the attempt to render skin as thick and oily to suggest barbarians. But sculpture of the Hellenistic period was still substantially dominated by metalwork. Marble carving of freestanding statuary came again to prominence only during the first century B.C., when the opening of the Roman market created a great demand for replicas and imitations of the classical masterpieces. Entire ateliers, in Attica, Asia Minor, and Magna Graecia, devoted themselves to the production of copies which, because of the patrons for whom they were made, are usually referred to as "Roman," often translating into stone, for economic reasons, a bronze prototype.

The Technique of Copying— Hellenistic Period (331–31 B.C.) Because of this ever increasing demand, a new technical factor comes to the fore: the making of plaster casts which could be distributed to distant workshops and enabled the reproduction in Italy or elsewhere of originals set up in Athens or Asia Minor. The exact date for the inception of this practice is controversial, for a passage in Pliny's *Natural History* (xxxv. 153) has been interpreted to suggest that Lysistratos, the brother of Lysippos and hence a fourth-century man, was the first to make plaster casts of the human body and to introduce the practice of taking casts from statues;[24] but Gisela M. Richter refers the citation to Pasiteles, who lived in the first century B.C.[25] In technical terms it is admittedly difficult to notice a sharp difference in the carving of the human body between the classical and the Hellenistic periods, as one would expect had the practice of making plaster casts of living models been extensively introduced at the end of the fourth century B.C. Pliny's passage is unclear, and, because it refers primarily to bronze casting, it is perhaps idle to speculate on its application to marble carving. It is, however, significant that foundries, as they had once supplied the stone sculptors with the inspiration and perhaps even the technique for making clay models, may later have provided them with the basic knowledge for the mechanical reproduction of earlier works, much more accurate than the approximate duplication of models in the classical period, by means of plaster casts or molds which could be sold to the various workshops of copyists catering to Roman patrons. Indeed, the same classical masterpiece could be copied so accurately by different masters at different times that frag-

10   Female head, showing
large hole for attachment
of metal ornament on
hair and smaller hole,
below hairline, for mea-
suring point. Fifth cen-
tury B.C. Courtesy, Rhode
Island School of Design
Museum, Providence, R.I.

11   Hermes from Olympia, Greece, showing unfinished area over shoulder
blades. Photo, N. Stournaras.

mentary replicas of different provenience have been completed
with plaster casts from other, better-preserved copies without need
for altering scale or single dimensions.[26]

The changes brought about in the Hellenistic period involved
primarily the reproduction of models or of earlier originals, hence
the phases preliminary to the actual carving of a statue. The
basic difference in technique consists in the fact that now, with
the greater degree of accuracy made possible by a perfected pointing system, the front of a figure could be almost entirely carved
before the back was tackled, so that no longer did a statue in
the making present the same degree of finish in all parts at a
given point. The latter approach, well attested for the sixth century, must have been followed fairly closely also during classical
times, even if preliminary models were used as general guidelines
for the carving. It is only with wholesale copying that the master
could concentrate on the most important aspects of a monument,
leaving for the end the invisible areas, or even neglecting them
entirely if he knew that the sculpture was to be set up in a
niche or in an otherwise sheltered position (Figure 11).

Roman The technical innovations of Roman sculpture, in some respects
Technique more sophisticated than the Greek, lie in a different field. The
vastness of the Empire gave the Romans access to different
quarries and varieties of marbles, so that many of their statues
were carved from stone of contrasting colors, eliminating the need
for much added paint. Roman taste seems to have delighted in
textural contrasts: juxtaposition not only of different materials
but also of different surfaces, obtained by tooling. Particularly
interesting in this respect is the high polish of fleshy areas during
Hadrianic times (A.D. 117–138), contrasting with the rougher
finish of hair and beard: a contrast exploited to the utmost in
later times (third and fourth century), when the rendering of
the beard is little more than a stippling of the surface against
the almost porcelainlike quality of the cheeks (Figure 12).

Coloristic contrasts started in Flavian times (A.D. 69–96) with
the peculiar use of the drill to penetrate the hair mass, so that
the final effect, in extreme cases, resembles a sponge. Greek masters had occasionally used drill holes for accents of shadow, and
in the first half of the fifth century B.C. even to mark the
center of curls, as apparent in the Olympia sculptures (Figure
13). But this last practice seems to have vanished with the severe
period, and henceforth punctuation with the drill was limited

12

Portrait head of Caracalla. A.D.
211–217. Courtesy, Metropolitan
Museum of Art, New York.

13   Head from Temple of Zeus, Olympia, 14
Greece, showing use of drill in hair and
beard. Photo, N. Stournaras.

Female head of the time
of Domitian (A.D. 81–
96). Courtesy, British
Museum, London.

to the diminutive holes at the outer corners of the mouth or, less frequently, the inner corners of the eyes. The Flavians emphasized also such holes, but especially delighted in burrowing into the hair (Figure 14), a practice which continued into the second century but without the same emphasis on basic round forms. The treatment of hair under the Antonine Emperors (A.D. 138–192) received one more technical enrichment. Ever since the second century B.C. long strands and locks had been separated from each other by channels cut with the drill; now these channels are spanned at intervals by small "bridges": interconnecting slivers of stone left uncarved from lock to lock.

Another technical feature worthy of mention is the rendering of the eyes. Starting late during Hadrian's reign, pupils were marked by a shallow hole, which was moved progressively closer to the upper lid, finally conveying to some portraits an almost moribund expression. Together with the single drill hole we also find, in the late second and early third centuries, instances of double holes with a small section of stone left in between, as if a light reflection were captured in the pupil (see Figure 12)—a mannerism repeated by Bernini, centuries later, in some of his sculptures.

Finally, as technique, one can include the treatment of rel'ef during the Tetrarchy (late third and early fourth centuries), as best exemplified by the Column of Diocletian in the Roman Forum, or the Arch of Galerius at Saloniki. Drill channels are cut not only into the drapery, like heavily inked lines but all around the figures in unbroken contours, so that even in places where the stone has weathered or broken off, the missing portions can be clearly visualized on the basis of their still preserved outlines against the background.

The Sculptor's Social Status In technical terms, Roman Imperial art added no new tools or methods, but simply different ways of exploiting technical effects. The range of Roman sculpture, moreover, varied so greatly from the capital to the provinces that any general statement is bound to find its contradiction somewhere. It is perhaps significant to point out here how different Roman sculpture was from the Greek, not because of purely stylistic or technical considerations, but because of its underlying approach. Roman sculpture consists mostly of historical relief and portraiture; cult statues existed, but they were patterned after the Greek and revered more for their function than for their appearance or the fame of the master who made them. The propagandistic nature of most Roman monuments prevented the name of the maker from prevailing over that of the sitter for the portrait or the protagonist of the relief, and we therefore find Roman sculpture curiously anonymous, as contrasted with the tradition of great masters prevalent for Greek art. The status of the Roman sculptor could never have been too exalted, and the ancient sources are singularly silent on this point, but a reflection of Roman attitudes can be found even in mentions of famous Greek artists, since not even the position of a Polykleitos or a Pheidias was considered enviable by the Romans.[27] The development of Roman sculpture must have depended on workshops and the impact of historical events more than on dominating personalities, and sometimes the strongest influence on artistic development might have originated from the Emperor rather than from a master carver.

The Greek picture, at first glance, appears entirely different. Literary sources credit single sculptors with daring innovations of lasting consequence, and traditional scholarship can still write treatises on Greek sculpture by masters and their schools. Obviously, single individuals attained great reputation in their own and in later times. For example, Lysippos became Alexander the Great's court sculptor and must have enjoyed considerable favor also with his successors. Yet we learn, significantly, that the master's production ranged from colossal statuary many times over life size to a simple vase to serve as emblem for a newly founded city.[28] Extant building accounts of the classical period do not suggest that masters were paid considerably more than apprentices, or sculptors more than stoneworkers, and often payment was made on the basis of number of figures rather than of complexity or excellence of performance.[29] It is therefore fitting to point out once again the fallacy of judging Greek sculpture exclusively through the literary sources: they name famous sculptors who for us are largely only shadows, and to whom attributions are made on the most tenuous and controversial grounds, while excavations have brought to light signatures of otherwise unknown artists and quantities of anonymous work. It is the excellence of this general production, the high competence of its workmanship, the accuracy of its finish which justify an enduring interest in ancient sculpture above and beyond the appeal of the great names and support the belief that every Greek who worked in stone was perhaps not an artistic genius but was invariably a master carver.

Greek vases were made to hold the three liquids essential to the Greek way of life: wine, water, and olive oil. Since their shapes reflect their function, it is easy to determine their use.[1]

Forms and The *amphora* for the storage of wine was one of the most common
Uses types of vases (Figures 1 and 2). It is a sturdy vase with two large serviceable handles near the mouth. The *hydria* for holding water is a large pitcher-shaped vase with three handles. Two small handles on the shoulder were used for lifting the hydria when filling it at a fountain house and the large handle at the back was used for pouring. Customarily the Greeks mixed water with their wine and for this purpose they used large punch bowls known as *kraters*. The krater had a large mouth to allow for the mixing of the wine and water and so that it might be ladled into the drinking cups.

There are two main types of drinking cups: the *skyphos* and the *kylix*. The skyphos is a large, deep, simple cup form with two small handles at the rim. It was not very elegant but extremely practical. On the other hand, the kylix while less practical was infinitely more attractive. The large, graceful, shallow bowl was balanced on a stemmed foot with two handles near the rim. Among the variations in shapes of the kylikes, one type has an almost continuously curved line from the lip of the bowl to the edge of the foot. Its delicate silhouette and gently curving shallow bowl is a triumph of the potter's art. An additional purpose of the handles on cups was to permit them to be hung on a peg in the wall when not in use.

Olive oil was stored in the *lekythos*, a tall cylindrical vase with a narrow neck, a cup-shaped mouth, and a single handle. The narrow neck allowed the oil to be poured in a fine stream. the mouth was constructed with a sharp edge on the inside to cut off the poured flow of oil without dripping. The single handle was for pouring. In addition to these principal vase forms, there were small flat plates, pottery boxes to hold trinkets, and cosmetics, small globular shaped vases designed to hold scented oils, and beakers, mugs, stands, funnels, lamps, and lamp fillers, all designed for utilitarian purposes.

Greek vases were functional and designed to be used. In all

1   Black-figured vases. *Left to right:* skyphos, amphora, amphora, hydria, stamnos. Courtesy, Joseph V. Noble.

2   Red-figured vases. *Left to right:* amphora, hydria, krater, kylix, lekythos. Courtesy, Joseph V. Noble.

Greek pottery there is an elegant balance between utilitarianism and beauty. Surprisingly enough the emphasis was on perfecting the existing designs rather than exploring the development of new shapes. This constant repetition in the production of standard shapes could have been disastrous, for it might have encouraged mass reproduction without artistic development. However, it was this faithful reiteration of shapes and the striving for perfection within the framework of the shapes that caused Greek pottery to develop in such a magnificent manner. The fact that the pottery was intended for daily use gave it a sense of a validity and forced it to be practical. Therefore it never degenerated into ostentatious bric-a-brac void of regard for function.

Origin The origin of clay-forming techniques seems to have occurred about seven thousand years ago at the beginning of the Pottery Neolithic period with the freehand forming of a vessel from a lump of clay. This was accomplished by pushing, pinching, and molding the clay until the desired shape was achieved. Examples of this earliest technique have been found in various sites in Asia Minor. Later the process was improved by winding strands of clay one on top of another to build a pot. A flat hand-formed base disc was made, and then a fixed strand was coiled around it. To consolidate the strands, they were pinched and smoothed to form a good joint. Additional strands were added and smoothed to build the pot to the desired height and shape. To help in the compacting and smoothing operation sometimes a rounded stone was held inside the wall of the pot while the outside surface was beaten with a paddle. Surprisingly fine pottery with walls of extremely uniform thickness was produced using this process. The coil process was used in the construction of plain utilitarian pottery intended for daily use. Unglazed cooking pots, simple water jars, and saucers were made for household purposes. Also, the extremely large *pithoi*, or storage jars, were always constructed by the coil method. The coil method has continued to be practiced widely in Greece even to the present day despite the invention of the potter's wheel.

A refinement of this technique involved forming the pot on a small piece of curved gourd or broken potsherd. These objects acted as a base during the building of the pot and as a pivot so that the vase could be rotated readily between the hands of the potter. This rotation was not the same as a potter's wheel but it did give the potter the opportunity to smooth the pot and adjust its symmetry as it was built.

Potter's The potter's wheel was invented near the end of the fourth mil-
Wheel lennium B.C., apparently in Asia Minor. Its use spread slowly throughout the Mediterranean. The earliest wheel-made pottery found at Troy dates from about 2500 B.C., and shortly thereafter its use spread to the Greek mainland.

The Greek potter's wheel was a heavy, sturdily built disc of wood, terra cotta, or stone about two feet in diameter. On the underside there was a socket which fitted over a low fixed pivot. The entire wheel was balanced to run true without wobble or vibration. It was customary practice to have a boy, presumably an apprentice, turn the wheel by hand, adjusting the speed to the command of the potter (Figure 3). The large size and weight of the wheel provided ample momentum once it was put into motion. The use of an assistant for the labor of the wheel-turning allowed the potter to use both hands in forming the vase and to devote his entire attention to it. The major invention involved in the potter's wheel and its principal advantage lies in the fact that in the rotation of the wheel the momentum transfers energy to the clay, which is then directed by the potter holding his hands virtually stationary. As he draws up the clay form, the clay is forced between his fingers, and he has but to direct it. The use of the kick wheel, or foot-operated potter's wheel, was unknown in classical times.

At the time of the earliest pottery making presumably each family produced its own pottery for its own use. In primitive groups most household tasks were performed by women. Therefore, they probably also made the pottery. With the introduction of the potter's wheel this work was largely taken over by a specialist, the professional potter, who for at least part of the year devoted his entire time to this business. Undoubtedly the potter was male because the use of machines was not usually considered a woman's work.

The shapes of most Greek vases were based on the cylindrical, conical, or spherical forms which are natural to the potter's wheel. The vases are forms in axial balance, symmetrically poised, held erect by a substantial base, and topped with a mouth and sometimes with a lid. The swelling curves, the practical handles, and the ample mouths take advantage of the capabilities, strength, and characteristics of the Greek clays. The proportions of a vase, the relation of the size of the mouth to the neck, of the neck to the body, and the entire vase to its foot, all fit together as a harmonious whole. For structural reasons, the handles widen at the point where they join the vase; this requ'rement for strength causes them to emerge gracefully from the vase and become organic parts of the composition of the entire piece.

The production of wheel-made pottery requires a high degree of manual dexterity and a continual application of artistic judgment. The form must evolve slowly but not too slowly, or it will collapse, and it has to be developed to its final state through a series of intermediate steps which must be anticipated by the potter. The tools of the potter are primarily his nimble fingers aided by a few simple implements. The vases were achieved freehand on the wheel with only a pair of dividers and a ruler as a guide. From a study of representations of ancient potters at work as seen on Greek vases, from an examination of Attic pottery itself, and with a knowledge of modern ceramic practice, it is possible to recreate the ancient methods of forming the vases.[2]

Clay Clay is an extremely abundant material formed by the continuing weathering and erosion of the surface of the earth. In the disintegration of the mineral feldspar, the alkali part is dissolved and carried away by water, leaving alumina and silica, which combine with water through hydrolysis to become pure clay. A clay which has remained at the site of the original feldspar from which it decomposed and has not been moved by water, wind, or glacier is termed a primary or residual clay and is uncontaminated and white. The whitish clay of Corinth is a relatively pure clay, whereas a clay that has been transported from its original location by the forces of erosion usually contains mineral or organic impurities acquired during movement. Attic clay is of this secondary type, and iron is present as an impurity; this accounts for its rich reddish-brown color. Clay deposits are found in many locations in Greece, but not all clays are suitable for making pottery; sometimes different clays are blended to vary the color or working properties. This practice was recorded in ancient times in *Geoponica* (vi. 3): "Not all earth is suitable for pottery, but with regard to potter's clay, some prefer the yellowish red, some the white, and others mix the two."

The clay as it came from the pit had mixed with it sand, small stones, decayed vegetable matter, and other foreign material, all

3   Potter throwing a vase on a potter's wheel turned by an apprentice. Glyptothek und Museum Antike Kleinkunst, Munich. Joseph V. Noble, *The Techniques of Painted Attic Pottery* (New York, 1965). This and the following items, as indicated, by permission of the publisher and The Metropolitan Museum of Art, New York.

4   Digging clay. Corinthian terra cotta plaque. National Museum, Berlin. Noble, *Painted Attic Pottery*.

of which had to be removed before the clay could be used (Figure 4). This was accomplished by mixing the clay with water and letting the mixture stand in large settling basins. The heavier impurities fell to the bottom, and the upper layer of clay and water was pumped or bailed into an adjoining basin. This process was repeated several times, and each settling purified the clay still further until the desired quality was obtained. Obviously, a purer clay was required to fashion a delicate kylix than for a large coarse-bodied pithos, or storage jar. When the clay reached the right degree of fineness, it was stored until needed. The storage of the clay over several months actually helped the working characteristics. It allowed the clay to take a "set" so that, while remaining malleable, the clay would hold its shape during the forming on the wheel.

The Greek potter had to know the properties of his clay in order to make the best use of it. The shrinkage of clay takes place in two distinct phases; the first occurs after the vase is formed during the thorough drying. The second shrinkage occurs during the firing process. On an average the total shrinkage is about $9\frac{1}{2}$ percent, or 9 percent in drying and $\frac{1}{2}$ percent in firing. The potter had to take this shrinkage into account when he was fashioning a vase. It is most probable that he made the lid for his vase at the same time he made the vase so that they would both shrink proportionately. In the manufacture of large pithoi, shrinkage was undesirable, and there was always the danger of the clay slumping during the forming operation. Therefore, temper was added to the clay. This temper consisted of sand and sometimes crushed rock. It not only minimized the shrinking but increased the stiffness of the clay during forming.

Forming The process of making a vase using the potter's wheel starts with the wedging, or beating of clay to remove air bubbles, to make it homogenous and to get the clay to the proper working consistency (Figure 5). A ball of clay is then centered on the rotating wheel and held firmly in cupped hands until it runs true without wobbling (Figure 6). Pressure of the thumb in the center of the ball of clay forms a thick-walled ring, which is slowly pulled up between the thumb and fingers, creating a cylinder (Figure 7). The cylinder can then either be opened into a bowl shape, drawn up as a long tube, flattened into a plate, or closed to form a sphere, at the pleasure of the potter (Figure 8). This process concludes the throwing operation and the vase is set aside to harden. The following day, when the clay has dried to a firm leather-hard state, the vase is centered upside-down on the wheel. As the wheel rotates, metal, bone, or wood tools are used to "turn" or refine the shape by shaving off unwanted clay (Figure 9). Then a wet sponge is used to smooth the vase. The foot of the vase or other sections may be thrown separately, turned, and joined to the body of the vase with clay slip (Figure 10). Finally, the vase as a combined unit is turned and the handles are added (Figure 11). The clay must still be in the somewhat plastic, leather-hard condition when the handles are applied with a clay slip binder or they will not adhere. The vase is now finished and ready for decorating and firing (Figures 12, 13, 14).

The marks of the tools used to form the vases were usually eradicated by the potter, but a careful examination will reveal some trace. The inside surfaces of vases with relatively narrow necks and mouths, such as the amphora, usually show the spiral ridges formed by the potter's fingers as he pulled up the clay during the forming operation.

At the completion of the throwing process the soft clay vase was removed from the wheel by cutting through the base of the vase with a cord or a wire (Figure 15). The wheel was allowed to rotate slowly while the cord was pulled through the clay. This left the characteristic pattern of spiral grooves on the bottom of the vase, which normally was removed during the turning operation (Figure 16). The body of a simple Greek vase, such as the deep cuplike skyphos, was thrown on the wheel and finished in one piece. Many others, like the kylix or the hydria, were thrown in sections, which were then joined with a slip of wet clay before being turned and finished on the wheel. The shape in many cases dictated where the joint was to occur. In the kylix it was at the point of juncture between the stem of the foot and the bowl. In the hydria, the joint occurs between the neck and the shoulder. The change of shape at these points tended to hide the joints. However, in the case of large hydrias, or kraters, the body of the vase was so large that it could not be formed properly in one piece, and it was necessary to throw the body in sections. These large bowl sections had to be joined on a continuous curved area where the joint could not be hidden by a point of articulation. Accordingly, after the sections were thrown and had become firm, they were assembled in their ultimate form and left to harden for a day. The hardening took place in a damp room to prevent too rapid drying and warpage. Later they were joined

5   Wedging clay. Noble, *Painted Attic Pottery*.

6   Centering the clay while the wheel revolves. Noble, *Painted Attic Pottery*.

7   A central hole is started. Noble, *Painted Attic Pottery*.

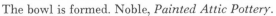

8   The bowl is formed. Noble, *Painted Attic Pottery*.

9

The bowl is turned
with a metal shaver.
Noble, *Painted Attic
Pottery*.

10

The foot is positioned
with clay ship.
Noble, *Painted Attic
Pottery*.

11

Handles are attached
to the bowl.
Noble, *Painted Attic
Pottery*.

12   Decorative elements are painted with a brush. Noble, *Painted Attic Pottery*.

13   Incised details are added with a sharp point. Noble, *Painted Attic Pottery*.

After firing, the kylix is finished. Noble, *Painted Attic Pottery*.

15

As the wheel revolves, a wire is drawn through the base. Noble, *Painted Attic Pottery*.

16

The base shows spiral wire marks. Noble, *Painted Attic Pottery*.

with wet clay slip, and the entire section was turned and smoothed so skillfully that on the outside of the vase, the joint was not visible.

Molds and Plastic Vases Almost all Greek pottery was made either by hand forming or on the potter's wheel. However, about one or two percent was produced using molds. Mold-made Greek pottery, a form of mass production, was little employed before the sixth century B.C. The manufacturing procedure began with the forming of the original model. The patrix, or master model, was made from clay by a sculptor, keeping in mind the ultimate use of the vase and the intermediate manufacturing steps.[3] In most plastic vases, the mold-made section was joined to a part, usually the mouth and sometimes a foot, formed on the potter's wheel. Therefore, the patrix was made for only the section to be molded. A patrix was usually made of terra cotta which was fired. A two-part mold was made over the patrix designed to separate on a line that would eliminate undercutting. The patrix was carefully covered on one side with clay. Then, after coating the edge of the clay which bisected the patrix with a substance that was probably animal fat or potash, the other side of the patrix was given a coat of clay. The animal fat ensured a ready cleavage of the two parts of the mold. When the two halves had dried slightly and had become firm, they were removed from the patrix and allowed to dry completely. The mold was retouched by hand and fired. Next a layer of soft clay was pressed into each of the two sections of the fired terra-cotta mold. Then the edges of the clay were scored and coated with clay slip for better adhesion, and the two halves of the mold were placed together and bound in position. Additional soft clay was smeared over the joint on the inside of the mold. Within a few hours the clay would have dried slightly and shrunk away from the surface of the mold. The mold was then opened and the piece removed. A mouth may have been formed on the wheel and attached with wet clay slip as was a hand-formed handle. This mold technique was used to make rather limited quantities of so-called plastic vases in the shape of animal heads and human figures (Figure 17).

Decoration The earliest Greek pottery being completely utilitarian quite understandably had little or no decoration. Gradually, incised lines were introduced as were slight decorative touches such as pinching the rim. It was discovered that a reddish clay could be fired to either a buff-red or a gray-black color depending on whether the fire was allowed to burn freely or was smothered. In Dimini ware, a Neolithic pottery from Thessaly, and in some types of Middle Helladic pottery, decorative lines of black and dark brown were applied by the use of natural mineral pigments. The lines and areas decorated with these natural pigments have a dull matte surface. Both on Crete and in the vicinity of Mycenae in the Helladic period there developed an extraordinarily finely decorated pottery in which naturalistic forms such as plants and marine creatures were used in highly imaginative patterns.

At this time there was invented the Greek black glaze which was of the greatest importance in the decoration of all subsequent Greek pottery. However, the destruction of the Late Helladic culture during the twelfth century B.C., including the deterioration of the pottery techniques, caused a dark age, from which Greek ceramics emerged anew about 1000 B.C. The decoration of the new pottery was based on geometric patterns which covered the ware with bands, concentric circles, and angular arrangements. By the eighth century B.C. human figures, drawn as simple linear silhouettes, were introduced into this geometric style.[4] In the following Proto-Attic ware the emphasis shifted from decorative patterns to human and animal figures, which were drawn in a more naturalistic outline technique. The potters of Corinth in the seventh century B.C. developed the incised line, adding detail and decisive clarity to their black glaze silhouette figures. From these techniques Athenian potters synthesized the Attic black-figure style by the end of the seventh century (Figure 18). Over the next one hundred years Athenian technology and artistic ability enabled Attic pottery to become unsurpassed in all Greece.

Shortly after the middle of the sixth century B.C., an Athenian potter invented a device which produced black glaze lines in relief. This made possible delicate black lines sharply contrasting against the red clay background. About 530 B.C. the vase-painting technique was reversed. Instead of painting the figures as black silhouettes with incised details, the figures were outlined and interior details were added using the relief line. The entire background around the figures was painted black. This red-figure style created a more realistic effect which presented human figures in the light red color of the clay against the black glaze background (Figure 19). For a generation, both black-figure and red-figure flourished side by side; however, the new technique eventually largely superseded the old. Red-figure vase painting continued in

17   Mold-formed vase. Courtesy, Museum of Fine Arts, Boston, MFA
Egyptian Expedition.

Athens until the last quarter of the fourth century B.C., when it was abandoned.

The subjects of the scenes represented on Attic vases also underwent an evolutionary development. The black-figure ware of the sixth century utilized to the fullest extent the rich lore of Greek mythology. Gods and goddesses, heroes and monsters illustrated the stories of Olympus and the Trojan War. Decorative elements, such as the palmette, lotus, and meander, were used to frame the panels in which the black-figure scenes were painted. Gradually, the theme of mortal man acting out his daily life was introduced. The soldier arming for battle, the activities in the gymnasium, and carousing and drunken revels began to supersede the divine myths.

This tendency continued in the fifth and fourth centuries in the decoration of the red-figure vases. Humanism became paramount, although mythological subjects continued to be used to a lesser degree. Battles, banquets, and athletic contests were drawn as were the daily chores of weaving, bathing, and dressing within the home. Real people were shown performing the actual tasks of daily life, less heroic perhaps, but a faithful portrayal of reality. Decorative elements were subsidiary; they were used to set off the drawing, or to add interest to the mouth or other parts of the vase which the artist wished to emphasize.

Colors The decoration of Attic painted vases was in the main based on the use of two colors, a reddish-orange and a metallic black. The reddish-orange was produced by the natural color of the fired Attic clay of the body of the vase and was intensified by a surface coating of yellow ochre. The metallic black, the color of the black glaze, was made by an ingenious process from the same red clay as was used for the body of the vase. Accessory colors such as white and a purplish-red were also employed, but the major colors were the painted black and the contrasting red-orange of the clay. This sophisticated, although restricted, palette was not limited as a matter of choice. These were the only pigments known to the ancient Greek potters that would withstand the firing of the vases.

Greek Black Glaze For understanding the use of the black glaze in decorating, it is important to realize that the vases were fired only once. After the vases were formed, they were kept in a damp room until they were ready to be decorated. The painting was then applied

18   Black-figured vase painting. Noble, *Painted Attic Pottery*.

19

Red-figured vase
painting. Noble, *Painted
Attic Pottery*.

directly onto the firm semidry clay surface. When the vases were completely dry, they were fired.

The process was rediscovered by Theodore Schumann in 1942 and was based on the fact that the iron oxide in the Greek clay was red in color when it had been fired in an oxidizing atmosphere and black when it had been fired in a reducing atmosphere. Both the clay, which was used to form the vase, and the black glaze material, which was made from the clay, contained the same iron oxides.

The chemistry of the process is as follows. Red ferric oxide (Fe_2O_3) is present both in the clay body of the vase and in the unfired black glaze matter. If the entire firing is done under oxidizing conditions, both the vase and the glaze will turn, and remain, red. In the middle of the firing cycle, however, the oxidizing atmosphere is changed to a reducing atmosphere by the introduction of green wood or damp sawdust and by closing the air vent. The smoke produced by this action is not important chemically, as smoke is largely composed of carbon, which is not the coloring agent present in the Greek black glaze. The carbon is consumed in the firing at 900–950°C.

The reducing atmosphere, with the kiln closed to the outside supply of oxygen, causes incomplete combustion of the green wood or wet sawdust and produces carbon monoxide gas (CO) instead of the carbon dioxide gas (CO_2), which would be developed during normal complete combustion. Carbon monoxide (CO) unites with any oxygen that it can obtain, in this case with part of the oxygen in the ferric oxide (Fe_2O_3) in the clay, turning it into ferrous oxide (FeO). This changes part of the carbon monoxide (CO) into the stable form carbon dioxide (CO_2), and the red ferric oxide (Fe_2O_3) into ferrous oxide (FeO), which is black. The reaction in this process is $Fe_2O_3 + CO = 2FeO + CO_2$. Now, the presence in the kiln of water vapor from the moisture in the pottery itself, from the green wood or wet sawdust, or perhaps from a vessel full of water placed especially in the fuel chamber produces a magnetic oxide of iron (Fe_3O_4), which is an even blacker oxide of iron than the mere ferrous oxide (FeO). The reaction in this process is $3Fe_2O_3 + CO = 2Fe_3O_4 + CO_2$. The hydrogen from the water (H_2O) is a powerful reducing agent. If the firing cycle is stopped at this point, the clay body of the vase and the glaze will be completely and permanently black.

The process is concluded by a reoxidizing phase. Through a small hole now opened, oxygen is permitted to enter the kiln and to unite with some of the black ferrous oxide (FeO) or magnetic oxide of iron (Fe_3O_4), turning it back into the red ferric oxide (Fe_2O_3). The vase, having a porous clay body, readily allows this to happen. Consequently, the body of the vase again turns red. On the other hand, the black glazed areas, composed of either black ferrous oxide (FeO) or the black magnetic oxide of iron (Fe_3O_4), or both, do not reoxidize at these temperatures. These areas remain black, and the result of this phase is the characteristic red and black coloring of Attic vases. The glaze does not reoxidize because it becomes partly sintered and is encased in a quartz layer, which does not permit the re-entry of oxygen into it and, therefore, prevents a chemical reaction from taking place. As a result, both physical and chemical factors inhibit the reversal of the process at 950°C. If the temperature is raised above 1050°C., the black oxides in the glaze will reoxidize to a red form and the black color of the glaze will be lost.

Invention The basic technique of producing a black glaze through the three-step firing was known as early as the Middle Helladic period. Possibly the glaze was accidentally discovered when local clay was being purified. It is a simple procedure to create a suspension of clay in water and allow it to settle, separating the coarse particles and the unwanted matter from the clay. A peptizing agent such as potash, or water in which wood ashes have been soaked, might have been used to facilitate the process. It would have been good practice to coat a coarse clay vase body with a slip of a more purified clay to give it a smoother finish. The Greek kilns, fired with wood and easily capable of changing from an oxidizing to a reducing and back to a reoxidizing condition as wood was added, could accidentally have produced the first vase in this technique. An observant early potter who was willing to experiment might have worked out the process on a predictable basis.

Another possibility is that the first peptized clay slip, made of very fine particles, may have come from a stream bed where it had been formed naturally. Later, the sedimentation process would have been used to produce a similar clay slip. Fundamentally, the decoration with black glaze consists of coating a vase of coarse clay with a finer layer of clay.

One may duplicate the ancient black glaze by using the following formula: In one pint of distilled water dissolve two and a half grams of Calgon (sodium hexametaphosphate). Calgon is the peptizing or deflocculating agent. The agent used by the ancient Greek potters may have been potash. Mix completely into the solution four ounces by weight of damp Attic clay, and shake until the entire mixture is homogenous. Not all red clays will produce a black glaze unless they, like Attic clay, are composed of minute platelets of varying sizes which can be separated by the deflocculating process. The mixture is allowed to stand in a tall glass container for forty-eight hours. During this time it separates into three clearly recognizable areas. At the top, a substantial quantity of very fine particles of clay hangs in a colloidal suspension. Between this top colloidal zone and the bottom zone, there is a clearly visible area of clay slip composed of particles of average size. At the bottom, there are sand and coarse particles which were present in the clay. The top colloidal suspension of fine particles is carefully removed with a siphon for the preparation of the glaze. The middle zone may be used for making the body of the vase and the bottom zone is discarded.

The suspension of fine particles has to be thickened by evaporation. Either the water is allowed to evaporate for a period of several weeks, or the solution can be boiled down without injury. Evaporation is continued until the liquid has the consistency of very heavy cream. The unfired glaze preparation is of a dark brown tone, deeper than the plain Attic clay. It already possesses, when dry, a slightly metallic sheen. Glaze matter which does not possess this metallic sheen in the dry state will not fire black, but will turn red in the same way as the unglazed clay body.

Vase Painters The vase painters sketched their subjects on the surface of the semidry vases probably with a thin pointed stick of charcoal or lead. Occasionally the vase was not as dry as it should have been, or the painter pressed too hard, so the stick left slightly indented lines which were preserved when the vase was fired. The painters often sketched their figures nude and then drew clothes over them in order to render their movement correctly. The charcoal or lead lines which were clearly visible to the painter vanished in the firing process.

Only a few simple tools were used by the painters, among them the caliper. It was used to compare and to transfer measurements. The compass, a modification of the caliper, was used to draw circles, as for shields and chariot wheels. A brush was used to paint the solid areas, figures, and designs on the vases.

The ancient paintbrush very closely resembled those in use today.

Scenes on Greek vases of potters and painters at work, while rare, do exist and are useful in the study of vase-painting techniques. The most representative scene extant of vase painters at work appears on a red-figured hydria, now in the Torno Collection in Milan (Figure 20). Four painters are shown: a man, two youths, and a woman. The reason for two vase painters, each having two cups of glaze, would appear to be that the cups contain glaze of different consistency. One cup presumably contains thinner black glaze matter, the consistency of heavy cream, and the other cup contains a much thicker black glaze substance which was used to produce the Attic relief line widely used in red-figure ware. An examination of Attic vases bears out this explanation. In examples where the black relief line goes over the black background glaze, the use of two glazes of different consistencies is clearly shown.

Relief There are no ancient illustrations of a vase painter drawing a
Line relief line. However, on a red-figured kylix fragment in the Museum of Fine Arts in Boston, there is shown a painter holding a brush in the fingers of his right hand and a pointed instrument in his left (Figure 21). It may be that this is a small syringe, which could have been used to produce the ancient relief line by extruding or trailing the glaze from the syringe in much the same way that a pastry chef decorates a cake by extruding the frosting from a pastry tube (Figure 22). A line produced in this way occasionally dries with a slight trough, or long ridge, very much like those that sometimes occur in Attic relief lines. When fired, the line adheres to the body of the vase with great tenacity. If the line is subsequently mechanically broken, it takes with it part of the clay body and leaves a groove in the vase; the same can be found on ancient vases. The drawing instrument used by the Attic vase painters was probably composed of a tapered nozzle made of bronze, bone, or ivory pierced with a very fine hole. To this nozzle a short piece of animal intestine filled with a heavy viscous glaze matter must have been attached.

The predominant colors of an Attic vase are the black glaze and the red clay of the body, but the Greeks made use of a limited range of additional colors. One of these was an ochre wash used to heighten the color of the clay body. This was burnished and polished to a firm smooth surface by the use of an agate pebble or a piece of bone or hard wood. The iron oxide in the ochre polishes to a very high luster. The color scheme of Attic black-figured vases calls for the addition of a white color for women's flesh, shield devices, etc. This white was produced from a very fine white clay, which was a primary clay. The other principle added color in black-figured vases was added red used for men's beards, clothes, wreaths, blood, shield devices, inscriptions, etc. This is a red oxide of iron pigment, or red ochre. The brown translucent line with which the Attic red-figure vase painters drew muscles, hair, other body markings as well as shadings, was produced by diluting the black glaze matter with water. The white clay was sometimes used to coat the body of Attic lekythoi which were used to hold tomb offerings of olive oil. It was applied while the vase rotated on the potter's wheel, and in that way a uniform coating was achieved.

The techniques of Greek pottery were exported to the Greek colonies, undoubtedly with the emigration of skilled workers. Even the Attic relief line found its way to Italy, where it was abundantly used. In Attica the application of the relief line made with black glaze continued until the end of the era of red-figure technique about 320 B.C., and in southern Italy and Etruria until a generation later. From the third to the first century B.C. the relief line technique degenerated, at which time a clay slip was substituted for the black glaze. Flowers, patterns, or a decorative series of dots were produced using a white or red extruded clay slip, quite often left unglazed to contrast with the black glaze of the balance of the vase. In Attic pottery this ware is known as West Slope ware. By the end of the first century B.C. West Slope ware was no longer produced; it was replaced by a coarser type of pottery known as Barbotine in which the extruded relief line was made from clay slip identical to the clay body of the vase. This ware was completely coated with either a black or red glaze. The relief line decorations were often in the form of animals or flower patterns in high relief. Barbotine ware was manufactured throughout the entire Roman Empire from the Black Sea to Egypt, Greece, Italy, Germany, France, and England. It continued until about the fourth century after Christ.

Firing The technique of treating dried clay with heat to change it from a soft friable substance to a hard vitreous useful material was discovered by man about seven thousand years ago at the beginning of the Pottery Neolithic period. The discovery was probably

20   Vase painters at work. Torno Museum, Milan. Courtesy, Metropolitan
        Museum of Art, New York.

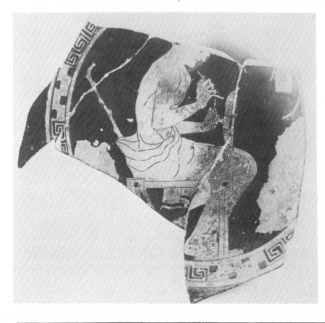

21

Vase painter holding brush
and relief-line instrument.
Courtesy, Museum of Fine
Arts, Boston, Pierce Fund,
purchased of E. P. Warren.

accidental, possibly as a result of building a campfire over a deposit of clay. The most ancient potters did not use a kiln; they arranged their dried clay vessels in a small pile and then covered them with whatever fuel was available, like wood, charcoal, twigs, straw, or dried dung. The temperature was not uniform in this mound of pots, and some did not reach the proper temperature for the vitrification of the clay. The color of the pottery was rather unpredictable because some areas of the fire were oxidizing in character and others reducing; therefore, some of the pottery was a brownish-red in color and some grayish or black. Kilns were utilized in Greece at least by the Middle Helladic period. In order to allow the potter more control over the process, a kiln usually had an area for burning the fuel which was separate from the area in which the pots were located. Openings were provided for tending the fire, for placing and removing the pots, for observing the fire, and for controlling the flow of air through the kiln. There are a few excellent representations of kilns on Greek pottery. A Corinthian kiln shown on a *pinax* (plaque) is a large one requiring the potter to use a ladder to reach the vent on top (Figure 23).

A schematic diagram of the interior of a kiln is shown on another Corinthian fragment (Figure 24). Less than half of the plaque is preserved; the scene did extend to the left and has been restored here showing the stoking tunnel and a potter tending the fire. In the part of the pinax that is preserved, the vases are shown inside the kiln chamber, which is isolated from the fuel chamber by a perforated floor. The burning embers are represented by the dots on the lower left-hand corner of the scene. Vases would have been nested and carefully stacked in an actual firing, but here the artist has spread them out to show their shapes. At the top of the kiln is a venthole, or chimney, which was covered during the reduction stage of the firing and left open during the two oxidizing phases. The vase painter did not draw the door to the kiln through which the pottery was loaded nor the small spyhole in the door or kiln wall which was used to observe the progress of the firing. The two test pieces, which the artist has shown near the vent at the top of the kiln in his idealized depiction of the kiln interior, would have been immediately inside the spyhole. These two draw pieces were removed one at a time during the course of the firing to test the temperature and the condition of the black glaze. They have holes in them to facilitate their removal with a hooked stick.[5]

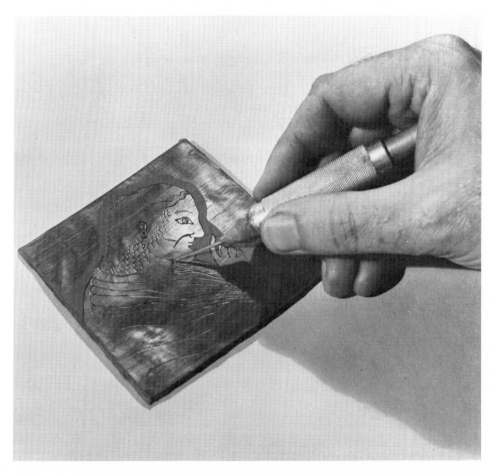

22   Drawing relief lines with a syringe. Noble, *Painted Attic Pottery*.

By analysis of ancient pottery and by tests of Greek glaze, it has been determined that the firing temperature in the kilns varied between 850°C. and 1000°C. Below 850°C. the black glaze will not properly sinter, and therefore it will reoxidize to red. Likewise over the 1000°C. the glaze tends to break down from the heat and reoxidize to a reddish-brown.

In loading his kiln, the ancient Greek potter was able to nest one piece inside another and stack them tightly in the kiln chamber. Since the black glaze did not melt in the firing process, the vases would not stick to each other. After loading, a fire was built in the firing chamber, and the temperature was slowly increased over several hours. Air was freely admitted to the kiln so that this first phase was under oxidizing conditions. Undoubtedly, wood was the principal fuel, although twigs, straw, and dung would also have been used when available. When the temperature reached approximately 800°C., the atmospheric condition was changed to that of a reducing atmosphere by closing the air vent at the top of the kiln and throwing into the firing chamber green wood and leaves. This produced smoke and, with the incomplete combustion, carbon monoxide gas. This condition was held for at least a half an hour, and then the temperature was gradually increased, still maintaining a reducing atmosphere until about 950°C. Then, while continuing to maintain the reducing atmosphere, the temperature was allowed to decrease slowly to about 900°C. At this point the last of the green wood was consumed, and a small amount of fresh air was introduced by opening an air hole in the kiln and removing the cover from the top of the kiln, which changed the atmosphere from reducing to oxidizing. The kiln was then allowed to cool slowly to the outside temperature while maintaining the oxidizing atmosphere, at which point the vases with their characteristic red and black colors were finished. The chemistry of the changes in color of the black glaze during firing was discussed earlier in this chapter.

Although the Greek potters sometimes used test pieces, which were removed from the kiln during the firing to judge the progress of the process, nevertheless the principal judgment of the time and temperature of the firing was based on the skilled eye of the potter. An experienced potter could rely on observations of the incandescent colors in the kiln to determine the proper temperature and be correct within a margin of plus or minus 25°C., which is satisfactory for this process.

23

Potter mounting a ladder to close kiln vent hole. Corinthian terra-cotta plaque. National Museum, Berlin. Noble, *Painted Attic Pottery*.

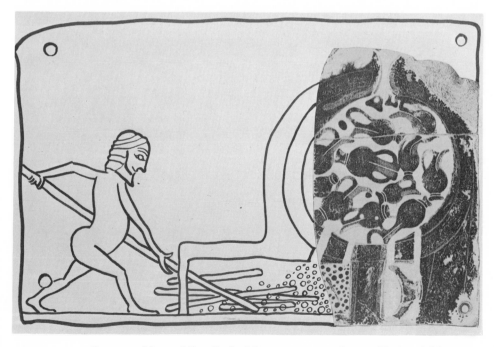

24   Potter stoking a kiln. Corinthian terra cotta plaque. National Museum, Berlin. Noble, *Painted Attic Pottery*.

Economics In the making of pottery the work divides itself readily into three areas of skill: the forming, the decorating, and the firing. Usually the potter owned and operated the kiln, and he needed the services of several vase painters to decorate his output.[6] The size of the potters' workshops probably varied greatly as ours do today. Undoubtedly, there was the tiny shop of the poor or highly independent potter, who shared his labors with his wheel-turning apprentice. The successful pottery owner most likely staffed his large workshop with a variety of laborers, skilled and semiskilled artisans, and most likely he himself served as the foreman or supervisor. Probably some Greek potteries employed as many as a dozen workers. However, the average number of employees would have been from four to six.

The potters and painters were craftsmen engaged in a hard but honest trade. They took their place among the other artisans and tradesmen who made the products and performed the services that were required for the business life of Greece. A sizable industry arose to supply the domestic needs which also required plain black unglazed serviceable pottery for use as inexpensive table and cooking ware. The output of the finer ware, first in the black-figure and later in the red-figure style, was extensive. The owners of the potteries, usually potters themselves, shared in the general prosperity and were apparently comfortably affluent. Evidence of this can be found in the existence of various dedicatory inscriptions in sanctuaries. The pottery was widely exported[7] and has been found at many sites throughout the Mediterranean area and beyond, including France, Germany, Italy, Corsica, Sicily, South Russia, Asia Minor, Mesopotamia, and in the Sudan as far south as Meroë.

The pottery of ancient Greece, now scattered throughout the world, stands as a witness to an era of perfection in the union of technique and beauty.

A Greek landowner, Xenophon tells us in his *Oeconomicus* (*Oec.* 15. 11),[1] once suggested that agriculture makes its practitioners generous. Persons engaged in other occupations, he claimed, tend to conceal the peculiar tricks of their trades; farmers, by contrast, are happy to have someone observe while they do whatever they do best. The good treeplanter, therefore, likes to be watched while he plants trees; the good sower, while he sows grain—all are ready to share their knowledge when asked the special basis for this success. The universal truth of the landowner's generalization can perhaps never be established, yet supporting evidence does exist: through the works of two poets who owned land and through a sequence of technical treatises prepared by Roman farm owners we probably possess more written information about running a farm than about the details of any other occupation in antiquity.

The two poets, Hesiod and Vergil, occupy a place of special prominence. Hesiod (8th century B.C.) in his *Works and Days* (*WD*) offers sundry proverbial advice and a schedule of farming operations adapted to the needs of his Boeotian peasant neighbors. His importance lies, not in the slender threads of technical information he presents, but in the fact that subsequent agricultural writers commonly acknowledged him as their earliest predecessor. Vergil (70–19 B.C.) is no such pioneer, for much had been written on farming by his date. Yet, in his *Georgics* (*G*) he breathed such a spirit of poetry into his subject and wrote with such genuineness and persuasiveness that his successors often quoted him and at least two, Columella and Palladius, imitated him by writing sections of their own manuals in verse.

But during the centuries between Hesiod and the Roman agronomists, countless volumes must have been written either upon agriculture or upon matters relating to it. The most useful survivors from this literature are the *Oeconomicus* of Xenophon (ca. 430–ca. 354 B.C.) a short essay on household duties, and two botanical works by Theophrastus (ca. 370–ca. 285 B.C.), the *Enquiry into Plants* (*HP*) and the *Aetiology of Plants* (*CP*).[2] The work from this period which may have exerted the widest influence, however, a twenty-eight-volume treatise by Mago the Carthaginian, has been lost. Mago's work, written in the Punic language, had been salvaged by order of the Roman Senate when the Carthaginian libraries were being given away to the petty kings of Africa, and was translated into Latin.[3] It was naturally appropriate to African conditions, so may have been translated largely to aid wealthy Romans who were buying African estates after the fall of Carthage,[4] but the Roman agronomists cite Mago with respect even when they seek to refute him.

The extant Roman authorities, our most valuable sources, begin with Cato the Censor (234–149 B.C.). His *De Agricultura* (*Agr.*) is utimately the product of jottings for personal use—recipes, prescriptions, checklists of materials and supplies, and highly specific notations about where to purchase certain items (as tunics, togas, blankets, and shoes at Rome; oil mills at Pompeii; pails and pitchers at Capua and Nola)—even dealers' names appear. Yet this very personal work owes debts: Cato twice (151. 1 and 152) mentions Latin sources for information, and Greek influences can be argued. However, when Columella, in his *De Re Rustica* (*RR* 1. 1. 12) says that Cato was the first to give Latin voice to agriculture, he is certainly right in principle, whether or not he is entirely so in detail.

The scholar Varro (116–27 B.C.), writing in his eightieth year, presents in his *De Re Rustica* (*RR*) a much wider range of topics than those offered by Cato, and his method is noticeably more systematic. His first book is devoted to farming in general; his second to livestock raising, for upland pastures were now more significant to the Italian economy; his third to the small livestock of the farmyard—poultry, game birds, bees, and fish. Cato would probably have regarded much of the new material as scandalous luxury, but Varro's thinking is that profit is equally sweet whether it comes from cattle, birds, or bees (*RR.* 3. 2. 11). The new topics reflect a social change; the organization into three books represents a new intellectual approach in Latin. Varro, a scholar enamored of categories, divides animal husbandry, for example, into three topics of three divisions each:

1. Smaller animals: sheep, goats, swine;
2. Larger animals: oxen, asses, horses;
3. Animals either kept for livestock raising or resulting from it:[5] mules, dogs, herdsmen [*RR* 2.1. 11–28].

These divisions then break into nine subdivisions: best age for purchase; points of a good animal; best breeds; legal form of purchase; pasturage; breeding; feeding; health; and proper number to a herd. Varro takes a scholar's pride in his eighty-one pigeonholes!

Columella's *De Re Rustica* (written shortly before A.D. 65) is the longest and most comprehensive Roman agricultural work. This author's concern for the morale and physical well-being of his slaves matches the best thinking of his contemporaries, and he is noticeably devoted to the social and national worth of a strong Italian agriculture.

The encyclopaedist, Pliny the Elder (A.D. 23–79), is not strictly an agricultural writer, but in excerpting for the botanical sections of his *Natural History* (*HN*) he collected great amounts of agricultural information. He occasionally inserts personal observations and at times preserves snippets of Celsus, Hyginus, and many other authors whose agricultural works have perished.

Most details of ancient Italian agriculture can be sketched pretty well from the five Latin writers here introduced—Cato, Varro, Vergil, Columella, and Pliny—but a few more can be recovered from three fourth-century authors. Only one, Palladius, is strictly an agriculturalist. His *Opus Agriculturae* (*Agr.*) generally recasts the materials of Columella in a simple style, although occasionally (as in his description of a reaping machine)[6] he provides the most important literary evidence about some topic. One Vegetius, presumably the tactician, compiled a treatise on veterinary medicine (a subtopic for all the agronomists), and Servius commented upon the *Georgics* of Vergil. Inevitably each supplies some minor information.[7]

These authors, together with the compiler of the late Greek *Geoponica* (*Geop.*) and all the poets and prose writers from Homer onward who allude to agriculture, contain the literary evidence about ancient farming. There are, of course, other kinds of evidence. Agricultural subjects at times appear, portrayed with great accuracy, in artistic representations, for example, manuscript illuminations, mosaics, sculptures, reliefs, and wall and vase paintings. Archaeological excavations have yielded many actual implements, and votive offerings from temples often represent in miniature elements from actual life. Inscriptions, too, record the thoughts of the persons who set them up (although inevitably adjusted to a style appropriate to a monument). Finally, much can be inferred with fair certainty from the forms of certain implements and machines still, or recently, used in the Mediterranean area, from processes still employed there or in primitive agriculture elsewhere, and from the techniques of "dry farming" anywhere. In the pages which follow, some details are adduced from Greece, North Africa, and Gaul, but owing to the weight of evidence from Italy and the works of the Roman agronomists, Italian agriculture is in effect the prime subject.[8]

The Men in the Fields Agriculture is not a simple occupation. Properly it is "The cultivation of the fields" (hence its prime concern should be grain-growing). Certainly farms have often become great commercial enterprises devoted to marketing single crops or products, but in practice farmers throughout most of human history have directed themselves toward a diversity of operations and products. Further, the farmer, living close to the ground he tills or the animals he tends, has normally expected to subsist on the products of his farm. These factors, combined with the demanding, time-consuming nature of many of the operations and the relative isolation of many farms, have tended to make agriculture not merely an occupation but in effect a way of life. It is appropriate, therefore, to see the kinds of people who farmed in antiquity before turning to the specific products, processes, equipment and problems with which they were concerned.

The men themselves belonged to several social categories (Varro, *RR* 1. 17. 2). Some were small landowners who tilled their own fields with or without the help of slaves or hired men. Some were tenants to whom land was leased. Some were debtors, obligated to work off their debts. Many, especially on the great estates of wealthy owners (*latifundia*), were slaves, some living in comfortable quarters and some chained in the workhouses. There is space to sample the situations only of the small landowners and of the slaves.

Hard work and independence are keynotes of the small farmer's life again and again in classical literature. Hesiod advises (*WD* 405–409) starting out with a house, a plow-ox, and a woman—"a slave, not a wife, one who also can follow the oxen" and to prepare everything needful, "so that you need not ask another, and he refuse, and you be in need and the proper time go by, and your effort be wasted." In New Comedy Menander's farmers are a hard-working lot. Old Cleaenetus from the *Georgos* leads a stark life, using the two-pronged hoe in the fields in company with his slaves (Figure 1). The best that can be said for such a miserable existence is that there are few witnesses to a man's misfortunes. But Menedemus, the Self-Tormenter,[9] enjoys less privacy, for his neighbor observes him hoeing, spading, plowing, or carrying loads at whatever hour he starts out in the morning and however late he returns in the evening. Both these farmers had slave crews, but the misanthropic old Cnemon in the recently discovered *Dyscolus,* despite the considerable size of his property, works it all alone, without household slave, hired man from the community, or the assistance of any neighbor. Only his daughter at times helps him in the fields. In like fashion the old Roman farmer-soldier Cincinnatus is plowing alone[10] in his little field when, as Livy reports (3. 26), the delegation from the Senate comes to call him as Dictator. These are all typical literary pictures.

But Cato has some of the same realities in mind although amid different circumstances. He, too, could boast, "Right from the start I governed my entire youth by frugality, hard-living, and hard-work, tilling my farm—digging again and planting the Sabine rocks and flintstones."[11] He is even said to have sat down from time to time to eat with his slaves (Plutarch, *Cato Major,* 3. 2). But already great estates were growing about him, and he could see that their owners would soon be out of touch with actual operations. These estates would normally be run by a slave manager (*vilicus*), upon whom would devolve the problems and realities of farm life. Almost inevitably, then, Cato wants this manager to have some of the qualities traditional with farmers in literature.

The *vilicus* must not be a loafer; he must always be sober; he must not go out anywhere to dinner. . . . He must take care to know how to perform all types of farm work—and he should perform them often . . .; if he does this he will know better the thinking of the slave crew, and their morale will be better as they work [*Agr.* 5. 1–5].

Against the background of this advice it is easy to see that the farmers of literature do reveal traits of personality likely to have been common among the small independent farmers of the countryside.

But life on the farm as a matter of choice was inevitably very different from life there by compulsion. The manager, although supervising slaves, was still a slave himself and therefore not free to leave the limitations and hardships of rural life. To this problem there is also literary testimony, in Horace's verse epistle to his farm manager whom he had promoted from some menial role in town. The poem seems studded with echoes of the slave's complaints: he longs for the city, the games, and the baths; he misses the handy brothel, the greasy cookshop, and the taverns with wines and flute girls; worse, amid deserts and wastelands, he must keep working over the long-neglected fields, care for the ox after it has been unyoked, stripping fodder to fill it, and after a rain he must wearily go out to dike up the brook to keep it from damaging the meadow.[12] This is a rather whimsical indictment of the countryside, yet the obvious concern of the agronomists about the morale and moods of slaves on the farm suggest a strong measure of reality behind it.

The problem would be especially important on the great estates where, the elder Seneca reports (*Controv.* 2. 1. 26), there were "gangs of slaves, unknown personally to their master" and "workhouses resounding with whips." Varro (*RR* 1. 17. 3) wants slaves neither timid nor too high-spirited. The men in charge of the crews should be literate, actually somewhat educated, rather older, and certainly wiser and more experienced than their men to gain the respect of the younger workmen. Words from them are preferable to whips, when the results are the same. Good foremen should be rewarded with bits of property and should be given mates from among the female slaves to bear them children and attach them more closely to the estate. Likewise, outstanding workmen among ordinary slaves should be consulted about work to be done to show that they too are valued. Material rewards, again, cause these men to take greater interest in their work.

These attitudes, essentially of enlightened self-interest, are developed even further in Columella who is much concerned about the proper treatment of slaves. The manager, preferably country-bred, should handle his underlings well, administering without laxness or cruelty, encouraging the betters and showing mercy to those worth less. Columella is proud that he himself speaks personally to his better country slaves more often than to his town slaves; he finds this lifts their morale. Then he describes how responsible owners should check conditions in the workhouse:

. . . they should inspect the slaves in the workhouse, investigating whether they are carefully fettered . . . and whether the manager has bound or released any without his master's knowledge. . . . The *pater familias* ought to be all the more careful to investigate in behalf of his kind, since these slaves are subject to more superiors [e.g., to managers, foremen, and workhouse keepers], hence more exposed to suffering wrongs, and again they are the more to be feared once they have been harmed by cruelty or greed. And so the careful master not only inquires of the inmates themselves, but also of slaves not in bonds (who are more trustworthy), whether they are getting their proper allowances in accordance with his set policy, and he personally samples the quality of their bread and drink, tasting it himself, and he checks out their clothing, gloves, and foot coverings. Further, he should often give them the chance to register complaints about those who harass them by cruelty or deceit [*RR* 1.8 *passim*].

Columella ends this discussion with suggestions of rewards for the energetic. He himself grants exemption from work to female slaves who bear three sons and freedom to those who produce more. Then he turns (*RR* 1. 9) to the physical qualities of slaves for particular jobs, arguing that specialization is effective if only because it engenders a feeling of responsibility.

But humanitarian or not, and psychologist or not, Columella, like his predecessors, wanted to use his slaves efficiently to enhance profits. Cato (*Agr.* 2. 7) would sell old or sickly slaves, for they could be only superfluous mouths amid a hard-working staff; Varro, like certain Southern planters, preferred hired labor for dangerous or unhealthful tasks, lest a valuable slave be lost;[13] Columella wants the manager to store up in good repair twice the number of implements and iron tools required for slaves on the farm "because greater expense is lost in the labor of the slaves than in the price of implements of this sort" (*RR* 1. 8. 8). More importantly, he frequently itemizes in terms of *operae* (mandays) the precise time required for certain tasks, e.g., four days to plow a *iugerum* (two-thirds of an acre) of damp, level ground, three days for a lighter soil; 200 *iugera* can be worked (plowed, planted, cultivated, reaped) by two yoke of oxen, two plowmen, and six menials devoting approximately ten man-days to each *iugerum;* a good worker cuts a *iugerum* of meadow grass in a day (*RR* 11. 2. 40); and a single workman makes twelve planting holes that are four feet each way, or twenty that are two feet each way (*Arb.* 4. 3). These statistics and the standards of efficiency set by Columella and other authors prove, upon examination,[14] reasonably in keeping with standards which obtain in comparable medieval and modern situations. Their existence and the lists of indoor or yard tasks for inclement weather[15] suggest that slaves were doubtless as busy on well-run farms as any Cleaenetus, or Menedemus, or Cnemon on the small farms of literature. Since slaves, however, lacked freedom of choice, the Varros and Columellas were doubtless wise to be concerned about their morale.

The Size "Praise large farms, but cultivate a small one," says Vergil (*G.*
and 2. 412–413), and in so saying he gives voice to the best theoretical
Location judgment about the sizes of farms in antiquity. Columella, for
of a example, agreed for several reasons: the Seven Sages had surely
Farm had land purchases in mind when they had urged measure and
proportion in all things; a Carthaginian proverb about the farm
being weaker than the farmer had implied as much also, since
"one must wrestle with the farm, and if it gets the upper hand,
the owner will be crushed—there is no doubt but that a broad
field poorly cultivated is less productive than a small field well
tended" (*RR* 1. 3. 8–13). Further, the early Roman hero-generals
had small farms, and the state had later attempted to control
the size of farms by legislation.[16] In view of all this he announces:

> . . . we ought to acquire only the land we need that we may seem
> to have purchased what we can manage, not what we can be
> burdened by, or what we can keep others from enjoying, as do
> the excessively powerful who possess the territories of entire nations
> which they cannot even travel round, but which they leave to be
> trampled by cattle and wasted and preyed upon by beasts or else
> keep occupied by the financial obligation of their citizens or by chain
> gangs. . . . If you cannot cultivate the land . . . the desire to possess
> it is not enough.

But whether this advice was phrased in some allusion to the
Golden Mean, or in a figurative Carthaginian proverb, or in Palladius' epigrammatic "Well-tended meagerness is more productive
than neglected bigness" (*Agr.* 1. 6. 8), it often fell upon deaf ears.
Many owners, like Trimalchio, desired to have "estates as far
as kites fly"; to claim that on their Cumaean property on a certain
date, 30 boys and 40 girls had been born, 500,000 measures of
grain threshed, and 500 oxen broken to the yoke"; and to boast
that the dinner wine "comes from my suburban place I've not
yet seen. It's said to be adjacent to my properties at Tarracina
and Tarentum. Now I want to attach Sicily to my little tracts,
so that when I decide to go to Africa I can sail through my
own property."[17]

This is satiric exaggeration, admittedly, but analogous conditions are implied by Pliny, who complains that large estates have
ruined Italy and are now destroying the provinces, for "six land-
lords had owned half of the Province of Africa when the Emperor
Nero had them put to death" (*HN* 18. 35). This too may involve
exaggeration, since Pliny, in the context, is arguing, as had Vergil,
for a small farmstead, but it is scarcely a complete falsification.[18]

Solid facts are somewhat elusive, but the evidence, while documenting the existence of occasional gigantic estates, suggests many substantial, intermediate holdings from an early date.

Cato was thinking in terms of the latter when he detailed the manpower and equipment for an olive yard of 240 *iugera* (160 acres) and a vineyard of 100 *iugera* (67 acres), although the ideal farm, he said, consisted of "100 *iugera* of land, of all types of soils and in an excellent location" (*Agr.* 10; 11; 1. 7). Even Horace's "little farm" (*agellus*), as he called it,[19] in the Sabine hill district was of intermediate size. It was manned partly by a manager with eight slaves, while the balance was farmed by five tenants (*coloni*) with their families. But perhaps the best evidence comes from inscriptions, and from the size and nature of certain farm dwellings about Pompeii. The latter suggest estates of rather modest size (intensive farming being quite possible on fertile volcanic soil).[20] At Veleia, however (in northern Italy, near Piacenza), and at Beneventum (north of Naples) inscriptions[21] (recording state mortages) suggest some larger holdings. The lands seem to have been concentrated into relatively few hands at Veleia, and one estate at Beneventum had been compounded from eleven smaller farms, but in neither location is a true *latifundium* to be found with, for example, the 1,500 *iugera* (1,000 acres) of olive orchards visualized by Columella.

Large holdings can be documented from different periods. Pliny reports that a freedman had executed a will in 8 B.C. in which, "although he had lost heavily in the civil war, still he was leaving 4,116 slaves, 3,600 yoke of oxen, and 257,000 head of other livestock . . ." (*HN* 33. 135). In the reign of Claudius, according to Tacitus, "troops of slaves" (belonging to Domitia Lepida) in Calabria were described as "troubling the peace of Italy" (*Annal.* 12. 65). In the third century after Christ the future emperor Aurelian assembled, on a private estate of Valerian, "500 slaves, 2,000 cows, 1,000 mares, 10,000 sheep, and 15,000 she-goats."[22] But such holdings are noted by the authorities probably in part because they are exceptional.

In Italy, then, from the Punic Wars onward, the fairly substantial farm is likely to have been typical, with occasional extremely large estates in some areas. But there is no positive evidence that all small farms had disappeared in any area at any time. Therefore it seems safe to assume that, while the advice about small holdings was often ignored, at least some farmers lived in terms of it in all periods of antiquity.

But the agricultural writers are concerned about the situations of farms as well as their sizes. Location, of course, cannot be changed for any individual farm, but the authors do offer suggestions about *desirable* sites. Cato sets the tone of this advice:

When you are thinking of buying a farm . . . observe the prosperity of the neighbors: in a good district they ought to prosper well. . . . [The farm] should have a good exposure to the sky, not subject to damaging weather, and good soil. . . . If you can get such a site, it should be at the foot of a mountain, looking toward the south, in a healthful location; there should be a supply of day-laborers, a good water supply, and a flourishing town nearby, or else the sea, or a navigable river, or a good, well-travelled roadway. It should be among farms which do not often change owners and where former owners regret that they have sold their land [*Agr.* 1. 1–4].

Varro and Pliny echo this advice, mentioning Cato as an authority;[23] Columella both concurs and disagrees. Cato, convinced that the farmer should be essentially a seller, would like him near a city (or at least a means of inexpensive transportation) to assure him an accessible market. Columella also wants the farm near a city, but for a very different reason. He recognizes that the owner's presence[24] is the most important guarantee that an estate will be run properly by its manager, and he would gladly subscribe, like Pliny (*HN* 18. 35), to the injunction of Mago that the first act of a new farm owner should be to sell his city residence. But he also recognizes the realities of Roman political and social life which would discourage any prolonged absence from the city. All this argues for a handy location.

The site and size of the farm buildings also occupy the attention of the writers. Cato (*Agr.* 4.) wants the owner's house (*villa urbana*) proportionate to the size of the farm, comfortable, and in a good location. If the owner enjoys residing in it, he will come often and stay long. Varro (*RR* 1. 11. 2–12. 1–4.) wants a location with a good water supply. The steading should stand at the foot of a wooded hill, facing the most healthful winds, but on high ground rather than in a hollow. Here, especially if a swamp is near as a source of infections, the breeze will carry the *bestiolae* (presumably "insects") away. Besides, the higher ground offers more protection against suddenly rising streams and the attacks of robbers.[25] Columella, as usual, amplifies many of these details, being especially concerned about the dangers from swamps, including the insects (*animalia*) "armed with dangerous stings which attack us in very dense swarms" (*RR* 1. 5. 6–8). He is also opposed to building on military highways since passers-by pillage and those who constantly turn in for hospitality lay waste the household supplies. This understandable comment reveals how even a wealthy landowner could share something of the mood of the misanthropic Cnemon, who resented the intrusions of passers-by.

A farm's location and size, and the site of its *villa*, are, for most owners, specifics determined for them by the act of purchasing. One buys a farm in this place or in that. Presumably, then, their treatment in these manuals means that the authors were writing in part for persons who were on the verge of buying land or who, like Varro's wife (*RR* 1. 1. 2–4), had just recently acquired a farm. Many such new owners, particularly if they had just combined two or more smaller holdings in forming a larger, new estate, would feel it appropriate to build a *villa* in proportion to the size of their new holdings and so would be in a position actually to implement some of the counsel about where to place a farm home.

Products of Ancient Farms "Agriculture is a source of joy," says Cicero, "not only from its fields of grain, meadows, vineyards, and groves,[26] but also from its gardens and orchards, as well as from its feeding of livestock, its swarms of bees, and the variety of all its flowers" (*Sen.* 15. 54). These words, intended to sketch some of the pleasures of an old man in the country, can serve incidentally to outline the principal sources of farm income in Italy (and most of the Greco-Roman world), for Cicero's list readily expands into a brief catalogue.[27]

The grain fields yielded various wheats and spelt, barley, and millet; other field products included flax (which came gradually to be used in clothing) and hemp, and various legumes as food or fodder and to fertilize the land (notably lupines, but also lentils, peas, beans, and chickpeas). The legumes often served as a quick crop on fallow land, to be grazed upon by livestock and serving as a green manure when plowed under. The meadows could be sown with various fodders: alfalfa (*medica*) was regarded as the best, but vetches, fenugreek, oats, shrub trefoil, and a mixed forage which included barley are mentioned.[28]

The vineyards naturally yielded the grapes used for raisins and a multiplicity of wines. Woodlots, planted boundary lines, and forests produced oaks, beeches, ilex, pine, fir, birch, ash, linden, maple, elm, cypress, willows, and cork. Many of these were valued for their wood (as maple for furniture); from many the leaves or fruits were prized (e.g., the leaves of elms and poplars as fodder [Cato, *Agr.* 6. 3] and the acorns from oaks as mast for swine); from others by-products were sought (e.g., tar and resin from pines and the bark from the cork tree).

Gardens produced many vegetables familiar to modern tables (e.g., lettuces, asparagus, onions, garlic, cucumber, beet, celery, turnips, radish, parsnip, artichoke, and cabbage) and herbs and seasonings (e.g., rue, all-heal, elecampane, dill, cress, and mustard). For Italy, at least, many of these were importations through efforts of Roman officials and travelers who had found them growing in the provinces or in more distant parts of the world. The orchards of fruits and nut trees likewise bore testimony to such travels.[29] Fruits included figs, apples, peaches, pears, plums, apricots, and cherries, among others (but not lemons and oranges which did not appear at least until late antiquity in the Mediterranean area).[30] In antiquity the principal nuts were walnuts, chestnuts, hazels, and the almond. The olive, of course, could be grown in most localities of moderate elevation.

Livestock raising was important both on large ranches and around the villas. Oxen were the principal draft animals, but cattle were raised also for beef and milk (hence cheese). Sheep and goats were valued for wool, meat, and dairy products. The finer horses, mules, and asses were commonly bred in considerable numbers on large ranches. The horses seem to have been used primarily for the cavalry, racing, and rapid travel, although geldings were, like mules and asses, used as pack animals. The horse was presumably inefficient as a draft animal in antiquity because the soft leather collars employed until about the tenth century after Christ interfered with the animal's breathing. Besides, the climate was drier and more predictable than in northern Europe; so the speed possible from a workhorse was less in demand. Swine were popular for their meat, the oak forests of Cisalpine Gaul being one of the principal sources, although presumably most farmers kept a few to be swilled from the kitchen and to provide bacon for the household.[31]

Almost every farm had a poultry yard as well, from which came chickens, geese, ducks, pigeons, thrushes, peacocks, guinea hens, pheasants, or other fowl, according to the predilection of the owner and the demands of the market, since poultry men obviously catered to the tastes of gourmands.[32] Cicero might have added fishponds at this point in his sketch of country delights, for Varro (*RR* 3. 17) and Columella (*RR* 8. 16–17) both write of them, but instead he continued with the bees. These were a topic dear to the agronomists at least from Vergil (*G.* 4) and Varro (*RR* 3. 16) onward. He concludes with garden flowers, a product important then, as now, near the larger cities. Pliny (*HN* 21. 1–69) has much to say about garlands and flowers which may be grown for them (e.g., roses, lilies, violets, crocus, valerian, iris, narcissus, hyacinths, and others).

This compressed list could be elaborated endlessly. But there are also special problems that would have to be faced, since ancient botanical terms are often difficult to equate with modern popular, let alone technical, names. British and American readers have further difficulties arising in part from unfamiliarity with certain of the plants in question, but their traditional dictionaries and textbook vocabularies have not helped them much in this. Latin *apium,* to cite but a single example, is usually identified as "parsley," whereas it is actually "celery." Further, these dictionaries are commonly in British literary English (and that of the last century) so that *frumentum* and *seges* appear as "corn" and "cornfield," rather than as "grain" and "field of grain," as they should in American (if not also Canadian and Australian) English of the twentieth century. But this problem exists for other languages, too. *Cytisus* ("shrub trefoil"), *medicago arborea* (apparently an importation from North Africa),[33] found in Greece and southern Italy, seems to lack an established popular Italian name, at times being styled *citiso virgiliano* in tribute to the poet's mention of it, since the original name *citiso* has long since been transferred to the toxic laburnum.[34]

Regardless of such problems, however, any systematic study of the agricultural products of Italy (and doubtless of other parts of the Empire) would bear testimony to the positive contributions of the forces of experimentation and of demand. Farmers and landowners did constantly try to raise strains of plants and animals native to other areas in the effort to improve the efficiency of their own efforts at home. But in this they were strongly abetted by the increasingly sophisticated demands of at least an influential section of the populace—persons interested in foods and other products both of finer quality and of a more exotic nature.

Scheduling The essential operations of farming, sowing and harvesting, are inevitably tied to the growing season. Grain planted too late may not grow and ripen before frost, drought, or other inhibiting forces kill it; grain planted too early may be stunted by cold weather, insufficient moisture, or other causes; again, the failure to start either operation in time may let inclement weather block its completion. As Cato says, in farming "if you do one thing late you'll do everything late" (*Agr.* 5. 7). And, as Columella phrases it, when a task is behind schedule, "the manager should believe that he has lost, not just twelve hours, but rather an entire year (*RR* 11. 1. 29–30).[35]

The situation is not always that serious, of course. Most plants do not need the benefit of every possible day in the growing season in most localities, but the importance of being approximately right about planting time in particular must have dogged man from his first prehistoric ventures into sowing and transplanting.

The principal difficulty in this inevitably relates to the problem of evolving a satisfactory civil calendar. Plants grow according to the solar year; man tends to measure his year in terms of lunations called months—cycles of the moon which, unfortunately, do not coincide in any obvious multiple with the 365 and a fraction days of the solar year.[36] The phases of the moon, therefore, cannot signal accurately the days for planting grain, nor can any civil calendar, unless it has been carefully adjusted and remains tolerably anchored to the solar year.[37]

As a result of this difficulty the early authorities do not use the civil calendar to assign dates for agricultural operations.[38] The proper times are indicated, rather, by recurrent patterns in the lives and development of certain plants and animals, or by meteorological phenomena like the start of the spring breezes, or else by recurring movements and positions of the sun and stars. But authors like Columella and Pliny, writing a century or more after the introduction of the Julian calendar, rely primarily upon the civil calendar. In fact, both authors, if they mention the stars, are likely to confirm the dates in question by the civil calendar, as when Columella (*RR* 2. 8. 1–2) quotes a Vergilian allusion to the setting of the Pleiades and then asserts that this constellation generally sets on October 24.

The Julian calendar, then, it would appear, largely replaced stars, solar signs, and cycles of weather and zoological and botanical phenomena in instructions for farmers in later centuries. But it doubtless never quite crowded out the homely use of swallow, crane, or thistle blossom. It never can. Conditions vary radically from one locality to another in Italy, Greece, or any other coun-

try. Further, spring may come early or late anywhere in any
one year. The natural phenomena which normally accompany
spring plowing or the fall sowing may indeed be the best practical
indications that the soil is ready for the next stage in the cycle
of the farmer's labors.

Techniques Soils, terrain, and climate all created difficulties for the ancient
and Greek or Italian farmer. Certain soils were adapted to certain
Equipment crops: the farmer had to learn what each could best support;
the olive, Columella implies (*RR* 5. 8. 6), prefers calcareous, but
well-drained, soil. Terrain dictated general uses: as Varro suggests
(*RR* 1. 6. 5), the plains were thought best for grain fields, the
hills for vineyards and orchards, the mountains for forests and
summer pasturelands. These problems involving soil or terrain
had fairly obvious solutions—plant what experience shows will
grow best or use the vegetation naturally present.

Climate created more complex problems, for in many areas
the annual rainfall was barely adequate to bring crops through
to maturity, and unusually dry years could be disastrous. This
inescapable fact committed the farmer, in any area where irriga-
tion was impossible, to mastering the techniques of "dry farming"
(some of which, incidentally, were subsequently brought to the
western United States by the Spanish and which are still employed there).[39] These techniques seek to limit the loss of the
little available moisture either through excessive transpiration by
plants or through excessive evaporation from the soil itself. The
latter could be greatly reduced by constant plowing to break up
the capillarity of the surface layers; the former could be reduced
by allowing the land to lie fallow in alternate years during which
it would be kept bare of vegetation, since weeds or a second crop
would themselves transpire moisture. Lupines or similar fertiliz-
ing vegetation could be grown early in the fallow year, but after
they had been plowed under, the land would be kept bare until
the autumn plowing and sowing.

The essential operation under this system is constant plowing
(Figures 2 and 3). The "thrice-plowed fallow field" seems to
have been the norm in early practice, but dense soil might require
five plowings, while the hard clays in Etruria might need nine.[40]
Yet despite the importance of plowing and despite many partial
descriptions of plows in the agricultural writers, no ancient account of the implement allows a complete reconstruction to the
general satisfaction of modern investigators; no Roman plows sur-

1   Digging with the two-pronged hoe. Mosaic, Palace of the Emperors, Istanbul. *The Great Palace of the Emperors*, 2nd report, ed. D. Talbot Rice (Edinburgh, 1958), Pl. 47.

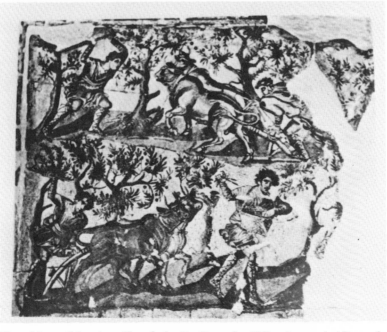

2   Ploughing. Mosaic, Cherchel. J. Berard, "Mosaiques inédites de Cherchel," *MEFR*, LII (1935), Pl. III.

vive, and the monumental representations usually give only an imperfect impression of certain details.

The Roman plow (*aratrum*), however, was surely a symmetrical "breaking plow," rather than a "turning" or "mould-board plow." The latter is valuable for the deep, moist soils in northern Europe and for most in eastern North America, but in a dry farming area it would turn up the earth too deeply, exposing it to the drying action of wind and sun, thereby wasting valuable moisture. The breaking plow, therefore, which disturbs chiefly the surface, generally served the purposes of the ancient farmer. Besides, if soil needed to be ridged over seed (or for drainage), "ridging-boards" or "ears" could be attached.[41]

If the ground had to be worked deeply in an orchard or vine-yard (either to blend in manure or to increase the bed of subsoil, which might retain moisture), trenchers, often members of the chain gang, were likely to be assigned the task. They used a *bipalium* (foot-rest spade), by which they could turn or stir soil to a depth of two and one-half feet.[42] Such deep spading is reported from Greek sites also. The Megarians, according to Theophrastus (*CP* 3. 20. 4), turned over the subsoil every five or six years, digging down as far as the water penetrated, since the "nourishment" would have leached to that depth.

The olive and fig orchards and vineyards presented the farmer with other special problems, although wild olives, figs, and grapes are equipped with extensive root systems which enable them to survive the drought of summer. The olive is typical. Young culti-vated varieties had to be raised in a nursery[43] for three years to develop a satisfactory root system. Then they were trans-planted. Thereafter the digging and hoeing continued, sometimes to ensure proper channeling of water during rains, occasionally to work manure into the soil, and at times preparatory to sowing grain, for intercultivation was practiced in some olive orchards. The necessity to cultivate the soil between the trees, whether it was used or not, and the desire for a variety of products on small subsistence farms must both have encouraged this practice.[44]

The vineyard required even more attention. Columella (*RR* 4. 5) says there is no limit to the number of times vineyards should be hoed, but most people do it every thirty days from March to October. All weeds and grasses should be rooted out. After mid-October, he says (4. 8), the surface roots must be cut away (annually for the first five years) to encourage deeper growth. Both actions relate to dry farming. To pulverize the soil by hoe or by plow would shut in more subsurface moisture; to pull out weeds and grasses would reduce transpiration; and deep roots could reach moisture long after the surface layers had dried. Cato (*Agr.* 33. 3) will allow clover between the rows of vines, and Columella (*RR* 2. 10. 1) lupines, but both intend these plants as fertilizers in exhausted vineyards and not as crops to be harvested.

Intercultivation can be observed from the highways of contemporary Italy, although chiefly perhaps on irrigated land. Wheat amid fruit trees is not uncommon, and even corn (maize) can be observed planted between rather widespaced rows of vines. In dry farming the shelter of taller vegetation is at times advantageous, but yields suffer from the double commitment of water and nutritional resources. The most spectacular attempt to use such shelter is reported from Tabace in Africa,[45] where grain grew under vines, vines under figs, figs under olives, and olives under palms.

Weeding and pulverizing were not the only care for vineyards. The vines needed staking, or even tying to trees (up to the limit of a man's height)[46] in regions with sufficient moisture. In more arid regions, or where damaging winds might harm the grapes, the vines might grow on the ground, despite the danger of foxes and mice, their leaves actually helping to slow the loss of soil moisture. The leaves and fruit might even be dusted to slow transpiration.[47] But perhaps the best known labor of the vineyard (apart from the vintage) was the constant task of pruning vines to guarantee proper growth, encourage fruit, and speed the ripening (by trimming away excess leaves—which again reduced the demands upon moisture in the soil).

Virtually everything described here has pertained to dry farming in the Mediterranean world. The persistence of devices and techniques there into modern times suggests both their efficacy and perhaps that the Roman world was incapable of further technical advances. But this is scarcely true. In the rich wheat-growing region of Gaul near the common border of France, Belgium, and Luxembourg, Pliny (*HN* 18. 296), Palladius (*Agr.* 7. 2. 2–4), and certain reliefs make clear[48] a reaping machine was devised to shorten the work of the harvest. The representations (Figure 4) of its various forms show it propelled from behind by a pack animal or ox between the poles of a cart, the body of which is a box or basket, and the front edge of which is a reaping comb which slices or tears off the heads of grain. An attendant uses

3   Six-pronged drag-hoe. Courtesy, Field Museum of Natural History, Chicago.

4   Reaping Machine. K. D. White, *Agricultural Implements of the Roman World* (Cambridge University Press, New York, 1967), Pl. 15.

a stick to push the heads back into the catchbox. While this is far removed from modern reaping machines, it does suggest that the comparative stability of techniques within the Roman world was in part the product of rather uniform conditions. Had the Romans exercised wide control outside the dry farming areas of the Mediterranean, numerous additional innovations might be known from antiquity.

But how successful were the ancient methods in practice? That is hard to estimate, since we lack satisfactory statistics, but shreds of evidence suggest that the farmers of Italy and Sicily, at least in the first century B.C., obtained yields comparable to some of recent years.[49] Cicero says (*Verr.* 2. 3. 113) that in one part of Sicily wheat under favorable circumstances yielded eightfold when sowed at the rate of one *medimnus* a *iugerum*, and under the best conditions might yield tenfold. This crop of about 70 B.C. (11.2 quintals per hectare) is just slightly greater than the average yield of wheat for 1959 in Sicily (10.6 quintals per hectare). Varro (*RR* 1. 44. 1) regarded tenfold as a typical yield in Italy (presumably about 11 quintals per hectare), a trifle under two-thirds of the present average of 18 in Italy in 1959. But the modern figure would be increased by the rich yields of Lombardy and Venezia, where modern machinery is more widely used. When Varro implies that in parts of Etruria the ancient yield was fifteenfold, he suggests a yield of 17–21 quintals per hectare, a figure quite comparable to the 19.9 quintals per hectare of the official regional statistics for Tuscany in 1959.

But another question arises. The authors obviously echo each other's work. Did they thereby gradually get out of touch with reality, creating virtually a literary tradition of agricultural writing? Palladius (*Agr.* 1. 1. 1–2) certainly thought their literary style had grown too ornate. To phrase the question another way: Would any ancient farmer regard the instructions of Varro, Celsus, or Columella as usable?

Occasional shreds of evidence, again, attest to agreement between the instructions and actual daily practice. Pliny, for example, who knew the Neapolitan area well, said (*HN* 17. 171) that, while vines ought normally be planted five feet apart, in rich soil they could be four feet apart. And Columella before him had recommended that the vineyard be set off by footpaths breaking it into units of about half a *iugerum* each. There were several advantages to this, he had observed: "It offers the vines more sun and wind, grants easier entrance to the eyes and feet of the owner . . . , and it provides a sure basis for judgment in exacting labor . . ." (*RR* 4. 18. 1). Whether or not these advantages impressed one owner of A.D. 79, his vineyard, currently the only ancient vineyard of some size that has been identified in the course of excavation,[50] conforms to certain of these instructions quite well. Footpaths divide it into Columella's half-*iugerum* sections, and in the fertile Campanian soil of Pompeii the vines were set at Pliny's minimum of four Roman feet apart. Further, the high productivity of the plot, perhaps about 1,375 gallons a *iugerum* (to judge from the capacity of the storage jars in the *cella vinaria*), would match notable yields mentioned by Cato and Varro.[51]

This is slight evidence, but, like the slight evidence about yields of wheat, it suggests that solid facts of daily experience stand behind reports from antiquity. And even some confirmation of the so-called "inferential evidence" of modern methods and practices is gained from the Pompeian vineyard under consideration, for at the time of their discovery the excavated vine roots had three or four depressions around them, recognized by modern "workmen as similar to the depressions that they put around their vines to hold water."[52]

The The preceding pages sample what can be said about the personnel,
Successful sites, products, processes, schedules, and tools of ancient agricul-
Farmer ture, chiefly as reconstructed for Italy, but occasionally as they obtained in other parts of the Mediterranean world. The processes, schedules, and tools are ultimately the results of human ingenuity. They originate from long experience over many generations during which men learned to produce, in handy sites, the essentials for life and at times surplus enough to insure some of its comforts and luxuries. They reflect, therefore, specific solutions to specific problems in one part of the world. Consequently, while many techniques and tools seem "old-fashioned" or ineffectual to observers familiar with the methods of farming the heavier, better-watered soils of northern Europe and in much of North America, the techniques of dry farming in the western United States and the contemporary techniques employed in parts of Italy, Spain, and southern France suggest that ancient farmers had indeed a practical knowledge of the agricultural problems of their part of the world and had worked out highly appropriate solutions.

Those ancient farmers, as we meet them in literature, are often typed as crusty, hard-working, frugal men, anxious to get out into the fields, and often downright hostile to intruders upon their privacy. Their unremitting efforts to maintain enough moisture in the soil to grow their crops can well have made them so. But what did they say of themselves in actual life? To this we have at least one answer from an inscription and perhaps the outline of a second from Pliny.

According to Pliny, a freedman, one Gaius Furius Chresimus, had obtained yields from his small farm so superior to those of the very large estates adjacent that his neighbors felt he must be using magic to entice crops from their fields into his own. He was therefore summoned into court on a charge of practicing black magic:

> . . . and he, fearing a guilty verdict . . . brought all his farming equipment . . . , taking along his husky, well-tended, neatly attired slave staff, his well-made iron tools, his heavy mattocks, his hefty plowshares, and his well-fed oxen. Then he said, "Fellow citizens, these are my black magic. I cannot, however, show or produce in this court my nighttime work, or the hours I have kept watch, or my heavy labors [*HN* 18. 41–43].

The story may be apocryphal—Pliny uses it as an instance to illustrate the importance of work in farming—but Chresimus' justifiable pride in the results of his toil is surely akin to that expressed in a genuine inscription set up by the famous "Harvester" at Mactar in Numidia sometime during the third century after Christ.[53] In this monument to his own career the Harvester explains, "I was born of a poor family and an humble father who had neither property nor a house of his own. From the time of my birth I have lived cultivating my lands. Neither the countryside nor I have ever had rest." Then he tells how he had hired out his services as a reaper in the fields of Numidia around Cirta, reaping for twelve seasons in the hot sun, with eleven years as a contractor and foreman for crews.

> This toil and a life content with little made me a landowner—I acquired a home and a farm, and my house itself lacks no wealth.
> My life has received the rewards of public offices, and I myself have been enrolled among our senators. Chosen by the Order, I have sat in the shrine of the Order, and I who was once a peasant (*rusticulus*) have become a censor.

The Harvester[54] is telling himself, "Well done, good and faithful servant," but he also bears proud testimony to the material and spiritual rewards of that life of toil and frugality which characterizes the farmers of literature from the caricatures of comedy to the idealization in Vergil's *Georgics*. Ancient literary motifs have a way of conforming to reality.

Columella (*RR* 1. 1. 1) felt that the successful farmer calls upon three essential resources: technical knowledge, sufficient capital, and a will to work. Pliny's Chresimus, and much more the Harvester, testify to the importance of that will to work, while they proudly describe the productiveness of their toil. The Harvester, too, testifies to the importance of capital, for by his constant toil and frugality as a custom reaper he had been able to amass the means to purchase his house and farm. Countless other farmers in antiquity could have testified to this point from bitter personal experience. When civil or military disturbances had damaged their property, or when changing markets had dictated a change to new crops, they had lacked the capital to rebuild or to convert their farms, hence had been forced to sell and to move to town.

Finally, the handbooks from antiquity testify to the importance of technical knowledge. The authors of these treatises themselves probably best illustrate what Columella has in mind. All clearly know their subject well; all are obviously men of means; all seem to write with the flush of success as they prescribe how to farm profitably. If this is a true estimate, these authors are appropriate successors to Xenophon's tree planters and sowers who were ready to share their skills. And of course they are part of the continuing tradition of agricultural education exemplified by experiment stations, schools, the Peace Corps, and all other training missions still active in every part of the modern world.

"The sea! The sea!" cried Xenophon's Greeks with heartfelt relief after their grueling march overland. They had their bearings once again, they were back upon the familiar shores of the sea "in the middle of the land" whose level expanse offered a swift and convenient path from one end of the ancient world to the other. Men had begun to go down to the Mediterranean in ships as early as the fourth millennium B.C. From then on, the trader, the pirate, the naval commander, each in his own way, worked to perfect techniques and vessels that would enable them to take best advantage of this superbly located means of communication.[1]

When the weather is good, no body of water is easier to sail on than the Mediterranean, particularly the eastern half, which was the scene of ancient civilization's earliest maritime activity.[2] The air is clear, and the shores in most places are steep and high, so the ancient mariner had little trouble following any course along the coast. When traveling over open water, he could pick his way from the stars at night, and during the day he was helped by the frequent lofty islands, visible for miles in the clear atmosphere. The introduction of the compass made little change in the habits of Mediterranean sea captains.

But the clear air and clement weather unfortunately do not last all year round.[3] From October through April the Mediterranean gets its fair share of cloud and mist, winds and storm. The ancients found a simple remedy: they knocked off for the winter. During the months in question, all craft, from the fisherman's skiff to the trader's big-bellied merchantman, slumbered on the beaches or in the harbors; ports shut down; and only a bare handful braved the elements—freighters carrying essential goods to relieve some emergency or government vessels with urgent dispatches.

Even during the summer, all was not always clear sailing. "The smiling sea that seduces" is Lucretius' phrase for the Mediterranean,[4] and it has much truth in it. Like a whore, the Mediterranean can lead a boatman on with clear skies and then turn on him with a tigerish squall. In the eastern half, the prevailing winds are northerly; this means that a southward trip is swift and easy, but the return slow and arduous. During the hottest months, calms are a frequent plague. The Mediterranean, thus, was a superbly convenient waterway—but only for half a year, and even during those months the mariner had to be ready for some slow and hard sailing, and had at all times to keep a weather eye to windward.

The *Earliest* *Sailors* The records of ancient man's first attempts on the water come from the three great rivers where so much of civilization started. Along each, ingenious adapting to local conditions and available materials took place.[5] The upper Tigris and Euphrates, where wood was not only scarce but any craft made of it was liable to be smashed in the stony rapids, saw the development of buoyed rafts, light platforms of saplings or boughs held up by numerous inflated skins. In the smoother lower waters, boatmen turned to coracles, bowl-shaped cockleshells of hides stretched over a light frame; these in time grew to sizes large enough to transport chariots and horses. Along the Nile, where wood was equally scarce but reeds grew in abundance, the Egyptians lashed bundles of them into rafts, which they soon perfected into sophisticated, boat-shaped affairs. Elsewhere, in forested regions about the Mediterranean, the dugout canoe came into being.

The true boat—a craft that would not only carry men across water but keep them dry at the same time—arose in different ways in different places. In Egypt, the boat-shaped reed raft was copied in wood; even as bundles of reeds had been bound together to form a boat-shaped raft, so planks were fastened together to make a wooden craft. In areas that used dugouts, boatmen learned to raise the sides of their canoes by adding planks as washboards. The planks could be fastened to each other by pegs or joints, or could be sewn together with twine; the Egyptians preferred the first technique,[6] their neighbors to the east the second.[7] True boats made in either of these fashions are attested as early as the second half of the fourth millennium B.C.[8]

The end of the fourth millennium B.C. marks a milestone in naval technology: this is when men learned to use the wind.[9] Now they were truly ready to take to the open sea; it is at this point that the story of the ancient sailor in a very real sense begins.

The early nautical achievements we know best are those of the ancient Egyptians.[10] By 2500 B.C., they were building vessels well over one hundred feet long and powered by a tall, oblong squaresail; these traveled as far as the Syrian coast for timber or down the Red Sea for incense and ivory. Yet the Egyptians were never in the mainstream of ancient naval technology. Throughout their history they favored lightly built craft designed first and foremost for the Nile.[11] The great strides which produced ships able to withstand the rigors of sailing the open water were taken elsewhere—along the coasts of Asia Minor and the Levant, or in Crete, lands that conducted a far-flung and active trade with one another. We have only miniature pictures on seals or the like to tell us of the craft used,[12] yet they are enough to reveal that, by the middle of the second millennium B.C., these countries had developed the types of vessels which were to become standard throughout ancient times: the slender, many-oared galley, primarily for war and piracy but available also for commerce; and the sturdy, big-bellied merchantmen driven by a large squaresail amidships.

Men of War A warship must be, above all, maneuverable. In the Mediterranean, beset during the summer season by frequent calms, there was only one way to guarantee this—by using galleys.

An ancient oar-driven warship was totally different in nature and behavior from what most of us imagine a warship to be like. It was, in effect, an overgrown racing shell (Figures 1–5), light enough, even the bigger types, to be run up on a beach or into a ship by its crew. It generally ventured forth only when the seas were placid. Its benches filled with oarsmen and its decks with marines, it had no room for stockpiles of provisions; it rarely stayed at sea but returned to land at night to allow the crew to prepare meals on the beach and spend the night there. All naval battles necessarily took place right off the coast and lasted but one day, closing when night sent both sides hurrying home. Such naval activities as patrol and blockade have a very limited meaning in ancient contexts: a group of galleys was perhaps able to bottle up a harbor mouth, but the blockading of a whole coastline was utterly out of the question. A group of galleys could patrol the waters in front of known pirate nests, but conducting wide-ranging sweeps over open water was equally unfeasible.

About 1290 B.C., Ramses II of Egypt threw back an attempt at a large-scale invasion by sea. So proud was he of the victory that he had a huge picture of it carved on the walls of one of his temples, thereby giving us the earliest representation of a sea battle and our first clear idea of what ancient warships looked like.[13] His were slender galleys (Figure 1), powered by ten or so men on either side, each pulling a single oar. Every ship carried

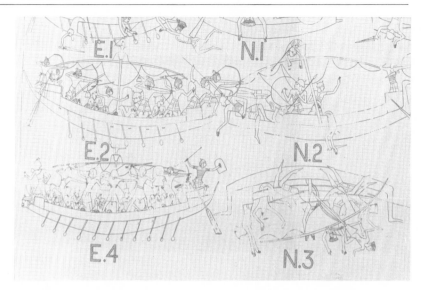

1   Egyptian warships of ca. 1300 B.C. H. Nelson, "The Naval Battle Pictured at Medinet Habu," *Journal of Near Eastern Studies*, Vol. 2 (1943), Fig. 4.

2   Two-banked Phoenician galley of ca. 700 B.C. Palace of Sennacherib. Courtesy, British Museum, London.

a complement of marines and archers on the decks, and the method of fighting was to bring these to the point where they could inflict damage on the enemy, perhaps even board him and take possession of his craft. Ramses' galleys could not have been very different in basic nature from the celebrated craft described in the poems of Homer. The prime purpose of both was to transport fighting personnel. Homer's heroes, having greater distances to cover, used much larger ships: even their small dispatch boats had ten rowers to a side, while the normal galley had twenty-five or even more.[14]

Sometime in the ninth century B.C. came a dramatic innovation, one that gave a totally different turn to ancient naval architecture and warfare—the ram. The credit for its invention goes either to the Greeks or the Phoenicians—we cannot be sure which. Shipwrights now designed vessels with the bow prolonged into a sharp, massively reinforced point shod with bronze (Figures 2, 3, 5). Crews no longer sought only to bring the marines and archers near enough to damage or even board an enemy; a quicker, more final decision could be gained by slamming the ram into him at a vital point. The warship had become a self-propelled projectile.

The introduction of the new weapon quickly brought in its wake a second all-important change. The harder the ram's stroke, the more effective it was; and the one way to make it harder was to increase the number of rowers. During the seventh and sixth centuries B.C., the standard galley was the penteconter, the "fifty," that is, a ship with twenty-five oarsmen on either side. So long as the rowers were seated in one line, their number could not well be increased, for the result would be a craft overly long and slender. By the beginning of the seventh century B.C., shipwrights had come up with the solution, one that was to have an effect equal to the introduction of the ram: the arrangement of rowers in superimposed banks.

The first step was, naturally, to use but two rows of oarsmen (Figures 2 and 3); for example, the designing of double-banked penteconters with thirteen men in the upper and twelve in the lower. But improvement went ahead with such speed that, by the end of the sixth century B.C., the climax had been reached with the emergence of that famed product of Greek naval engineering, the trireme.[15]

The trireme, or *trieres* to give it its technical Greek name,

3   Two-banked Greek galley of the 6th century B.C. Tarquinia Museum.
           Photo, Anderson.

4   Reconstructed cross section of an Athenian trireme of the 5th century
           B.C. National Maritime Museum, Greenwich. Photo, John Morrison.

had three superimposed lines of rowers, each of whom, as in all previous types of galley, wielded his own oar (Figure 4). Deep in the hull, working their oars through ports, sat the row of thalamites, twenty-seven to the side. Just above them, working theirs through ports just below the gunwale, sat the zygites, also twenty-seven to a side. Slightly higher than, and outboard of, the zygites, working their oars through an outrigger set upon the gunwale, sat the thranites; there were thirty-one of them to a side, since the gracefully rising curve of the vessel aft left room for four more oars than in the other banks. The word *trieres* means "three-equipped"; it refers to the cluster of three oarsmen who sat each above the other, the thalamite, zygite, and thranite, in a vertical, or nearly vertical, line. There were twenty-seven such clusters on either side; these plus the four extra thranites on each quarter made a total of 170 rowers. To fit everybody in, triremes ran 120 feet in length, with a beam of slightly over 15 feet. On a short afterdeck sat the helmsman, guiding the ship by means of a pair of steering oars, one slung on either quarter; alongside him the captain took his station. Forward of the bow oars was a foredeck on which crowded the spearmen and archers who formed the fighting force; forward of this stretched the massive timbers that ended in the bronze-shod point of the ram. Since the oarsmen were to be saved for battle, every galley carried sailing gear. The working rig consisted of a mast amidships that could be lowered, on which was mounted an ample, broad square-sail. Since this was stowed away during action—or even, when convenient, left ashore—each ship at all times carried an emergency rig, a short mast and small sail that could be set up easily and swiftly.[16] In Roman times the working rig was augmented by a little sail placed in the very eye of the ship, like a bowsprit-sail (Figure 5).

The trireme was a light craft, extremely so, and, to be effective, it had to be kept that way and not allowed to get waterlogged. When away from port, crews ran their ships up each night on the beach. In port they were housed in special slips which held them raised out of the water and which were roofed to keep off rain. Despite their light structure, triremes lasted an average of twenty years, and some hardy Methuselahs stayed alive as long as twenty-five.[17] For those built in regular course and not thrown together to meet an emergency, the materials were select logs of fir, pine, or cedar, and the method of construction—we unfortunately lack any information—may very well have involved the same superb craftsmanship that characterized the building of merchantmen (see pp. 191–195).

By the beginning of the fifth century B.C., the trireme had become the queen of the sea. It retained this distinction unchallenged during the fifth and fourth centuries B.C., and again during the long heyday of the Roman Imperial Navy, from the first to the third centuries after Christ.[18] Only during the three hundred years from 300 B.C. to the beginning of the Christian era did it lose pride of place, yielding to a widespread predilection for larger units. Toward the beginning of the fourth century B.C., *tetrereis*, "fours," and *pentereis*, "fives," made their debut in warfleets. Then, within a hectic sixty to seventy years, from ca. 320 to 250 B.C., the successors of Alexander, in possession of far greater resources than the individual Greek city states which they had conquered and consolidated, entered into a frantic naval race that produced ever greater and greater units: the "fives" were followed by "sixes," "sevens," "eights"—right up to a pair of "twenties," a "thirty," and a "forty."

Unfortunately, no certain pictures of these craft have survived, nor even useful descriptions of them.[19] Of one thing we can be sure: they did not have four, five, six, and so on, tiers of oars. The trireme marked the limit so far as superimposed banks were concerned; there were never more than three. In designing these larger units, the naval architect's key break with the past was to abandon the practice, so carefully maintained hitherto, of putting one man at each oar. The ancients had a weakness for this system, for it enabled a rower to work from a seated position. Even two men can operate an oar this way, which makes it very likely that the first "fours" were merely triremes expanded to take two men on each upper oar, and the first "fives" triremes expanded to take two men on each oar in the two upper banks. Perhaps, similarly, the first "sixes" were triremes with two men on each oar throughout. But for units larger than this, naval architects perforce had to turn to the long sweep manned by three or more men. Once they did this, they had to give up the seated stroke for one in which the rowers rose to their feet to dip the blade and threw themselves back on the bench to deliver the stroke. This brought, in compensation, one important advantage: in a trireme, every oarsman had to be skilled; in a ship powered by multiple-rower sweeps, only the man at the head of the loom had to be, and the others supplied merely muscle.[20]

All larger units from the "sevens" upward must have been

driven by one, two, or three superimposed banks of such sweeps. Since we know no details, we can only offer reasonable guesses. A "seven," for example, could very well have had an upper row of four-man sweeps and a lower row of three-man sweeps, an "eight" could have had two rows of four-man sweeps, a "ten" could have had two rows of five-man sweeps, and so on.[21] Indeed, once the multiple-rower sweep came into widespread use, it was then introduced even in the smaller units. For example, alongside the "fours" and "fives" which, as suggested before, may have been oared like expanded triremes, there were designed and launched single-banked versions using four-man and five-man sweeps respectively,[22] as well as two-banked versions using, perhaps for the "five," two-man and three-man oars.

These larger units, heavier and less maneuverable than the trireme, though always fitted with the ram, were intended primarily for grappling and boarding. The increased size supplied room for bigger contingents than ever of marines, and the greater stability allowed the mounting of catapults on the decks, so that the firing of missiles to open battle could take place while the combatants were still a considerable distance apart. Most ships of the line were constructed in "cataphract" fashion, as the Greeks put it, that is, closed in by a fighting deck above and by protective screens along the sides. In this way the rowers were kept safe from spears, arrows and catapult missiles.

Big war galleys were relatively short-lived. By 250 B.C., the great superdreadnoughts, those ranked as "thirteens" or higher, had all but run their course. The others lasted somewhat longer; Mark Antony, for example, had "tens" at the Battle of Actium in 31 B.C. And that just about marked the end. Though the Roman Imperial Navy used a "six" as flagship and had a certain number of "fours" and "fives," its standard ship was, as half a millennium earlier, the trireme.

The complement of a trireme at full strength amounted to no less than 200. In addition to 170 rowers, there were 25 hands to work lines and sail and 5 officers. In command of the ship was the trierarch. In many Greek navies he was a rich man of the community who for one year assumed certain expenses in connection with a galley and was given its command, at least in name. The ship itself was built and fitted at public cost; what the trierarch took on was the financial burden, often very heavy, of keeping it manned and running for a year. This system, started by the Greek city states early in the fifth century B.C., was carried on even by the great maritime powers of the third and second centuries. On the other hand, the Roman Imperial Navy, established by Augustus toward the end of the first century, was run entirely on government funds.[23]

Second to the trierarch was the *kybernetes*, the executive officer, when a trierarch was in command, and the actual captain, when the trierarch chose not to take command. His station was aft, alongside the helmsman. Under him was the *proreus* or *proretes*, "bow officer," who held down the foredeck, and the *keleustes*, literally, "time beater," who had complete responsibility for the rowing personnel. In more primitive times the *keleustes* no doubt actually beat the time; now this was done by the *trieraules*, "trireme flutist." Then there was the complement of fighting personnel; in navies that went in for ramming tactics these could be as few as ten to fifteen; in those that preferred grappling and boarding, it could be four to five times that number. "Fours" and "fives" and other larger units, as might be expected, carried additional personnel, such as a ship's doctor and a carpenter, and, of course, special crews to work the catapults.

Greek navies were innocent of any elaborate logistic or commissary arrangements. When cruising, a Greek admiral's sole responsibility was to pick a spot for beaching his fleet near enough to a town so that the men could go off and buy food. It seems incredible that a casual town market could take care of a sudden influx of thousands of customers, but the system apparently worked. The Roman navy, with its more sophisticated organization and its network of bases, very likely was less haphazard on this score.

The crew of a trireme, 170 men pulling 170 oars to exact coordination, had to be perfectly trained—"beaten together," to use the Greek phrase. This meant long hours of extended practice. Occasionally fleets were built from scratch in a hurry, and green hands had to be turned overnight into rowers; wooden platforms were then set up on land to accustom the men at least to the movements of the stroke while they waited for the ships to come off the stocks.[24] Practice was essential not only for teaching the stroke but for putting the crews into proper physical shape. In 494 B.C., the Greek cities of Asia Minor, in an attempt to throw off the Persian yoke, organized a fleet and turned over the training of the rowers, citizens who had eagerly volunteered, to a hard-bitten old navy hand. The volunteers took just one week of the punishing regime he put them through and then quit en masse

(Herodotus 6. 12). Anyone who has nursed a set of blisters and sore muscles from a few hours in a rowboat can appreciate how they felt.

For the crews of navies that specialized in ramming tactics, proper training was of the essence. Ramming was not only a most delicate maneuver, but a one-shot or at best a two-shot affair: a captain could not afford to miss more than twice, for by then his rowers were too exhausted to go through the grueling procedure all over again. At the moment of impact his ship had to be traveling at an intermediate speed: if too slow, the enemy could back water out of range; if too fast, the thrust would embed the ram too deeply in the enemy hull, and his men would not be able to back water in time to get clear before the opponent's marines could grapple and board. If the first thrust missed or was not mortal, his men had to be ready to back water at full speed just enough to get into proper position again and then resume forward movement at the appropriate ramming speed. It was this need to fight a battle in a sort of slow motion, as it were, that made marines an essential part of the complement of all vessels, even those designed chiefly for the use of the ram. Without such fighters to rake the enemy's deck during the approach or to stand by to repel boarders after the impact, the attacked vessel's marines could grapple, board, and stand a fair chance of taking over the attacker.

Besides training, the crews needed courage. In the days of the single-banked open warship, a rower of a defeated vessel might count on survival: a wooden galley, when holed, does not sink but either goes awash or capsizes, and, in either event, the men stood some chance of getting clear and swimming off. But any such chances were incomparably less on a cataphract, closed in as it was on top and all sides. Some of the rowers of the upper bank might be able to scramble out to safety, but surely the others, particularly the lowermost in a trireme, were doomed. And we can only guess at the havoc caused internally, for example, by a maneuver like that in which an attacker passed close enough to an enemy to shear off his oars.

On vessels using multiple-rower sweeps, the standard of training could be a good deal less demanding. For one, these ships were intended more for boarding than for ramming. For another, as indicated previously, only the rower at the head of the loom had to be experienced. He guided the stroke; the others along the oar just added muscle.

The introduction of the multiple-rower sweep was very likely connected with the increasing difficulty that nations began to experience in recruiting crews. In the earliest times, such as those described by Homer, there was no problem: the fighting men of the army doubled as rowers. When Odysseus or Agamemnon or Achilles boarded their ships, their men took their places at the oars; on landing, the men dropped the oars to take up shield and spear. As galleys grew more sophisticated, the oarsmen came to require special skill, particularly aboard a trireme, which, by the fifth century B.C., was the universal ship of the line. Rowers were now drawn chiefly from among the poorer citizens: those men who could afford armor and weapons performed their military service in the ranks of the infantry; those who could not, on the benches of the galleys. Except on certain extraordinary occasions, slaves were never used as galley rowers at any time during the ancient world—the widespread misconception to the contrary, the galley slave did not make his appearance until the fifteenth century after Christ.[25] As more nations built up naval forces, and as the fleets got bigger in numbers and adopted larger types of galleys, the need for rowers skyrocketed. Athens, for example, lost some 200 triremes with their crews at the famous siege of Syracuse in 415–413 B.C., a loss, in other words, of no less than 34,000 rowers. Greek city states were simply not populous enough to supply the manpower required. As a result, in the fourth century B.C. there came into prominence the mercenary rower, the man who hired himself out to pull an oar for whatever state offered him the most attractive salary.[26] Some smaller Greek navies continued to depend on their citizens, notably the island of Rhodes which boasted a long and proud naval tradition. In most, however, from the fourth to the first centuries B.C., the benches were manned by a mélange of citizen and mercenary rowers. The Ptolemies of Egypt, for example, who had no maritime population to draw on, had to hire most of their skilled oarsmen. The Roman Imperial Navy broke with the past in this respect as in so many others: having available to it the populations of its far-flung possessions, it manned its units with provincials. Since the Romans themselves had no taste for the sea, they turned for the officers to the maritime cities of the Greek east, and, for the men, to the less developed or the more exploited provinces in the empire. The fleet based at Ravenna had large contingents from the coastal towns and villages of Illyria and Dalmatia; that based at Misenum near Naples had numerous Egyptians. Both, set up on a permanent and well-organized basis, had the time and facilities to convert this raw material into trained oarsmen. Boys from the provinces in question did not hesitate to sign up for the twenty-six year hitch required. They had scant hope of getting ahead in their local villages, while a career in the navy not only opened new horizons but gave them a chance to earn Roman citizenship along with their honorable discharge. By a lucky accident there has survived to our day a letter[27] from a young boot who, sometime in the second century after Christ had left his home town in Egypt, been shipped to Italy, and there received word that he was assigned to the fleet at Misenum. He writes to his father full of enthusiasm, mentioning his "hope to get quick promotion, if the gods are willing." He adds that he has given "Euctemon a picture of myself to bring to you"; in those precamera days it had to be a miniature—but, just as in postcamera days, it unquestionably showed him in his new sailor suit.

A long road had been traversed. Over a thousand years earlier, in Homeric times, the able-bodied men who could afford to own arms and fight in the army doubled as oarsmen. By the fifth century B.C., in most Greek city states it was those citizens who could not afford arms who reported to the harbor at regular intervals for rowing practice and, when the call came, for the hazards of actual battle. A century later, groups of outsiders were to be found living about the naval installations, professional oarsmen who shared the benches with whatever citizens could still be persuaded to serve. And then the Roman Imperial Navy introduced the system familiar to us, the use of conscripts or volunteers for a fixed hitch—a good long one, so that the navy would be served by professionals who dedicated a lifetime to it. At the great naval bases in Italy were garrisons of Greeks, Dalmatians, Illyrians, Egyptians, Levantines, Corsicans, Sardinians, and others, who spent the best part of their lives in the service, often married local girls, and, if they lasted, retired as Roman citizens. But their sons did not often replace them; with a better start than their fathers, they were able to enlist in the choicer service of the legions, while fresh young recruits from all about the Mediterranean flocked in to replenish the naval ranks.

Merchant-
men In the ancient world the galley was not limited to warfare or piracy (which can be considered a kind of warfare). There were also merchant galleys, heavier and slower than their slender, war-

5   A Roman trireme of ca. A.D. 100. Fototeca Unione, Rome.

6

Roman merchantman of ca.
A.D. 200, entering the harbor of
Portus. Torlonia Museum, Rome.
Fototeca Unione, Rome.

like sisters and making far more use of sail. The merchantmen par excellence, however, were sailing ships.

It is often stated that the ancients were for long timid sailors who clung to the coasts and consequently used craft of relatively small size. Galleys—of war and commerce—clung to the coasts because, as explained above, they had no alternative. But as early as the third millennium B.C., sailing ships were striking boldly across open water.

The earliest craft were rigged with a single broad squaresail amidships.[28] In the sixth century B.C., perhaps even before, a square foresail was added (Figure 6). As time went on, this was reduced in size and converted into a bowsail, the *artemon*, a small squaresail set on a short mast that slanted over the bows (Figures 5, 7, 8); it served not as a driver so much as to aid maneuvering and to give lift to the bow and keep it from digging in. For added drive, a triangular topsail was flown over the mainsail (Figure 6).

This three-sail rig—*artemon*, mainsail, and topsail—was standard throughout the ancient world for all but the biggest ships, which added a square mizzen on the afterdeck (Figure 8). It was neither fast nor efficient. Since drive was provided largely by the mainsail, this came to be a broad, unwieldy expanse hung from a yard that often ran nearly as long as the ship itself. The world had to wait until the fifteenth century after Christ before sailors took to breaking the canvas up into more easily managed, superimposed units.

Yet the absence of superimposed sails allowed the ancients to introduce one unique feature which no later age has matched.[29] In all subsequent times, the standard way of shortening canvas has been by means of reefpoints, short lengths of rope pinned at intervals across the sail. When the need arose to shorten sail, a few hands would slack off the appropriate lines from the deck, while most would swarm aloft and, perched precariously along the yards, gather in the billowing canvas, bunch it, and tie it securely with the reefpoints. The ancients' system of shortening sail was totally different. Instead of reefpoints it used what we call brails, lines which, guided by fairleads, ran from the foot of the sail vertically up the forward surface to the yard and then from the yard aft to the deck (Figures 5–8). By hauling on all simultaneously, the crew could quickly bunch the sail together up to the yard like a venetian blind, and hands would have to go aloft only to snug it down. By hauling on certain brails to a given extent the crew could shorten any part of the sail the

7

Greek
merchantman of
500 B.C. Tomba
della Nave.
Courtesy of
Dr. M. Moretti,
Superintendent
for Antiquities
of Lower Etruria.

8

Roman
merchantman of
ca. A.D. 200.
Mosaic from the
office of the
Shippers of
Sullecthum. Foro
delle
Corporazioni,
Ostia.

desired amount. Had the ancients used superimposed sails, they very likely could not have introduced this convenient system, for it would have involved too many lines. But with their simplified rig it was ideal, not only permitting more accurate and quicker control than reefpoints but also avoiding the hazards and effort of going aloft.

The ancient rig, offering no great expanse of canvas in relation to a vessel's size, was slow.[30] Moreover, the big mainsail, made to catch the wind from behind, was of scant use against it; on such a course, a ship was lucky to log two or three knots. This was not too serious, since ordinarily no sailing ship sailed against the wind unless there was absolutely no avoiding it. On the other hand, even under ideal weather conditions and with a wind steadily from behind, conditions under which the crack clippers of the last century used to log eighteen to twenty knots, the best an ancient merchantman could do was six. Voyaging long distances, thus, was a tedious business. Rome to the Levant or Egypt, a crossing that could generally count on a fair wind all the way, took two to three weeks, while the return could take two to three months. The situation was somewhat better in the western Mediterranean where the winds were more variable and more usefully slanted. Rome to the Strait of Gibraltar or vice versa, for example, could be done in less than two weeks.

When the breeze was light, the ancient mariner slacked off the sheets and brails to let the great mainsail balloon out to the forestay.[31] The moment the wind freshened, he could meet the danger in an instant by taking up on the brails; since his rig was so low, the wind rarely could exercise enough leverage to put the ship in peril of capsizing (Seneca *Epistles* 77. 2). If the wind grew still fresher, he either brailed in further or dropped the yard to a lower point on the mast, thereby lowering the center of pressure. On the occasions when he could not avoid sailing into the wind, he braced the yard sharply round and brought the weather sheet forward of the mast (Seneca *Medea* 321–322). With his excessively broad mainsail, this probably let him sail no closer to the wind than seven points, that is, with the wind just slightly ahead of the beam.

If the ancient mariner's rig was not too efficient, his steering apparatus, despite the common belief to the contrary, was supremely efficient.[32] It consisted of two oversize oars, hung slantwise on either quarter and fixed in a protective housing (Figure 6). They were fastened to the hull in such a way that they rotated on their axis, and the helmsman made them turn by means of long tiller bars socketed at right angles into the upper part of the loom. The axis of turning did not bisect the blade: there was a carefully worked out variation in the width of the blade abaft and forward of the axis,[33] and it was precisely this variation that made the blades so effective as rudders. The steering oars were remarkably easy to handle, and the ship responded swiftly and obediently to their slightest motion. The stern rudder, which replaced them in the thirteenth century of our era, was brought in for reasons other than efficiency alone.

Hulls took two general shapes (Figure 8). Most ships, as we would expect of beamy cargo carriers, were tubby affairs with well-rounded bow and stern. But alongside this was a second type whose prow was convex, ending at the waterline in a ramlike point. The reason for this and its advantages are anybody's guess. It could not have been intended as a weapon, for it is found not only on huge lumbering freighters but even on tiny skiffs.

The hulls ran the gamut of size, depending on their purpose.[34] For ordinary overseas hauling, the smallest craft the ancients considered useful were from 70 to 80 tons burden. From the fifth century B.C. on, carriers of from 100 to 150 tons burden were common, while those of from 150 to 500, though considered big, were by no means rare. When it came to passengers, vessels could take as many as 600 on long voyages. The building of oversize warships in the third century B.C. apparently affected merchant marines: not long after the middle of that century the biggest freighter known from the ancient world, a brobdingnagian grain carrier of some 1,700 to 1,900 tons burden, came off the ways under the eye of Archimedes himself. In subsequent centuries, great grain freighters of perhaps 1,300 tons plied between Alexandria and Rome. The dimensions of one of these has been preserved: 180 feet long, 45 wide, 43½ deep in the hold—as big as Britain's largest East Indiamen, those in use just before the coming of steam. The dimensions that went along with the other tonnages varied according to the cargo the ship was built to carry: for example, a 250-ton craft for hauling building stone would be shorter and sturdier than one for hauling grain. As it happens, our information about dimensions is limited to carriers of heavy loads such as wine, which was shipped in ponderous clay jars, or building stone. These vessels commonly ran 60 to 100 feet long and 25 to 33 broad, while larger types reached 130 by 33. The figures may not seem impressive by nineteenth- or twentieth-century standards, but they are by those of any other century. Indeed, Rome's merchant marine in the first or second centuries after Christ surpassed in the number and size of its units any that sailed the waters subsequently until practically the end of the eighteenth century.

Shipbuilding, Accommodations, Crews   And the ships of these fleets must have been remarkably long-lived and sound, for they were built in a special way, unique to the Greco-Roman shipwright, that was a model of craftsmanship.[35]

There are basically two ways to construct a wooden boat. The one that has been most widely used, particularly in the West, begins with the setting up of a sturdy skeleton of keel and frames (ribs); then, to this, is fastened a smooth skin of planks. The other, favored by southern Asia and some parts of northern Europe, is just the reverse: first a sturdy shell of planks is erected by pinning each plank to its neighbors, and then a certain amount of framing is inserted to stiffen the shell.

The shipwright who starts with a shell of planks may join these to each other in any of three ways. One, best known to us because it was used in northern Europe and can be traced from pre-Viking times to our own day, produced the clinker-built boat: each plank overlaps the one below for a certain distance, and pegs or nails or rivets driven through where the thickness is double hold the two securely together. In the other two methods, the planks are set edge to edge to make a smooth skin; what differs is the means for fastening. In the waters from the east coast of Africa to India and in many other areas as well, the planks are sewed to one another with twine made from coconut husk or split bamboo or whatever fiber is available. This was, for example, the favored practice of Persian and Arab shipbuilders: we hear of boats so made as early as the first century after Christ; Marco Polo reported seeing them; and the technique was widely practiced in the Indian Ocean, Red Sea, Persian Gulf, and elsewhere until the coming of Westerners brought in the more flexible keel-and-frames system. In other parts of India, notably eastern Pakistan, in parts of Egypt, and in certain other regions, the planks are pegged together or nailed together. Whichever of the two systems of fastening is used, the frames, if any, are always inserted later. They are not necessarily of any great strength: in some makes of boat the number depends simply upon how much money the shipwright wants to spend; he often adds frames only after the boat has been in long use and the shell has started to weaken.

As mentioned before, far back in primitive times the Mediterranean knew the sewn boat, and ancient Egypt had learned by the third millennium B.C. to build craft of planks edge-joined by means of joints. The great forward step, however, was taken by Greece and Rome. The Greco-Roman shipwright, as we are now aware through the discovery of numerous ancient wrecks, created his own form of shipbuilding, one so refined that it more resembles cabinet work than carpentry. In a sense he combined the two basic ways of putting together a planked boat. Like the Egyptian (from whom he may have gotten the idea), he started with a shell of planks. But instead of using casual joinery he locked these together with mortices set as close as the joints in a piece of furniture; and into this tightly knit structure he inserted framing as complete as that in hulls made with a pre-erected skeleton. So far as we can tell, the building of ships in this impressive fashion was peculiar to, and the sole method used by, the Greco-Roman world; it very likely goes back at least to Homer's day, and it was still employed well into the Byzantine period. The technique of pinning a skin to a pre-erected skeleton, which was to become standard in Western shipbuilding, came into use no earlier than the Middle Ages.

The Greek or Roman shipwright's first step was to lay the keel. He added stempost and sternpost, probably scarfing them to the keel, and very likely set up a number of temporary mold frames to guide him in giving the shell the proper lines. His very next step was to begin on the planking, setting the garboard strakes into a rabbet in the keel and edge-joining the succeeding planks with an appropriate number of mortices and tenons. Sometimes he planked up to the gunwales before turning to insert the frames; sometimes he planked only a certain distance up the sides and then inserted frames, finishing off the planking later. The strakes ran in thickness from two inches to four inches as a rule; a wide variety of widths appear in the same vessel, reflecting no doubt whatever could most economically be sawn from available logs. The garboard strakes were morticed to the keel rabbet, and sometimes they and other bottom planks were doubled, the outer layer being spiked to the inner. For edge-joining strakes, tenons two inches broad were most common, but they could run as wide as four inches; in depth they could penetrate halfway into the plank (Figure 9). On seagoing ships the mortices

seem never to have been more than eight inches apart, most often
they were but two inches to five inches (Figure 9), and sometimes
by being staggered so that one was nearer the outboard surface
and the next nearer the inboard, there was hardly any space at
all between them. It seems likely that the mortices were cut into
the upper edge of a plank already in place, and the tenons inserted
into the lower edge of the plank to come next; this plank could
be clamped temporarily in place while the carpenter marked
where the tenons were to go. The wood for the strakes, because
of the many joints each had to take, was selected with great
care, not too green and not too dry; too green, on drying out,
would leave the joints with too much play; too dry would involve
the risk of splitting when the plank was knocked into place and
the joints driven home.[36] There is some evidence that the tenons
were greased to make them slip easily into their slots (Plutarch
Moralia 321d). Once the joints were driven home, each was transfixed by a wooden peg to make sure it would never separate
(Figure 9).

When the shell had been completed or nearly so, the shipwright
turned to the insertion of frames, scoring lines on the inner surface of the shell to show where each was to go. On seagoing craft
he placed them not over ten inches apart (Figure 10), and most
were often much closer. Some vessels had frames that were all
one unit, a floor timber spanning the bottom of the vessel scarfed
to futtocks; other vessels alternated this type with frames that
had no floors, descending on either side to rest on the keelson.
The shipwright secured each frame to the planking with treenails,
and often, to wedge them in as tightly as possible, transfixed
the treenails with bronze spikes; on occasion spikes longer than
the thickness to be spanned were used so that the part protruding
through the inner face of the frame could be clenched. Over the
frames, made fast to them by nails, was laid a lining (Figure
10). A keelson rested on the keel, appropriately notched to pass
over the floor timbers. On some ships, at the point where the
mainmast was stepped, there was fixed over the keel a massive
piece of timber with a socket hollowed out in it to receive the
heel of the mast.[37] Below the keel was a false keel, of resistant
beech if it had to withstand the wear and tear of hauling on
to shore or across seaways.

With planks edge-joined by close-set mortices, caulking was
hardly needed, and, on the wrecks examined so far, evidence
of it has yet to be found. When the joints were relatively widely

9   Planking from an ancient wreck of the 2nd century B.C., split from edge to edge, revealing the mortices and tenons, the latter about $2\frac{3}{4}''$ wide. F. Benoit, *L'épave du Grand Congloué à Marseille*, XIVᵉ *Supplément à Gallia* (Paris, 1961), Fig. 82.

spaced, however, caulking was essential, and it was done with whatever was locally available. Most hulls, but not all, were protected against marine borers by a sheath of lead sheets set over a layer of tarred fabric and held in place by multitudinous large-headed copper tacks.

Since the sea floor for the most part preserves only the bottoms of ancient wrecks, we know much less about the construction of the upper part of the hull. Sometimes all the deck beams were brought through the sides, a practice that is attested in the third millennium B.C. in Egypt and remained characteristic of Mediterranean shipbuilding up to at least Renaissance times; sometimes only massive through-beams, inserted aft and amidships and forward to add to the lateral stiffening, came through the sides (Figure 6). Powerful waling pieces girdled the hull horizontally (Figure 6), held in place by spikes or even long bolts that passed through the frames and the lining; matching these were heavy stringers on the inside. The upper part of the hull was brought out on either quarter into winglike projections for housing the steering oars (Figure 6).

It was usual to smear the seams or even the whole hull with pitch and wax.[38] Ship's paint was encaustic, that is, wax melted to a consistency that could be applied with a brush and to which color had been added. The colors available, mineral derivatives, were purple, white, blue, yellow, green, red; the brighter shades, such as red or blue or purple, were used for bow-patches and decorative effects. The hull could be either painted or left the black color it took on from its coat of pitch.

The woods preferred for planking, frames, and keel were fir, cedar, and pine, but cypress, elm, and alder saw service as well, the choice most likely being determined by what was available locally. Oak was freely used for frames and false keel, and particularly for tenons and treenails, but apparently not for strakes.[39]

In the hold of an ancient merchantman, the floor was given over to ballast and bilge. Floor timbers had limber holes to allow free passage of bilge water, which was such a problem that often a hand—generally the least able in the crew—was detailed to stand by and keep an eye on it. On larger craft bailing was done by sophisticated devices, such as an Archimedean screw operated by a treadmill, on smaller with buckets. Ballast was usually sand or stone. Cargoes of wine jars, building stones, tiles, ingots, or the like, were loaded right on the lining (Figure 10), but more perishable wares, such as sacks of grain, were no doubt stored well

10   The floor of the Chrétienne A wreck of the 1st century B.C. Bottom
          planking, frames and lining are clearly distinguishable. Photo,
          F. Dumas.

above the bilges. The commonest form of dunnage was twigs and branches, and stowage methods were employed that utilized every inch of space. Once the hatches had been battened down, additional cargo could be loaded on deck. Deep in the hold was the water supply, at times carried in a single, large receptacle rather than numbers of smaller. In one wreck that has been particularly carefully examined, the aftermost 'tween-deck area was entirely given over to the galley. The port half was the hearth, consisting of a grid of iron bars on which rested a floor of flat tiles, the whole set at a level of about two feet above the floor proper of the galley. The starboard half was the work space; probably the bulkheads were lined with shelves and cupboards. The galley was roofed over with standard clay rooftiles; one of these over the hearth was pierced by a large smokehole.[40]

The main deck on freighters of any size ran from stem to stern. Bigger ships had a lower deck, and the biggest, two. Whether the lower decks were complete or partial is not known.

There was never a foredeck but always a poop deck—or rather an ample platform formed by the roof of a superstructure at the stern (Figure 6). This usually took the form of a deckhouse with doors to port and starboard. Further aft an inclined overhanging gallery girdled the stern. On larger craft the overhang was great enough to allow for a small shelter suspended over open water behind the sternpost, perhaps a latrine to judge from its position. The choicest accommodations were in the deckhouse: here were the quarters for the owner or his agent, for the captain, and for a few select passengers traveling, as it were, first-class. On very special ships, particularly royal yachts, these accommodations could offer genuine luxury: lavishly fitted cabins, promenades, exercise areas, baths, lounges, chapels. Most passengers, as in medieval times, camped on deck, living either in the open or under tiny temporary shelters (Achilles Tatius 2. 33. 1). There were also some steerage accommodations in the bowels of the ship (Lucian, *Jup. Trag.* 48).

The names of ancient merchantmen as a rule were indicated not in writing but by a symbolic carved or painted device on each side of the stempost (Figure 6). Near the sternpost were poles for mounting streamers or banners. The sternpost itself ended in the distinctive mark of the sailing ship, a gracefully curved goose-head (Figures 6 and 8), which, for added effect, was often gilded.

A well-fitted ship carried a full range of equipment.[41] The captain had available good coast pilots, which supplied brief notes on distances, landmarks, harbors, anchorages, and so on, but there is no evidence for the use of charts. There was a leadline to sound depths, and the lead had a hollow on the underside which, filled with tallow or grease, brought up samples of the bottom. Signaling and identification gear consisted of flags and lights; whether there were conventionalized running lights is unknown. There was at least one ship's boat, usually towed astern and with a hand stationed in it (Figure 6). Very large ships could have more than one, and could, by rigging lines from the masthead, haul them aboard. There were mooring lines and anchor cables (chain was strictly exceptional), and capstans and winches to help handle them (and to perform other functions, such as raising the main yard, which would unduly tax human muscle). For mooring at a quay, there were landing ladders (Figure 7) and gangways. For mooring offshore and for emergencies, there were a number of anchors (St. Paul's ship, just before it came to grief, threw four over the stern) kept at the ready both fore and aft, including the "sacred" anchor or what we call the sheet anchor. The commonest type of ship's anchor was totally different from those familiar to us, being mostly of wood.[42] It had arms of wood, tipped with metal, and a massive shank of wood. The essential weight the ancients put into the stock—the reverse of our practice, which is to put it into the arms and shank. Stocks were usually ponderous masses of lead; a 250-ton freighter, a ship, in other words, of moderate size, could carry an anchor fitted with stock 8 feet long and weighing 1,500 pounds.[43] Most stocks were fixed permanently to the shank, but some were so made as to be removable—a most useful form that was forgotten after the close of the ancient world and had to wait until the eighteenth century to be rediscovered.

So much for the ships; now for the crews.

Heading the hierarchy on a seagoing merchantman was the owner or charterer of the vessel. When he carried cargo for his own account, he or his representative was generally aboard. He might even be his own captain, though most often the captain was a hired professional. The Greek term for captain was *kybernetes*. The Romans, to judge by a distinction made in Roman law, divided the authority somewhat: there was a *magister navis*, or captain, who had over-all responsibility for the ship and particular responsibility for its administration and condition, and there was a *gubernator*, or sailing master, who seems to have had

pretty nearly complete charge of its handling once it had cleared
harbor.[44]

The captain had two chief officers under him, the *proreus*,
who was first mate, and the *toicharchos*, a combined purser and
supercargo.[45] There is mention of quartermasters, ship's carpenters, and guards, and there must have been the usual other
specialists. Though slaves played no role in navies, they played
a considerable one in merchant marines:[46] it was common, both
in Greek and Roman times, to man cargo vessels with slaves.
Indeed, in Roman times the officers, including the captain, could
be slaves, as well as the men. Unfortunately we have no way
of telling how extensive the practice was, what the proportion
was of slave crews to free.

Coastal,   Such names as York lugger, Venetian bragozzo, Adriatic trabac-
Harbor,   colo, Maine gundalow, Long Island sharpie are reminders of how
River   much the sailor likes to design his own style of craft, nicely
Craft   adapted to local conditions and individual purposes. There are
hundreds of examples of such varied types still alive even in
this homogenized age. And the ancient world had its fair share.[47]

Off the Breton coast, as Caesar noted, the locals used a type
of vessel that, with its ponderous oak timbers and leather sails
and chain anchor cables, was peculiarly adapted to withstand
the rigors of the north Atlantic. The pirates of the Black Sea had
developed a small fast galley which was double-ended, so that,
by a split-second shift, it could be rowed in either direction. On
the Tiber, rivermen worked out a particular style of boat for hauling upstream to Rome. There must have been similar local types
in every corner of the Mediterranean, along every river that emp-
tied into it. Through a unique accident we happen to have rather
full information about daily life in Greco-Roman Egypt; we hear
of at least a dozen different kinds of boats that plied the Nile.

A seagoing merchantman either takes off with a favorable wind
or waits around until one springs up. Local craft generally cannot
afford to be so leisurely. They must try to go about their work
no matter which quarter the wind is from and, in the course
of a single day, flitting about a harbor or stitching their way
up and down a coast, may sail in a multitude of directions. The
ancients fitted most of their small craft with squaresails, usually
hung for convenience's sake on a retractable mast. This was a
serviceable rig and the best there is for winds astern—but not
too effective when working against the wind, as a small boat

often has to do. For this purpose, as we have only recently learned, they knew at least two versions of the fore-and-aft rig.

In the square rig, the sail sits athwartship. In a fore-and-aft rig, on the other hand, the sail lies parallel to the keel, runs "fore and aft." A sail so set, though not as good with a fair wind as the squaresail, is far superior to it with any wind forward of the beam. By the second century B.C. at least, one version of the fore-and-aft rig, the spritsail, had come into being, and there soon followed a second, the lateen. Both represent milestones in naval technology: the lateen was to become the sail par excellence of the Arab world, while the spritsail made its way into every corner of Europe and America, powering all sorts of craft from Turkish coasters to the boats in which Yankee whalemen gave chase to their prey. The credit for the two rigs, often given to the Arabs and Dutch respectively, goes to the Greco-Roman sailor.[48]

Harbors A sound ship is only half the sailor's need. He must also have a safe place to put it when a voyage is over.

Harborworks are attested as far back as the second millennium B.C., and there is ample evidence that, by the fifth century B.C., the Greeks had become highly skilled port engineers.[49] They knew how to construct massive walls, generally of undressed stone but sometimes of squared stone, to form breakwaters that would guarantee a smooth and untroubled body of water behind at all times. Often, to ensure protection against man as well as the sea, they worked the breakwaters into the defensive perimeter of the town. As time went on, they introduced such refinements as openings through the breakwaters to permit a wash from one side to the other which would flush the harbor clean.

Our fullest information about harbors dates from Roman times. A major port, such as Portus, near Ostia, which served the city of Rome, had an impressive series of installations.[50] Breakwaters were of solid concrete, the lower portions poured in caissons to set underwater, as well as of squared stone. Near the entrance was a lighthouse, a lofty tower at whose summit a blazing fire was kept going all night through (Figures 6 and 8). Within the harbor the shores were lined with stone quays fitted with massive stone rings to which ships, nosing up, could make fast their mooring lines. On the quays stood powerful cranes, strong enough to lift 40-ton blocks of marble out of a ship's hold. Back of the quays were lines and lines of warehouses, some boasting such sophisticated devices as central heating to keep contents like grain properly dry. Over the harbor waters swarmed various kinds of specialized craft.[51] There were tugboats, stumpy affairs that carried a spritsail and a crew of well-muscled oarsmen; they would sail out to meet an incoming freighter, throw a towline aboard, and then the oarsmen would bend to the oars and warp the new arrival into a berth. There were lighters to unload ships that moored at anchor. There were skiffs of all sizes to carry messages or ferry sailors and workers. And, for the haul upriver, there was a fleet of specially rigged craft: these carried a mast somewhat forward of amidships, and a long line made fast to the stern and carried to the tip of this mast ran to the hauliers trudging along the towpath that followed the bank. (This primitive system remained in use until the coming of steam—and is still in use where labor is cheaper than power.)

Every harbor had its variegated groups of workers. Some of these, like stevedores or caulkers or shipwrights, belong to every age. Others were peculiar to the ancient world, like the "sandmen" who handled the sand used as ballast, or the *urinatores*, the corps of divers who were kept on hand for recovering merchandise that had fallen overboard.

Thus by the time of the Roman Empire elaborate facilities had been developed to handle the complex and varied trade of the Mediterranean. The great harbors and the specialized personnel who worked in them were a far cry from the shelving beaches and the daring Phoenician and Greek sailors who had worked out the lines of long-distance trade in its waters.

In the chapters of this book we can read much about the activities, workaday and recreational, of the peoples of ancient Greece and Rome. The individual studies describe both the technical methods of their crafts and artistic production and the manner in which the people worked and lived. Their life was primarily urban, for the form of community characteristic of Greek and Roman civilization was the city. Urban communities provided the chief markets for craft work. The cities were the setting for the important creations of architecture and of sculpture, and both music and the theater were intimately associated with urban life.

The life of the cities depended in large part on the use of their land in agriculture. From the beginnings of historical Greece in the eighth century B.C. through the long history of Greece and Rome the land was the chief source of wealth, and possession of land tended to determine social status. Yet from the earliest period, too, basic products, such as metals, were exchanged. As we have seen, many centers of craft and artistic production depended on imported materials. In turn, the goods of these producers were distributed far beyond their own region. As wealth grew, luxury products were sought in trade, and, as population increased, foodstuffs were imported from producing regions to major urban centers. Much of this trade moved over long distances by sea. The chapter on sailing has traced the development of shipping and of ship types by which the manufactured goods such as metalware and pottery, stone for building and sculpture, wheat, olive oil and wine for food were carried.

The framework for this Mediterranean commerce was laid in the early period of Greek history, between the time of Homer in the eighth century and the Athenian Empire of the fifth century B.C. During this same period, aided by the stimulation of trading, the rural villages of Greece were transformed into cities. It is the role of the Greeks in this early trading which I discuss.[1]

Two Greek writers, in particular, who lived in Athens in the latter part of the fifth century B.C., realized the vital role which sea trade had played in the growth of Greece and in the primacy of their own city. For, before the Athenians were defeated by Sparta in the Peloponnesian War (431–404 B.C.), Athens was the great sea power of the eastern Mediterranean and the veritable "capital" of Greece. To it came writers, craftsmen, artists, and philosophers, as well as traders and businessmen from the other cities of Greece. Thucydides, who wrote the history of the Peloponnesian War, well understood this relation of trade, sea power and political domination in Greece:

The land now called Hellas, it appears, was not stably settled until recent times. The inhabitants were migratory, readily abandoning their land when oppressed by greater numbers. For there was no regular trade nor safe intercourse among one another, either by land or sea. Each group cultivated its own land only for subsistence and had no accumulation of capital [Thucydides 1. 2. 1–2]. . . . And Hellas began to build ships and take more to the sea. The Corinthians are said to have been the first [in the late eighth century] to deal with marine affairs in somewhat the present fashion and the first to have built triremes [1. 13. 1–2]. . . . Those who paid attention to navies gained greatly in power by addition of revenues and control over others [1. 15. 1].[2]

A contemporary of Thucydides, called the "Old Oligarch," because of his trenchant criticism of the Athenian democracy, forcefully expressed the rewards Athens enjoyed from her control of the sea:

It is through the control of the sea that the Athenians discovered luxuries of life by intercourse with other countries. So the desirable products of Sicily and Italy, of Cyprus, Egypt and Lydia, of the Black Sea, of the Peloponnesus, or wherever, are all funneled to one center by control of the sea (Pseudo-Xenophon *Athenaion Politeia* ii. 7). . . . For, if a state is rich in timber for shipbuilding, where will it market the timber, except by persuading the ruler of the sea? If rich in iron, bronze or hemp, where will it find a market except by permission of the great seapower? [ii. 11].

While both writers stress the political role of the Athenians as controllers of sea-borne trade, rather than as a trading people, both emphasize the vital significance of trade to Greece as a whole. Athens had taken over the intricate system worked out by various Greeks in the preceding centuries and was exploiting it in her Empire.

The Start of Greek Trade During the ninth and eighth centuries B.C. Greece was a complex of small villages and towns on the shorelines and islands of the Aegean Sea. We can get some notion of their character from the poems of Homer and from the excavation of Old Smyrna in Turkey,[3] where one tradition, at least, placed Homer's career. If our eyes are not dazzled, like Homer's memory, by nostalgic reminiscences of an earlier Greek civilization, that of Mycenaean

Greece, four hundred years earlier, we can see the Homeric communities as poor and drab hamlets. The house of the ordinary man seems to have been a one-roomed, mud brick hut. He had little to keep in it beyond a few tools and personal possessions. His king's house would have been larger, but still constructed of timber and mud brick. The Homeric community was almost self-sufficient, living from its farms and flocks and on the fish of the sea nearby. Yet the people had two needs which were to turn them to the sea for trade: metals, for their weapons and tools, and a taste for luxuries and exotic products. The Homeric heroes boasted mainly of their wealth in land and animals, but they were sensitive to the flashing beauty of good armor and weapons, of gold and silver cups, of ivory carvings and of fine textiles. Most of these were acquired in primitive fashion: by war, piracy, the ransoming of prisoners or as gifts of hospitality made with a keen eye to the value of an exchange. One of Homer's rare personal comments in the *Iliad* (6. 236) is on the folly of one hero who exchanged his armor, worth one hundred oxen, for another's worth only nine. Some goods, also, were purchased by the exchange of hides, cattle and the like, from wandering Phoenician traders. Yet the Homeric Greeks themselves were already beginning to take to the sea.

In the *Odyssey* (6. 262–272) Homer sketches an ideal community—the first of those which the Greeks were so fond of creating. It is the island city of the Phaeacians. The Phaeacians had colonized their island far from men who lived by grain, that is, by toil on their farms. They erected houses and temples and divided the fields—evidently some grain was needed. The city was built, Homer tells us, on an easily defended peninsula, at the base of which lay harbors where ships were drawn up and where the place for housing and preparing gear stood. Homer calls the Phaeacians oar-loving and seafarers. Some cities of the Aegean islands and of the coast of Asia Minor, like Lindos on Rhodes or Old Smyrna,[4] fit the description well, but surely Homer is describing a Greek city as it would have liked to be: defended primarily by a peninsular position, the entrance to which could be walled off, drawing its livelihood partly from the land nearby, but increasingly from the sea.

Elsewhere in the poem familiarity with the sea is apparent in the ease and rapidity of the lines which tell how Telemachus set out from Ithaca to seek news of his father Odysseus:

The men loosed the mooring lines, climbed on board and sat down on the benches. Athena sent them a fresh west wind singing over the wine-dark sea and Telemachus called to his men to lay hands on the stays. They raised the mast and set it firm, hauled up the white sails with twisted ropes of hide. The wind filled the belly of the sail and the dark waves hissed round the stern of the running ship as she sped over the water on her way. They made all fast in the swift black ship and set out the bowls brimming with wine, poured drink to the deathless gods and, above all, to Athena, Zeus' daughter. All night long and through the dawn the ship cleft her way [*Odyssey* 2. 418–434].

Like Telemachus, the Greeks were on their way out of the Aegean to establish themselves along the shores of the Mediterranean and Black Seas.

Direct connections with Syria, Cyprus, and soon with Egypt, which had been tenuous for four hundred years since the fall of Mycenae, were restored. In Sicily and South Italy the Greeks found a congenially familiar landscape and built cities modeled on those of their motherland. New links with the unknown lands of the western Mediterranean, Spain and France, and with the shorelines of the Black Sea to the northeast were forged. In the space of about two hundred and fifty years the geographical horizons of Greece were widened from the Aegean to the whole basin of the Mediterranean. The new colonies and trading posts were tiny settlements, at the outset of no more than a few score persons, set on or near the shore line. Many were picked with an eye to the fertile fields in the neighborhood, but in most the settlers were careful to choose a shelving beach on which their light ships could be drawn or a sheltered roadstead and potential harbor. Some were very plainly selected with access to trade routes into the interior in mind: Al Mina, near the mouth of the Orontes River in Syria, and Naukratis in the Delta of the Nile; a group of settlements near the Rhone River in France, one of which, Massalia, was to become Marseilles; Olbia, near the Dnieper River, down which wheat was to come from the fertile black earth of South Russia. In this manner the Greeks established direct contact with both the barbaric West and North and with the highly civilized countries of the Near East. The network of colonies gave them access to far more wealth than their own Aegean area could produce, and the transformation of the agrarian towns of the Homeric period to city states began.[5]

Even in those towns which tended to remain essentially agrarian in character the effects of trade were soon apparent. In Homer's own city, Old Smyrna, the process of urbanization was accelerated. In the seventh century larger and better built houses of stone appeared and the city was laid out in a plan of rectangular blocks with substantial houses.[6] The problem of a growing population and a static food supply was solved, in part at least, by the import of wine from the nearby island of Chios and of olive oil from Athens across the Aegean, as the pottery jars which carried them attest.

Trade in Pottery   It is, of course, mainly through the distribution of pottery that the lines of trade can be traced in this early period, for it alone has survived in great quantity in the graves and shrines and in the earth which covers the buildings on archaeological sites. The style of decoration, the type of clay, characteristic shapes, all these enable fabrics from different places of manufacture to be distinguished from one another—and from the imitations which the best of them provoked. While almost every Aegean town made pottery for its local use, only certain fabrics were widely distributed in export. In some cases a city, active in early colonization, supplied the pottery for newly founded colonies until their own industry was able to compete. For example Corinth almost monopolized the market in Sicily and South Italy. Rhodes and some cities in Ionian Greece shipped their wares in quantity, partly to this market, but much more to the trading posts on the Black Sea, to Al Mina in Syria and to Naukratis in Egypt. Quality, too, was an important factor in marketing. During the eighth and seventh centuries Corinth and Rhodes were the important centers of export, but, from about 575 B.C., the beautifully decorated and well-made Athenian ware drove them from the export markets. Thus pottery distribution offers material evidence of the lines of trade, for it seems proper to assume a well-established trading connection between exporter and importer when a considerable mass of pottery, from one city extending over a long period of time, is found in another.[7]

The use of pottery, however, as evidence for trade raises further questions. Were vases imported as objects of art? as objects of use? as happy examples of both in the one piece? to carry other materials—as containers?

The fine pottery of Greece, as the chapter on pottery making indicated,[8] is characterized by an unusual union of beauty and technique. Its shapes were highly specialized and functional: to

1   Black-figured amphora, apparently priced at two obols. Ca. 540 B.C.
Courtesy, Metropolitan Museum of Art, New York.

hold and pour olive oil and wine; to carry water; to mix wine and water; to provide plates and cups for various uses. The common pottery, too, for ordinary household use, which was left undecorated or entirely covered with black glaze, was generally well made and pleasing in appearance. Many potters and painters of fine vases evidently took a special pride in their work, for numerous vases are signed. To what degree beauty or utility determined the price of a particular vase we can scarcely say. Yet, on some, so much skill and care have been lavished that we may assume they were regarded by maker and purchaser as an artistic prize in their own right. They are given primacy of place in a modern museum gallery, and presumably they found a special market in their own time: for display and occasional use in a wealthy home or for special dedication by the wealthy in a sanctuary like that of Athena on the Acropolis in Athens. It is striking that many of the finest pieces of Athenian workmanship found their market in non-Greek Etruria—they had been made for export.

While all the fine pottery is not to be placed in this category of "objets de luxe," a very large part of it is pleasingly decorated and of very good quality. It might have been the good household china of the wealthy, the prized piece of the ordinary man or his special dedication for a grave or temple. Can we form any estimate of the cost of such vases?

Take the Athenian amphora represented in Figure 1.[9] It is rather small in size, the quality of decoration routine, but the scene has some distinction. Apparently it represents a victor in the footrace for heavy-armed soldiers, hoplites. Beside him, on the reverse, is the inscription, reading in translation: "Two obols and you have me"—an example in advertising of Greek moderation. The inscription was written in the workshop and fired on the vase at the time of manufacture. This, then, would have been the price in Athens. The vase was presumably purchased by a trader for export abroad, however, for it was found in an Etruscan grave. It is very difficult to determine the real value of the amount in its own period, about 540 B.C., for there is very little evidence for prices in classical Greece. Possibly, however, the price represents almost half of his week's earnings for an ordinary worker.[10] Yet, if he purchased the vase, it was not simply a useless indulgence—he could store olive oil or wine in it and display it to gratify, quite properly, his sense of possession. But the very fine pieces were beyond his means. The ordinary workman could see

2

Corinthian aryballos.
Ca. 580–575 B.C. Mary C.
and Carl Roebuck, "A
Prize Aryballos,"
Hesperia, Vol. 24
(1955), Pl. 63. Courtesy
of the American School
of Classical Studies at
Athens.

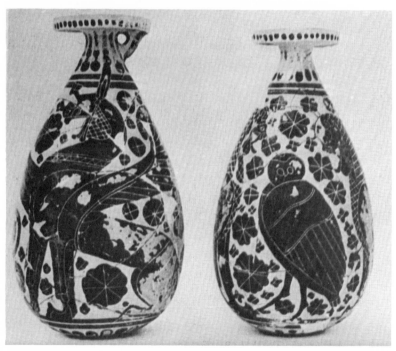

3   Corinthian alabastrons. Ca. 600 B.C. Saul S. Weinberg, "A Cross-Section
of Corinthian Antiquities," *Hesperia*, Vol. 17 (1948), Pl. LXXIX.
Courtesy of the American School of Classical Studies at Athens.

some of them in a temple, as his medieval counterpart saw the treasures of a cathedral.

Some pottery very neatly combined the function of packaging a special product with a very attractive appearance. The vase might be treasured for itself after the contents were used. The vases pictured in Figures 2 and 3 are a round aryballos and an alabastron, shapes characteristic of Corinthian pottery.[11] They were used to hold perfumes or liquid salves for which there was a continuous demand in the hot, parching weather of a Mediterranean summer. The Corinthians were principal exporters of these products from the Black Sea to Spain, in addition to making the vases.

For liquids carried in bulk, olive oil for cooking and wine, large jars of coarser fabric and with simple decoration were used. Those with striped decoration in Figure 4 were made in Athens but found discarded in a housewell in Corinth,[12] perhaps the wreckage of some disaster in the pantry. Those on the lowest row were from the islands of Chios and Thasos and reveal the source of some of the wine drunk in Corinth. Thus the pottery is sometimes an article of trade for its own sake, sometimes reveals a trade in other commodities.

Greek pottery, however, could not find a market among all the peoples of the Mediterranean from whom the Greeks wished to purchase goods. In the colonial areas of the West, particularly in Sicily and South Italy, and in the trading posts on the Black Sea large quantities of imported pottery have been found in excavations. Then, too, much fine pottery found a market in native Italy among the Etruscans from whom the Greeks apparently obtained metals. But in Egypt the finds of Greek pottery are almost wholly limited to the Greek trading center at Naukratis. The same is true of the Near East; there the Greek pottery comes mainly from Al Mina and other Greek trading posts, used by the Greeks themselves, but little has been found in the native towns and cities of the interior. In both regions, of course, the local industries were well established and experienced, so that Greek pottery could not compete with the native wares. Yet Greeks wished to import certain types of luxury goods from Syria, such as textiles and metalware, which were an inspiration in techniques to their own burgeoning industry. When trade began with Egypt on some scale in the last quarter of the seventh century B.C. the availability of Egyptian grain for export to the Aegean became apparent. A means of payment was needed. This was found in silver, in the forms of bars, ingots, and coins, of which the Greeks were the first regular users, if not the actual inventors. Apparently about 650–625 B.C. precious metals, particularly silver, began to come into regular use for the purpose of exchange.

Early Greek Exchange It is apparent from the distribution of Greek pottery in the ninth and eighth centuries B.C., the period of Homer, that some Greeks were beginning to trade. They sailed from the islands of the Aegean as far as the Bay of Naples in the West and to the Syrian coast in the East. Yet in the Homeric poems there is little mention of the professional trader, the middle man, who distributed goods from the producer to the customer.[13] The professionals of Homer's period were Phoenicians who peddled about the Aegean, bringing valuable luxuries for the rulers of the Greek towns and cheap trinkets for the ordinary people. There was also some "amateur" trade among the Greeks themselves. In the *Odyssey* the goddess Athena disguised herself as a prince, Mentes, and pretended she was carrying a cargo of iron. In the *Iliad* Euneos, son of King Jason of Lemnos, traded wine to the Greeks encamped before Troy. Presumably great landowners thus disposed of a lucky find of metal or some agricultural surplus from their own lands. Presumably, too, ordinary farmers, as they are represented by the poet Hesiod (*Works and Days* 630–634) at a slightly later time, might build a small boat and trade their own farm surplus in the off-season of farming.

It was evidently customary to obtain the privilege of trading in a community by making a generous gift to its ruler—a primitive form of the tolls which Greek cities later demanded of traders. For example, Euneos gave Agamemnon and Menelaos one thousand measures of wine before trading with the Greek warriors (*Iliad* 7. 467–475). This sale of food to soldiers was also a precursor of later Greek practice, for it became customary for commanders to establish a regular market for their men while on campaign. The warriors before Troy exchanged what they had on hand, bronze, iron, hides, cattle, slaves for the Lemnian wine. The wandering trader, however, was usually regarded with dislike. When Odysseus came to Phaeacia the nobles of that community commented insultingly: He looks like "a man who sails on a many-oared ship, a ruler of sailors, mindful of his cargo and of his wares, grasping after gain" (*Odyssey* 8. 159–164). Such suspicion was justified, for the early trader might also be a kidnaper and a pirate, and, above all, he was a stranger to the tightly knit, rural communities of Homeric Greece.

In the era of colonizing which followed these early essays in trading the professional ship captain and trader emerged. On the long runs to the western Mediterranean and to the Black Sea the men would have been away for weeks or months, and their livelihood depended on the success of their ventures. Most of the early captains and traders remain anonymous. Their stories must have furnished the romantic material for myths and legend, like the tale of the Voyage of the Argonauts to the land of Colchis. Their observation and experience made it possible for a Greek writer, Hecataeus, to compile a virtual sailing guide of the Mediterranean about 500 B.C.

Some famous voyages, however, were remembered in tradition, like that of Colaeus, a sea captain from the island of Samos. He was blown, Herodotus (4. 152) tells us, by a great storm from the Libyan coast of North Africa to Tartessus beyond Gibraltar in Spain. There Colaeus obtained a rich cargo of metal, which he brought back to Samos, where, very properly, he dedicated a tithe to the goddess Hera in the form of a large mixing bowl of bronze. The story marks the inception of the very important Greek trade to Spain for metals.[14] After Colaeus the chief carriers were the sailors of Phocaea, a small Ionian Greek city on the east coast of the Aegean. The route was long and dangerous not only because of storms and unknown waters but from Carthaginian piracy in the seas west of Sicily. To avoid the latter the Phocaeans usually followed a long coasting route from the Straits of Messina up the west coast of Italy, along the French Riviera, then down the east coast of Spain to Tartessus. Along the way Greek goods could be peddled to the Greek colonies and to the Etruscans, while at the end were the metals, probably silver and tin, or bronze, made in Tartessus. From the profits of the trading the city of Phocaea was able to provide itself with a new city wall.

The activities initiated by such men as Colaeus and the Phocaeans gradually established a complex organization of trading and commerce. We know little of the detail of its growth, but by the end of the fifth century B.C., when literary evidence is abundant, we can see the result.[15] Distinctions were made between internal trade, exchange inside a community, and foreign trade, trade with other Greek or barbarian states; the Greeks, as usual, had names for the men engaged in trading. The *kapelos* was a local trader, usually a retailer, but the term includes whole-salers, who sold their goods within a city in some quantity. Retail-ing was also carried on by a great variety of peddlers and stall keepers, each with his own specialty. The *emporos* was the trader to foreign countries who might carry his goods on another's ship or overland by pack animal. The *naukleros* was the merchant ship owner who carried the goods of the emporos, as well as his own. Trading had become almost wholly professionalized, al-though farmers still brought their vegetables and other produce to market in the cities and towns. By that time, too, it was possible for traders to finance their more ambitious ventures through credit. Bankers and other wealthy individuals made bottomry loans and both backer and trader could make, or lose, a small fortune. Such activity, of course, implies considerable development toward a monetary economy, the result of almost two centuries of experi-ence with coinage since its invention in the latter part of the seventh century B.C.

It is currently a matter of argument whether motivation for the invention of coinage is to be sought in the need for a conve-nient medium of exchange to facilitate trade or in the increase of governmental operations of the Greek states.[16] The affairs of the latter had become more complex about 600 B.C. Cities were levy-ing tolls on trade, exacting fines from their citizens, paying for the erection of large public buildings, and hiring mercenary sol-diers on some scale. It is possible that coining, stamping the official mark of the issuer on a specific weight of metal as a guarantee, was designed to facilitate these operations. On the other hand, the earliest coins did appear in an area of intense local exchange of goods and services, in western Asia Minor, where the Ionian Greeks of the coastal cities dealt with the Kingdom of Lydia in the interior. Which issued the first proper coins, Lydian kings or Ionian cities, is not clear, but tradition assigns the invention to the Lydian kings. A recent suggestion for the practice is that coinage facilitated the payment of the Greek mercenaries hired by Lydia.[17] Presumably soldiers would find no difficulty in putting the money into circulation. Lydia had deposits of electrum, a natural alloy of gold and silver, and from the discovery of an early hoard of electrum pellets and coins in the Temple of Artemis at Ephesus it has been possible to trace the growth of coinage:[18] from small unmarked pellets, through stamped pellets to coins stamped with the national emblem of Lydia or that of certain Ionian cities. This process of development was apparently rapid, from about 640 to 610 B.C., and the practice was quickly adopted by other Greek states in the Aegean and across it on the Greek mainland.

The Greek states, however, did not have deposits of electrum in their own lands and were not in the same favorable position as the Ionians for acquiring it from Lydia. Accordingly they began to coin in silver. Those Greek and native areas around the Aegean which had deposits of silver or were able to acquire it in trade were in a very favorable position. Corinth and the island of Aegina themselves possessed no silver, but they were active in trading and could acquire it for their early and extensive coinages. Aegina probably did so from the small island of Siphnos, which experienced a boom in the sixth century and then almost dropped from history;[19] Corinth probably got its silver from the mining areas of Macedonia and Thrace, at that time in the possession of native tribal peoples with whom the Greeks had to trade manufactured goods and textiles for the silver. Ionian Greeks, too, had trading relations with this area and thus could use their own electrum in western Asia Minor but could also acquire silver for external trade. Athens, too, was able to get silver easily from the mines in its own territory of Laureion in southern Attica.

The new coinage seems to have had a limited use at first in internal trade within the cities, that is, in retail transactions, for issuance of coins in small denominations—to make change—was scanty. It is apparent, however, from the hoards of early coins which have been discovered, that they, as well as silver in bar or ingot form, were used in interregional trading and, in particular, in trading with Egypt and Syria. It will be remembered that Greek pottery could not find a native market in those lands. In Egypt a number of hoards of early Greek coins have been found, apparently hidden away by Egyptian merchants who dealt with the Greek traders.[20] During the sixth century B.C. the principal trading states of Greece, Aegina, Corinth, the Ionian cities of Chios and Miletus seem to have participated in this trade. It is striking that the early coins of Athens stamped with various heraldic devices (Wappenmünzen) are rare in these early hoards, but shortly before the Persian Wars the Athenians issued a new type of coin, the well known tetradrachms, pieces 'worth four drachmas. Soon these began to make up almost the whole of the hoards. Evidently Athens had deliberately made this new issue for purposes of overseas trade, for the coins are of excellent quality and are stamped with the advertising symbols of the city:

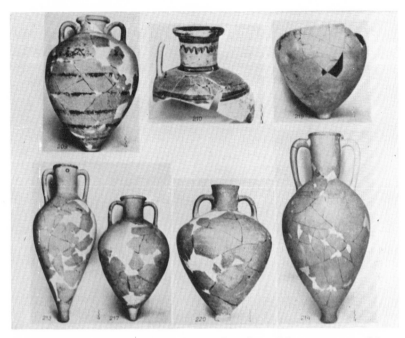

4   Amphoras for shipping olive oil or wine. Late 6th century B.C. Mary Thorne Campbell, "A Well of the Black-Figured Period at Corinth," *Hesperia*, Vol. 7 (1938), Fig. 29. Courtesy of the American School of Classical Studies at Athens.

5

Greek silver coins, mainly Athenian, ranging in denomination from a tetradrachm (upper left) to a fraction of an obol (lower right)—about $\frac{1}{8}$" in diameter. Private collection.

the head of the patron-goddess Athena, her tiny owl, and an olive twig (Figure 5). By the early fifth century B.C. Athens had the silver, the goods for trade—fine pottery, olive oil and wine—and, after the Battle of Salamis, the sea power to take over control of trade in the eastern Mediterranean. The move into the Egyptian trade was evidently to acquire wheat for Athens' own population. For a century grain had been one of the most important imports into the Aegean for the growing population of Greece.

The Grain Trade In our dicussion of the pottery trade in early Greece it was at least possible to point to the material evidence of trade, for the pottery itself was traded or used as a container. For trade in grain and metals, however, we have to proceed largely by inference. First of all, there seems to be an amazing imbalance of trade in early Greece. In the colonial areas and in Etruria imported Greek pottery can be counted in the thousands of pieces. But in Greece itself very few imports from Etruria have been found, and it is hardly possible to identify any object as from the Western or Black Sea colonies. From Egypt and the Near East there is only a scattering of cheap jewelry and bric-a-brac, little scarabs, charms, beads and the like, many of them probably from the Greek trading post at Naukratis. Evidently, then, the articles sought abroad by Greek traders were perishables. We can assume that these included costly textiles and metalware, for the eastern motifs which appear in early Greek art were obviously imitated from such objects. Presumably, too, as indicated above in the case of the Phocaean traders, the metals which Greece itself did not produce were sought: tin, copper, and iron. But these would have come from a relatively few mining areas. So it seems that it must have been grain which was imported in some quantity to feed the rapidly growing population of the Aegean area.

As soon as the population in Greece rose above a certain, and very low, level, imports of food must have been necessary, for about 80 percent of the land area of Greece is mountainous, unfit for cereal production, and ancient Greek methods of farming do not seem to have been as productive as those described for Italy.[21] It is usually held that this level was reached toward 700 B.C. and that emigration to colonies was one method of relief for draining off the surplus population. Certainly many Greeks did leave their homeland, but this main wave of emigration lasted little more than a century. During the sixth century relatively few new colonies were founded, but the population of the Aegean continued to grow as the extension of existing cities and the establishment of new towns in Greece itself attest. Evidently Greece turned to the importation of grain on some scale.[22]

There are indications that the trade was well established by the time of the Persian Wars. Herodotus tells a story of King Xerxes' advisors asking him why he let a Greek grain fleet from South Russia pass through the Dardanelles. Xerxes replied grandiosely that he was letting them carry his own supplies to Greece which he confidently expected to conquer. To Herodotus (7. 147) this was but one more example of the Persian king's arrogant presumption, but evidently the Greeks wondered why Xerxes had failed to block their grain supply from the Black Sea. Xerxes' successors, too, continued to allow Greeks to purchase wheat in Egypt and in Syria throughout the fifth century B.C., although no formal peace had been arranged after Xerxes' invasion. Even more directly revealing is a law passed in this same period by the Ionian city of Teos in western Asia Minor: "Whoever prevents grain being brought to Teos by any device either by land or sea or who re-exports it after it has been brought in, that man is to be put to death, both himself and his family."[23] The drastic penalty may reflect a temporary condition of famine in the city, but the decree does show that there were regular means of supply to add to a city's own production. The fields of Sicily and South Italy, of South Russia, and of Egypt were all sending their surplus to the city states of the Aegean. The specific case of the trade with Egypt, mentioned before, will illustrate the process.[24]

The Greeks established regular contacts with Egypt about 650 B.C. when the Saite princes were engaged in consolidating their authority in the Nile Delta. Previously Greeks had traded occasionally and perhaps made piratical raids when that seemed profitable. Odysseus, for example, in one of his tales, represented himself as a Cretan pirate who raided Egypt and made a disastrous bargain with a Phoenician trader. The latter got the better of the cunning Greek (*Odyssey* 14. 257ff.). Yet regular trade in some volume would have been possible only after the foundation of the Greek colony at Naukratis, where merchants found it worth their while to settle and to build warehouses. The trading colony was established between 625 and 600 B.C., when it replaced a slightly earlier settlement of mercenary soldiers hired by the Saite king, Psammetichus I. The king allowed the traders to settle on land granted for this purpose and to erect shrines to their own gods.

From the outset Naukratis lived by trade—its settlers were admitted by the Egyptian government for that purpose. The Greek merchants who called there found a double opportunity in the new town. They could provide the olive oil and wine, the fine and household pottery which the Greek residents wanted for their houses and temples. From the import of wine there developed an interesting side line. The wine jars were collected by the Greek authorities and sold to the Egyptians who used them for water storage along the desert route to Palestine across the Isthmus of Suez (Herodotus 3. 6). This trade with the Greek population, however, was relatively small and in return the Greeks produced some cheap bric-a-brac on the Egyptian model. The merchants' other opportunity, a much greater one, lay in organizing the grain trade, for which Egypt had a surplus of wheat from the intensive cultivation of the Nile valley.

The hoards of silver, by which the Greeks paid for the grain, offer a clue to the organization of this trade. Many of these, as mentioned before (pp. 214–216), have been found at scattered points in the Nile Delta, where Egyptian dealers apparently had concealed them. As chance finds the material in the hoards would represent only a small surviving portion of the silver brought in for large-scale purchases. Large-scale, because the coins themselves are of large denominations and mixed with them in the hoards are disks and bars of unminted silver. Both bars and coins are bullion exchanged for grain. Egypt itself had no coinage until the Macedonian Ptolemies, who succeeded Alexander the Great, began to mint, but the Egyptian rulers needed silver to pay their mercenary soldiers and for their jewelry crafts. Silver had always been imported from beyond Egyptian frontiers. The Egyptian dealers did not care from which Greek city or on what weight standard the coins came, for ultimately they were melted down. But a high standard of purity was required, and, even if the Greeks did not bring gifts, they were suspect. Accordingly the coins were gouged and clipped to find out whether they were solid or plated over an inferior metal. It did not matter that the coin was marred—both pieces and whole coins could be weighed and melted together.

A find of coins in Greece itself shows that Egyptian suspicion of Greek traders was well founded.[25] In the excavation of the sanctuary of the god Poseidon at Isthmia near Corinth scores of silver coins of this early period have been found. They were offerings in the temple by worshippers of Poseidon. On examination, some of them, of proper size and normal appearance, were found to be only a thin shell of silver with the interior of baser metal or filled with the dust of an original mud core.

The Greek cities which were interested in the trade in grain are indicated by the sources of origin of the coins in the hoards and of the pottery found in Naukratis. There is a neat correlation. The earliest coins are the very old pieces of Corinth and of the island of Chios, dating from the early sixth century B.C. About 500 B.C. after a century of mixed trading, the new Athenian tetradrachms began to appear in quantity and replaced coinage of the other cities as Athenians took over the trading. The same is true of the pottery used by the Greeks at Naukratis, and so the correlation enables the trading interest of particular Greeks and the time of their interest to be worked out. We can go a step farther from the evidence of the hoards. The cities of Corinth and of Chios, whose coins predominate in the hoards, had no silver deposits in their own territories, yet silver was the all-important article of exchange. The clue to another link in the chain is afforded by the presence in the hoards of a group of coins called collectively Thraco-Macedonian. They make up about 30 percent of the total. These coins were minted by the native tribal groups of eastern Macedonia where there were large deposits of silver. Unlike the coins of the Greek cities, they are of very large denominations and are particularly adapted to a trade in bullion. In fact, rather than coins, the pieces are a type of ingot whose makers, following Greek fashion, stamped them like coins. The Macedonian natives themselves had no need of grain nor the ships to carry it. Here, then, was the source of some of the silver which the carriers, Corinthians and Chiots, procured by trading with the people of eastern Macedonia.

At this point another check is possible. The excavation of Greek colonies and native towns in eastern Macedonia reveals that the Chiots were particularly active there. Chios had ships, its agriculture was specialized early to wine and olive oil production, and it had founded a colony, Maroneia, in a suitable location to trade with the Macedonian natives. The coin types of Chios itself influenced the choice of symbols and weight standards of the Thraco-Macedonian coins. As an article of exchange for the silver the Chiots could offer their famous Chian wine. Perhaps this contributed to the reputation of the natives of the silver-producing region as heavy drinkers—they were censured by the Greeks for drinking their wine straight, not in the usual proportion of four to one of water, which the Greeks favored.

From this reconstruction of the grain trade with Egypt a whole process has emerged, which is typical of the organization of trade in this early period. Those cities of the Aegean advantageously situated on the sea began to import grain for their own population and to carry it to other cities. To pay for the grain an intricate system of exchange was developed: the use of products of specialized agriculture, olive oil and wine, of local craft products, pottery, metalware and textiles, to purchase silver in the producing regions or from Greek traders. The silver, in its turn, went to pay for the grain in Egypt. In the Greek colonies of the West and of the Black Sea, however, grain could be procured by exchanging pottery and craft products. A net of trade connections had been woven from the Aegean throughout the Mediterranean.

In some cities and colonies the discovery of an unexpected local bonanza might provide a desirable trading commodity. Cyrene, founded by farmers from the Aegean island of Thera on the Libyan coast of Africa, is an example. Beyond the city stretched a high plateau which caught enough moisture for pasturing sheep, the fleece of which was woven into textiles for export, and for the growth of a plant called silphium.[26] Silphium became a medical staple in a region prone to stomach ailments. Since it seems also to have been used as a cooking spice, the plant may have helped to provoke the disorders which it purported to cure. In any case, silphium became a famous article of export from Cyrene, and the trade stimulated an artist in Sparta, far off across the Mediterranean from Cyrene, to paint the little picture represented in Figure 6 on the interior of a drinking cup.[27] The scene represents the ruler of Cyrene, Arkesilaos, supervising the storage of his silphium in an underground storage chamber. He sits, if not quite in his countinghouse, at ease under a large awning watching the bales being brought down and weighed by the Libyan natives.

Greek Trading Posts Although the Greek trade with Egypt can be reconstructed from the pottery found at Naukratis and from the coins in the hoards of silver, the buildings in which it was carried on are too poorly preserved to permit of a reconstruction of the warehouse and harbor area. It is apparent, however, that in Naukratis the Greeks

tried to live as they had in the cities of the Aegean from which
they came. They used their own Greek pottery, apparently preferred to cook in olive oil and to drink wine rather than use
vegetable oils and drink beer like the Egyptians. They built small
enclosed shrines to their own gods and made dedications in them.
From the names on the dedicated vases we can see the varied
origins of the traders and learn, too, that Greek *hetairai* came
to live in Naukratis. Among the Greeks was the brother of Sappho
and a famous courtesan, Rhodopis, who made a dedication to
the god Apollo at Delphi back in Greece.[28] Perhaps most important to the Greeks was the possibility of continuing to some degree
their familiar political life. Despite the mixed origin of the settlers
a feeling of unity grew among them, a consciousness of being
the people of Naukratis. As early as the second quarter of the
sixth century they established a common sanctuary, the Hel-
lenion. They chose their own officials, too, and Naukratis remained sufficiently Greek to be reckoned as one of the Greek
cities of Egypt, along with Alexandria, under the Ptolemaic
regime.[29]

At the more remote and smaller Greek trading posts in Syria,
however, to judge from the example of Al Mina, the Greeks were
more completely absorbed into the traditional life of the Near East.
Al Mina was well situated for purposes of trade. The town lay
near the mouth of the Orontes River. In the background Mt.
Kasios served as a landfall to sailors and along the river valley
lay the route to the long-established cities of Northern Syria and
the Fertile Crescent. From the eighth century B.C. down this road
and from the Phoenician cities on the coast came the metalware,
textiles, and ivory carvings which were so enthusiastically imitated
by Greek craftsmen in the Orientalizing phase of Greek art. Unfortunately the buildings at Al Mina used in this early period
of trade were largely obliterated by subsequent rebuilding in the
fifth and fourth centuries B.C. Yet the builders seem to have retained the type of warehouse developed in the earlier period.[30]

The warehouses (Figure 7) at Al Mina are unpretentious structures, one story in height, built around an open courtyard. The
foundations are of small roughly dressed stone on which walls
of sun-dried bricks were raised. The walls were faced with clay
stucco and the roofs built in Syrian fashion with layers of matting,
reeds and clay, laid on poplar poles. In the courtyards merchandise was unloaded and sorted, to be stored in the surrounding
rooms, while on the street side a row of small rooms served as

offices and retail shops. In them small hoards of coins and weights were found, and in the storerooms were stocks of pottery fallen from collapsed shelves when the building went out of use. In this latter period of trade there seem to have been separate quarters in the market section for the different types of goods handled, but we cannot tell whether this bazaarlike arrangement was true also of the earlier period. The pottery found was for use in the town itself, for in Syria, as in Egypt, the Greeks seem to have purchased native goods with silver. The Syrian hoards of Greek silver are similar in composition to those of Egypt.[31]

As the cities of Greece itself developed their monumental form regular provision was made for the operations of trade. The market places, *agoras*, were marked off as areas for public assembly and trading. We can do little but conjecture about arrangements before the time of the Persian Wars, for in Greek cities, too, early structures were destroyed and overbuilt when they became too obsolete to provide for the more complex life of the classical and Hellenistic periods. By that time, the form of the agora familiar in the ruins of the Greek cities in the Aegean had evolved—a great open square, often open on one side to allow access, surrounded by small temples, monuments, and public buildings to provide for the official life of the city. In the colonnaded porticoes were located the offices and shops for business and trading.[32]

Through this system of trade which we have described the Greeks of the period before the Persian Wars had remedied the lack of metals and of sufficient grain in their own land; also they had amassed at least some of that capital singled out by Thucydides as the primary weakness of early Greek society. Subsequently trading became more complex when the uses of money and credit were developed and the geographical horizons of the peoples of the Mediterranean were extended. Even before the campaigns of Alexander the Great the lands of the Near East were being brought into a meaningful economic relation with Greece. The rulers of the Hellenistic kingdoms, which succeeded Alexander's brief regime, began to develop further connections: to the Red Sea and the Persian Gulf, to northwestern India and to central Asia as they sought to reorganize the dismembered Persian Empire.[33] When the Roman Empire finally brought political stability to the Near East, these tentative lines of trade were developed into more regular routes. Then, the important centers of trade shifted eastward from the Aegean to the great cities of

6

The Arkesilaos kylix. Storing silphium at Cyrene. Cabinet des Médailles, Paris.

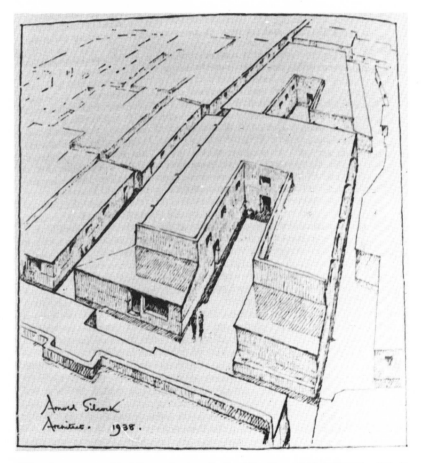

7   Warehouses at Al Mina, Syria. C. L. Woolley, "Al Mina-Sueidia," *The Journal of Hellenic Studies*, Vol. 58 (1938), p. 14, Fig. 3.

the Hellenistic East: to Ephesus, Seleucia, Antioch, Damascus and Alexandria. Some of the older cities of Greece became links to the new markets created in Italy by the rise of Rome. In its turn Rome's conquest of western and central Europe linked those lands to the economic life of the Mediterranean. The range of trade and the degree of interconnection were extended far beyond those of the early sailors who had ventured to the western Mediterranean past Sicily and South Italy and into the Black Sea but the Greeks and Phoenicians had started the process.

One of the greatest romantic stories of all time, and one of the oldest, is that of Orpheus and his love, Eurydice. Who has not heard of the mythical musician, whose sweet singing entranced not only men but beasts of the forest and fish in the sea, and who caused great oak trees to dance? Orpheus—who charmed even the hellhound Cerberus and the god Hades to rescue his bride from the Underworld, only to lose her by a fateful backward glance! When one thinks of Greek musicians, one thinks first of him. We tend to visualize him as a graceful figure draped and posed in the style of fifth-century Athenian sculpture, and to imagine his music in the alien anachronistic strains of six-teenth-century Italian opera. For who can bring to mind the Bachs, the Van Cliburns, or the Sinatras, for that matter, of Pericles' day? The Parthenon, though broken and profaned, sur-vives to testify to the genius of Ictinus and of Pheidias. But what music lover has praises for the composer whose works have perished utterly, or the virtuoso whose voice has been stilled for over two millennia? We shall never know what melodies Orpheus played or thrill to the songs that Circe and the Sirens sang so sweetly. But in the visual arts and the literature of the ancient Greeks we find much to feed the imagination—ample evidence for the spell that they and their human counterparts cast upon their audiences. And by invoking the archaeological muse, we can help to resurrect the musicians, if not the music, of classical Greece.[1]

Instruments Athenian vase paintings are especially rich in musical representa-tions and tell us much about the musical life of the ancient Greeks.[2] Many depict with clarity and detail their favorite instru-ments. This is most helpful to the archaeologist and musicologist since few actual examples of musical instruments have survived from antiquity, made as they were from perishable materials; those that have are incomplete and unplayable. In a lovely scene on an amphora in the British Museum (Figure 1),[3] we see, at the right, the simple *lyre*, its strings and tortoise-shell body intact; this is the favorite Greek instrument and usual accompaniment to song. Hanging on the wall above the central figure is a more elaborate form of the lyre, known as the *kithara*, a big, concert,

1   Muses and Musaios. Athenian red-figured amphora. Ca. 440 B.C.
British Museum, London. M. Wegner, "Griechenland," *Musikgesch-ichte in Bildern*, eds. H. Besseler and M. Schneider (Leipzig, 1963),
II, Fig. 22. Courtesy, Deutscher Verlag für Musik, Leipzig.

professional instrument constructed of wood. To the left a girl adjusts the reed mouthpiece of an *aulos*, chief among the wood-winds. The *trigonon*, a triangular harp played or tuned by the seated central figure, is a rarer instrument of Asiatic origin, some-times played by women in the home (here, by the Muse Terpsi-chore), but not considered appropriate for formal concerts.

The Greeks, in speculating about the historical origins of their main instruments, aulos and lyre (or kithara), claim Greek inven-tion for the latter, but see the aulos as an import coming from Phrygia or Lydia in Asia Minor about the seventh century B.C. Actually both instruments have very early Eastern ancestors, which, however, the Greeks developed and improved; even the word *kithara* is thought to have a Semitic root. To be sure, a recently discovered archaic Phrygian statue of the Anatolian god-dess Cybele, who later came to be worshipped also by the Greeks, shows her attended by musicians playing the aulos and the kithara,[4] and the music of her orgiastic rites may have been the first to feature the *harmoniae*, or "modes," which the Greeks called "Lydian" and "Phrygian." But in any case, despite gaps in our knowledge about the early development of instrument mak-ing in Greece, it is clear from numerous depictions in art that advanced forms of both aulos and kithara were already the favor-ite instruments of musicians in Bronze Age Crete and Greece, at least a millennium before the time of Pericles. If either or both were introduced to Greece from the East, this must have happened at a very early date.

Mycenaean epic, if it existed, continues to elude us. A My-cenaean minstrel, depicted playing the kithara on a fresco from Pylos,[5] looks suspiciously like later Apollos with long robe and tresses, but he might be King Nestor's court musician, singing an early lay on the woes of the Achaeans and the fall of Troy. By the time of Homer in the eighth century B.C., every king had a professional bard in constant attendance, who entertained at banquets and festivals, and provided music for sacrifices, danc-ing, and athletic contests. These men appear to have been sophisti-cated musician-composers, rather than simple folk musicians, and they were capable of singing lengthy epics of their own composi-tion to the accompaniment of the kithara. In this heroic age their favorite subjects were the adventures and tragic fates of heroes, glorified accounts of military exploits, and the loves of the Olym-pian gods. One suspects that the music for such long recitals had to be extremely repetitious, though the singer might elaborate some favorite passages if he chose to do so. (Tradition has it that most bards were blind, like Demodocus in the *Odyssey* and Homer himself. Perhaps their lack of sight resulted in the development of unusually acute hearing and an increased capacity for memorization.) The literary value of Homer's great epics, and his descriptions of the respect paid to these bards as musicians, suggests that we have already arrived at a period in which the art of music is highly developed, as indeed it may have been some five hundred years earlier in the Mycenaean courts. In any case we should think of the Homeric bards as virtuosi under the patronage of royalty, rather than as slave entertainers.

Of course, the educated, well-born professionals had their village counterparts and imitators, singing to a simple lyre, or perhaps even without accompaniment other than a staff to beat time. A pale ghost of this folk tradition survives in Greece to this day. The favorite epics can be traced back effectively only as far as the medieval period, but they contain many elements which can be paralleled in Homer, and which must have been perpetuated from antiquity.[6]

Where written literature is unknown, or books are rare, meter and melody act as mnemonic devices in preserving and transmitting oral compositions. Homer's invocations to the Muse were as much supplications for aid in a prodigious feat of recall as they were prayers for literary inspiration. It is not surprising that the earliest Greek literature is poetry—much of it *lyric*, that is, sung to the lyre. In this paperback age we forget to think of it as song.[7]

The nine Muses, divine patronesses of the arts, and attendants on the god Apollo, are often shown performing on various instruments (as in Figure 1), though with a casualness that suggests the music school rather than an Olympian chamber orchestra. They give us our own word for music, Greek *mousike*. This word seems first to have had a simple meaning comparable to our own definition, but by the end of the fifth century B.C. it had taken on wider, philosophical connotations.[8] Hence Socrates' dilemma in being commanded by the Delphic oracle to "make music," a typically ambiguous pronouncement. These mystifying "overtones" stem partly from the teachings of the great sixth-century philosopher Pythagoras, who maintained that the entire universe was literally "harmonized" according to a "music of the spheres"—a system of corresponding mathematical and harmonic relationships. The philosopher, in his quest for comprehension of the true nature of the universe, could perceive this system by the power of reasoning. The implications of Pythagoras' theory were manifold. Harmony, wedded to mathematics, gave birth to the science of astronomy, which is for us a field quite unrelated to music! And Pythagoras, almost incidentally to his philosophical investigations, became the founder of the science of harmonics. He worked out a logical system of musical intervals, employing eight-tone scales, based on experiments with measuring stretched strings of different thickness and tension. Following his lead, subsequent Greek philosophers favored stringed instruments over woodwinds for testing their harmonic theories, as the former lent themselves to more accurate measurement. Pythagoras' methods and hypotheses not only formed the basis for ancient musical thought but became the root of our Western musical tradition, which has clung persistently to Pythagorean octave-based scales and intervals for over twenty-five centuries! The long-shunned prospect of innovation is amusingly alluded to in an old J. Wesley Smith cartoon, depicting the philosopher struggling with his strings, while the ubiquitous onlooker protests, "But, Pythagoras, even if you *do* invent an eight-tone scale—what's to prevent some fool from inventing a *twelve*-tone scale?"

Pythagoras was said to have studied oriental music and astronomy in Babylon and Egypt, and he thus may have been influenced by Eastern musical theory, but of that we know almost nothing. The Greek systems of harmoniae, which are often translated as "modes" (the appropriate terminology and interpretation is disputed by musicologists), have been compared by some to East Indian *raga* and Arabic *maqam*, systems of scale patterns which have very ancient roots. But they do not seem to have been so strictly organized, or so limiting to composer and performer.[9]

Like the music of the Middle East and rural Greece today, ancient Greek music must have been primarily homophonic; this is partly suggested by numerous references to improvisation. Some experts have surmised that since the Greeks are known to have considered intervals of a fourth or a fifth consonant, they may have had a simple harmony comparable to, and perhaps ancestral to, the *organum* of the medieval West. Curious examples of songs with a primitive harmony which may be a survival from ancient times, unless it is a Western intrusion, exist in Greek folk music,[10] along with "ancient modes," which were also adopted, but apparently in altered forms, by the Byzantine church.

Accounts of the peculiar effects attributed to the different
Greek harmoniae remind one again, however, of the Indian raga.
To mention only the commonest—the Dorian is supposed to inspire virile and generally virtuous behavior, sometimes eagerness
for battle. The Lydian, by contrast, is soft, effeminate, intimate,
and suggestive—a trifle indecent. The Phrygian, useful for treating
illness both mental and physical, including sciatica, ranges from
enthusiastic to ecstatic, and may induce religious frenzy. These
effects, which are lost on us, are well illustrated in this ancient
anecdote:

Among the accomplishments of Pythagoras, it is said that once, with
the help of an aulos player, he quenched the angry raving of a
young fellow from Tauromena by means of a Spondaic song! The
young man, who was drunk, had gone on a binge on account of
a girlfriend at the entrance of his rival's house and was on the
point of setting it on fire. For he was himself inflamed and had
his fury constantly rekindled by a Phrygian aulos tune—a situation
which, however, Pythagoras ended most expeditiously. For it happened that he was up studying astronomy in the early morning hours.
And he requested the aulos player to change his tune to the Spondaic
hymn, through which the young man, immediately calmed, was made
to leave for home in a decent manner. But shortly before he was
so far gone that he could neither be restrained by force nor, in
short, would tolerate any advice from Pythagoras, and even snubbed
him in a belligerent manner when they met.[11]

The calming "Spondeian hymn" of this story was a libation
hymn, which would have been in the dignified Dorian mode.
This more sober type of song might well have had an effect comparable to that of playing the national anthem to quiet a crowd.
It is interesting that the same instrument could play both modes.
Changes in scale were effected by lengthening or shortening the
mouthpiece (as in Figure 1). Raising, lowering, or separating
the two pipes would also affect the pitch; as an aid to maintaining
control over the embouchure, professionals often used straps
which compressed the cheeks.

The aulos took second place to the lyre because of its unreliable
behavior. Like the oboe, its modern counterpart and descendant,
it was known even in antiquity as "an ill wind that nobody blows
good." Pindar's "Twelfth Pythian Ode" pays tribute to an aulos
virtuoso, a certain Midas of Akragas, who, in 486 B.C., competing
at the festival, accomplished a feat no less remarkable than
Paganini's celebrated one-string performance. The double reed
of his instrument cracked just as he was about to begin. Nothing

daunted, he discarded the broken reed and played on his aulos as if it were an open pipe! The audience was so charmed by his skillful improvisation and by the different sound that they awarded him the prize.

In myth the invention of the aulos is credited to the goddess Athena, who created it from reeds growing by a river. Enjoying her own music and feeling very pleased with herself, she chanced to catch a glimpse of her reflection in the water, whereupon, seeing her cheeks all swollen with blowing, she threw down the instrument in disgust. The satyr Marsyas, less fastidious, snatched up the discarded pipes and acquired such skill that he dared to challenge the god Apollo to a musical contest. Apollo, being an Olympian, and the god of music at that, was offended by the satyr's impertinence. With his divine voice and superior instrument, the lyre, he naturally won the contest. Poor Marsyas paid for his hubris by being flayed alive, and the Phrygian King Midas, a mortal spectator, who had foolishly applauded the louder and more exciting aulos music, was rewarded with asses' ears, a fitting ornament for an insensitive critic.

Many of the Olympians besides Apollo and the Muses play instruments, especially the lyre or kithara, which Hermes is sometimes credited with inventing. Dionysus, god of wine, seems constantly to perform or listen to music. He is often shown with the lyre, while his consort, Ariadne, may bang on a tambourine. Hymns to Dionysus, known as *dithyrambs*, were generally accompanied, as were Apollo's *paeans*, by the lyre, though the aulos became increasingly popular at his orgiastic rites.

A simple type of lyre, known as *barbitos*, was favored by folk singers, and might be compared to the modern guitar. Lyric poets, such as Alcaeus and Sappho of the sixth century, both utilized and composed folk songs, elevating them to the realm of great poetry for all their simplicity of form. Sappho, for example, has given us some truly unsurpassed love songs, such as this, on the effects of approaching one's beloved:

. . . my lips are stricken to silence, underneath my skin the tenuous flame suffuses; nothing shows in front of my eyes, my eyes are muted in thunder. And the sweat breaks running upon me, fever shakes my body, paler I turn than grass is; I can feel that I have been changed, I feel that death has come near me.[12]

What popular ballad has better catalogued the agonizing physical symptoms of desire?

In a formal concert of the fifth century, professional musicians of classical Greece played the kithara rather than the lyre, but as in less formal lyre performances, the singing voice was the main instrument. The kithara provided accompaniment, doubling and sometimes embroidering the melody carried by the voice, as in the lute accompaniments of Middle Eastern vocal music. A kitharode's repertoire might include anything from lyric songs and odes to epic recitations. Often he would be composer, singer and accompanist in one person. The importance of the human voice in Greek music cannot be overemphasized; song, with its inseparable companion, poetry, was held equal to the noble arts of sculpture and painting, which we can so readily appreciate. Singers of the fifth century B.C. were aristocratic, highly educated, and much respected for their talents.

Festivals and Perform-ances —The Virtuosi Most ancient Greek concerts were competitions held in connection with religious festivals and athletic contests, including the great Panhellenic games such as the Pythian. The competitive inter-national atmosphere is reminiscent of our present-day European music festivals. Athenian festival performances, held in connec-tion with the Panathenaia, are sometimes represented on vases.[13] In these depictions, one is often struck by the elaborately em-broidered dress and fancy hairstyles, not only of the aristocrats in the audience (as in Figure 2), but also of the performers. Greek kitharodes, in particular, are frequently shown wearing curious long robes, almost oriental in character (as in Figure 3, and on the aulos player in Figure 4), rather than the usual Greek *himation*. The cut of such garments may have been de-signed to free the musician's arms for playing, while the himation, a cloak which wrapped around the body and draped over one arm, might have hampered his actions. In any case, it is clear that Athenian virtuosi had a special taste for exotic and showy outfits. They also performed in a strange, many-columned build-ing, the original Odeion, which reminded Athenians of the tent of the Persian King Xerxes. It may have been built by Pericles, who is known to have been a great patron of music. Prizes, inci-dentally, seem usually to have been in the form of cash, though in the vase paintings a winged Victory often hovers over the performer to bestow a wreath or a jar.

Occasionally the aulos was used instead of the kithara as an accompaniment to solo singing, necessitating a second performer. However, though this instrument was considered helpful in keep-ing a beginner on pitch, it was not favored as an accompaniment by really fine singers, for it was relatively loud and competed with the voice. It is noteworthy that a rare representation of such a performance, on a black-figured vase, shows a young boy with an adult accompanist.[14] (Separate contests, incidentally, were held for children and adults.)

The aulos, as I have mentioned earlier, was also played solo in competition. On an early Athenian red-figured vase (Figure 2),[15] a vase painter contrasts a formal concert with the performance of a saucy little courtesan at a drinking party. The charming representation of the recital in the main scene, with each participant labeled by name, shows, instead of the moment of victory, the expectant hush which falls over the audience as the performer takes his place on the platform. One gets the impression that the audience sat on portable stools arranged quite close to the musician, probably surrounding him completely.

Instrumental duets seem to have been rare before the Hellenistic period, though several instruments might accompany a large chorus. We can speak of Greek chamber music, but not of real "orchestras" (in the modern sense of the word). "Citizen" choruses, however, were common, and some were fairly large. Choirs of men and boys trained and practiced for competition. Hymns sung to the gods at festivals and sacrifices, such as the Apollonian paeans and Dionysian dithyrambs, were choral, and of course there was that special development of the Dionysian choir, the theatrical chorus.[16] As performances were public these choruses were all male. They seem to have sung in unison, natural differences in voice register resulting in octave intervals; the usual accompaniment was a single aulos. The importance of choral competition is well attested by the impressive victory monuments set up by rich aristocrats who paid for the training of such groups. Perhaps the best known is that of Lysicrates in Athens; intended originally as a monument rather than a building, it was later used by that relatively recent bard, Lord Byron, as his study.

You may read further about Greek theatrical performance and performers elsewhere in this book (see pp. 250–269). But it may be well to emphasize here that Greek drama was sung, and included many forms of music, such as folk songs, hymns, and choral odes. They could be performed separately, and many became "popular classics." I might also mention the enchanting representations of fantastically costumed comic choruses in Greek vase painting, especially as tragic choruses and citizen choirs seem seldom to have been depicted. One scene from comedy, on a

2   Courtesans and aulos recital. Athenian red-figured krater. Ca. 510 B.C. Louvre, Paris. E. Pfühl, *Malerei und Zeichnung der Griechen* (Munich, 1923), p. 122, Figs. 393–394.

3

Kitharode and listener. Athenian red-figured amphora. Ca. 480 B.C. Museum of Fine Arts, Boston. Wegner, "Griechenland," p. 115, Figs. 73–74. Courtesy, Deutscher Verlag für Musik, Leipzig.

black-figured vase, shows men disguised as horses, carrying warriors on their backs—evidently a chorus of "knights," similar
to that in Aristophanes' play of the same name.[17] One wonders
if both horses and riders sang! A number of vases show men
in satyr costumes (as in Figure 4),[18] sometimes all playing accompaniments to their own singing. Others, picturing actors dressing
and practicing music behind the scenes,[19] show that these are
satyr suits rather than satyr skins.

Fifth-century music, theatrical or otherwise, was in every sense
classical, as it featured, to quote one writer, "perpetual competition of new music with recollected models and standards."[20] Because every educated person was trained both in harmony and
performance, subtle musical parody and criticism could be an
important feature of comedy, as it clearly was in Aristophanes'
Frogs, produced in 405 B.C. The competition there between
Aeschylus and Euripides in the Underworld was not simply literary—it was a contest between the then "classical" and conservative music, which in the play wins by reason of its weight, and
the innovations of the "modern" Euripides. Even though we cannot hear Aristophanes' musical parodies, which must have been
sidesplitting to the Athenian audience, we have many hints from
the text as to what they were like. For example, the "tophlattothratt, tophlattothratt" represents Aeschylus' monotonous lyre-
plucking refrains.

In the following year, 404 B.C., Athens had fallen to conservative
Sparta; both music and criticism suffered. By the fourth century
it was no longer considered proper for a gentleman to play an
instrument well—a curious snobbery which has since been very
persistent in the West. Plato and his pupil Aristoxenus were the
last philosophers to understand fully and appreciate Greek classical music, of which they witnessed the decline. Being musically
ignorant, late classical audiences demanded nothing very serious
in theatrical music; criticism, no longer appreciated, died, and
the plays of Aristophanes' immediate successors featured simple
musical interludes by cheap artists, comparable in skill and intel-
lect to those we now endure on television variety shows.

Serious concert music suffered a comparable decline, being in
the hands of uneducated, tasteless professionals, who even invaded
the "citizen" choruses. These men, concerned mainly with putting
on a diverting show, were more actors than musicians. One interesting new feature is program music, criticized by implication
in Plato's *Republic* (3. 396–397); this must have developed in

part from theatrical sound effects. A lyric by a certain Timotheus, entitled *The Persians*, represented the battle of Salamis, with orchestral imitation not only of battle noises, but even of such natural sounds as birds singing, dogs barking, thunder, and windstorms! Meanwhile the classical tradition was abandoned and even forgotten. A late production of a play by Aeschylus or Sophocles might well not have featured the original music. The ancient Greeks, regrettably, had no conservatory to perpetuate musical tradition.

The Amateur Musician To return to the happier time of the fifth century B.C., which is my principal concern in this brief survey, we should consider the role of music in the life of the average citizen, as opposed to the virtuoso. We may safely presume that the amateur musician would still feel a kinship to the heroes of epic, such as Achilles, who were not ashamed to sing and to play the lyre. In Pericles' day, as in Homer's, only boors admitted to musical ignorance. All young Athenians were taught to play musical instruments, usually the lyre, but sometimes also the aulos, at school. Even Plato in the fourth century considered this musical education essential, and lamented its passing. A young boy would begin on a simple lyre. Lessons seem to have consisted largely of demonstration, imitation, and memorization (note the boy and his teacher at the left in Figure 5),[21] and would have overlapped with literary studies when long classical poetic works were memorized. If a young man were especially gifted, he might hope to graduate from the lyre to the kithara. At singing lessons the pupil might be taught melodies or accompanied by his teacher on the aulos; he would stand to sing or recite (as the boy at right in Figure 5).

Sometimes in school scenes on Athenian vases the teacher holds a scroll on which a few lines of poetry may be read (as in Figure 5), or a pupil who appears to be singing or reciting may hold such a scroll. However, no musical notation appears in any of these depictions. If indeed a song is being taught, the scroll must be used only for learning the words.

Ancient Greek musical notation did exist and can be read. Between the lines of an ancient hymn from Delphi, carved on marble, one can make out various symbols, based on the alphabet; these represent notes. A small number of musical fragments have preserved this notation,[22] notably snatches of theatrical music on papyri, unfortunately all late and obscure. We have not a single

musical masterpiece from the fifth century. These late samplings
tantalize, but even they are difficult to interpret, and have been
variously transcribed into our system of notation. None of the
versions has aroused much critical enthusiasm.

In the fifth century it would seem that Greek musicians, both
professional and amateur, largely did without musical notation.
We need not conclude that most pieces were short and simple.
Many young Athenians could recite the entire *Iliad* and *Odyssey*
from memory. So trained, they were surely capable of mastering
long musical works. Greeks scales, which featured semitones difficult for the modern ear to distinguish, could be very richly ornamented, as in Near Eastern music; lacking harmony, at least
in the developed form that we know it in the West, the Greeks
concentrated on the elaboration of the melodic line. Nineteenth-
century classicists concluded that we should probably not like
classical Greek music, could we hear it, and that we need not
mourn its passing. I doubt that we of the twentieth century should
dismiss it so smugly. Now, for the first time, most Westerners
have listened to Indian and Arabic music and have been subjected
to all kinds of modern innovations from twelve-tone to electronic
music. Greek music should certainly be at least equally appealing
and comprehensible.

By now you will have noticed that women have been conspicuously absent among the Greek musicians, professional and amateur, that I have discussed. Great poetesses, like Sappho, are rare,
and respectable women did not participate in the more highly
competitive musical contests. They could, however, sing, play,
and even dance at some religious festivals, and they might enter-
tain family and friends at home. Many households, even in the
fifth century, had Oriental slave girls who played exotic instruments. And Athenian vase painting is rich in depictions of the
courtesans, more skilled in love than in music, who enlivened
Athenian stag parties (Figure 2).

Theocritus gives us a humorous description of two Syracusan
ladies elbowing their way through the crowd to get a good place
at a musical contest. It has a curiously modern sound, until we
realize that what they have come to hear is a dirge to the dead
vegetation god, Adonis! When the two women have finally secured a good place, Gorgo says to Praxinoa:

Listen, Praxinoa, she's about to sing, the daughter of that Argive,
you know who—that versatile young vocalist, what's the phrase—the
prize singer of the dirge last year. She's sure to give us something

4   Satyr chorus. Athenian red-figured krater. Ca. 420 B.C. Metropolitan Museum of Art, New York. Wegner, "Griechenland," p. 65, Fig. 37. Courtesy, Deutscher Verlag für Musik, Leipzig.

5   School scene. Athenian red-figured kylix. Ca. 480 B.C. National Museum, Berlin. Pfühl, *Malerei*, p. 165, Fig. 468.

well worth listening to. There now, she's preening, ready for the song.[23]

This concert chatter is relatively late, Hellenistic, but one imagines that women in the fifth century, lacking the rigorous musical training of their menfolk, would have sounded equally frivolous.

Our modern fad for special music to eat, drive, and do the dishes to has a counterpart in the ancient Greek use of music as an accompaniment to all kinds of activity. The ancient listener, however, was less passive than we. Music, usually played on the aulos, helped to regulate and speed up the monotonous motions of outdoor work, in addition to entertaining the workers. There were folk songs for many different occasions, perhaps sometimes sung to the aulos. As in the Moslem East, music was a must at Greek athletic contests, and seems to have been important for the athlete's timing of his movements. On one black-figured vase two ill-matched boxers advance in spirited fashion to the sound of the aulos, their exaggerated steps reminiscent of the ceremonial approaches of Japanese wrestlers.[24] Discus throwers, javelin throwers, and jumpers—all performed to the aulos. The Athenian aristocrat exercised to music while the peasant and craftsman worked to it.

Instrumental music and song accompanied any important occasion in the life of an ancient Greek, just as they figure in the lives of Greeks today. Traditional hymns and folk songs were an important part of the wedding ceremony. Dirges, sung by female relatives and professional mourners, accompanied the ancient Greek to his grave. Some dead hero-musicians are pictured in art with a lyre on their deathbed, as if intending to take it with them! You may be amused by this late verse on the funeral of some popular musician-poet, as commemorated by a rival or critic:

Eutychides is dead, and what is worse (fly wretched shades!) he's
    coming with his verse.
And listen! they have burned upon his pyre two tons of music,
    and a ton of lyre,
You're caught, poor ghosts. But what I want to know
is where in hell, now he's in Hell, to go.[25]

The trumpet (*salpinx*) was used for signals in battle, and was sometimes fitted with cheekstraps, as was the aulos. Not a very refined instrument, it sometimes figured in a game popular at drinking parties, in which the first man to chugalug his cup of wine while the trumpeter blew one long blast would win a prize. The aulos, too, was used in war. The Spartans, who were peculiar (by Greek standards) in that they marched in time, always had aulos players with the army, and actually went into battle to the sound of music. Their John Philip Sousa, the poet Tyrtaeus, has left us the words of numerous marching songs, such as this:

Up, in free-born hardihood
Soldiers born of Spartan blood!
Guard your left with shields a-swinging;
High the gallant spear-shafts flinging.
Hoard not life nor stint to pay,
Such was never Sparta's way.[26]

A warrior's dance, the *pyrriche*, imitating combat and performed in armor, was also popular. Some modern Greek folk dances, such as the *Sousta* and *Pentozales* of Crete, and the *Hassapiko*, are said to be its descendants. Perhaps the closest is a warlike dance from the Black Sea region, the *Serra*, which features a fight with swords.[27]

Of a completely different character would be the music performed by shepherds in the country. Some of these solitary musicians favored a simple form of the aulos; others a reed pipe, easy to fashion, but frail and liable to crack. Some may even have played an end-blown flute without any kind of mouthpiece; the hero of Pindar's ode, mentioned earlier, must have had experience of such an instrument.[28]

The *syrinx*, or "Panpipes," is first represented on an archaic vase of the early sixth century B.C., and may thus be a relatively late arrival in the Aegean; we tend to think of it as typical of Greece, though actually it was never used by professional musicians, and was probably considered uncouth. This truly primitive instrument, which for us evokes the fauns of Debussy, is associated with the goatish god Pan, who springs upon the unwary traveler in wild mountain glens. The instrument is really nothing more than a bundle of reeds of different lengths and diameters, closed at one end. Each gives a tone when blown, bottle-fashion, across the aperture. Though the syrinx is a rural shepherd's instrument, the arrangement of pipes invites comparison with the water organ, an invention of late Hellenistic times.

Country music has a long tradition in Greece. A Minoan vase of 1500 B.C. shows a party of harvesters, their voices raised lustily in song.[29] The leader of this farmers' chorus shakes a kind of metal rattle, the *sistrum*, an exotic instrument imported from

Egypt. Folk song types are amazingly consistent over the long span of Greek history, as is attested by the snatches of verses preserved in ancient literature. An interesting example is the traditional spring song, sung from house to house by village children to welcome the first swallow in March. An ancient text of this carol corresponds remarkably to the versions sung all over Greece to this day.[30] The survival of such songs parallels the persistence of folk customs in rural Greece; shrines and attributes of the pagan gods have been shifted to the Christian saints. Festivals marking seasonal changes were especially important to the farmer and have also survived in altered form.[31] These would always have been celebrated with music.

An important part of any Greek festival, then as now, was the dance. Participants held hands and moved in a circle, an accompanying musician at the center. Sometimes men danced alone, sometimes women; often both together in alternation. This type of circle dance was known in Bronze Age Greece, and is described vividly by Homer. The folk dances of modern Greece are based on the ancient types. The favorite is the *Syrtos*, a simple circle dance, whose very name is ancient, as is its curious 7:8 rhythm. Another, the *Tsakonikos*, is said to have been invented by Theseus, and danced by him and the seven youths and maidens whom he rescued from the Minotaur.[32] Its steps represented their tortuous escape route from Minos' labyrinth. Other ancient circle dances featured a cross grip. A modern counterpart of very great antiquity is danced every year at the little town of Megara during the week following Easter.[33] It is called the *Trata*, or "fishnet," from the interwoven arms of the dancers and their slow movements, recalling fishermen pulling in their nets. But the words show that it is really a spring song. It has a weird, sinuous melody, which may itself be a survival from an earlier age. The Lenten dance held at the Temple of Zeus in Athens seems also to be a remnant of ancient custom.

The average educated Athenian of the fifth century might not qualify to perform as a soloist in competition, but he would know much more about music than the average American, having studied it until he was thirty, and he would be expected to sing and play on informal social occasions. Music was an important feature of the dinner party, or *symposion*, of which we have so many vivid ancient descriptions, including Plato's dialogue. These affairs were often very boisterous, and respectable women were not invited. Professional entertainers, such as flute girls (see Figure

2) and acrobats, took their place. In addition to animated and witty conversation, guests also entertained each other by singing drinking songs, called *skolia*. Some of these were the compositions of famous lyric poets. There were also others for which guests improvised verses on the spot, like the modern Cretan Pentozales. We actually have the music of a very short, late, anonymous drinking song, preserved on a Greek tombstone in Asia Minor. Appropriate for its secondary use as an epitaph, it translates: "So long as you live, be radiant, and do not grieve at all. Life's span is short, and time exacts the final reckoning."[34]

Any drinking party began with a libation of wine to the gods. This ceremony was accompanied by a special type of song, the *Spondeian*, which figured in the Pythagorean anecdote recounted earlier. (The word *sponde*, literally "libation," survives today as a metrical term in poetry. Similarly, the poetic "foot" refers to the rhythmic beat of ancient dance steps.) As the party proceeded, the music might change in character. There probably would have been more and more requests for aulos tunes and songs in the lascivious Lydian or frenzied Phrygian modes, to correspond with the mood of the guests. Dancing—solo, rather than the festival group dancing—also figured in the entertainment. Dancing girls in Greek vase representations often use a pair of clappers, similar to castanets, called *krotylai*. Their often scanty, sometimes topless, costumes make one think of belly dancers, who are actually mentioned in Roman sources as a feature of Greek parties, presumably in late antiquity. But perhaps some Asiatic slave girls in the fifth century also went in for exotic dancing.

As the evening wore on, and the effects of the wine began to be felt, the guests themselves, no longer content with singing and being entertained, usually began playing and dancing themselves. These dances bring to mind an amusing story told by Herodotus. Cleisthenes, a tyrant of Sicyon in the sixth century, has been looking over prospective suitors for his daughter at a dinner party, and has been inclined to favor a young man named Hippocleides:

[When dinner was over, the suitors began to compete with each other in music and in talking on a set theme to the assembled company. In both these accomplishments it was Hippocleides who proved by far the doughtiest champion, until] at last, as more and more wine was drunk, he asked the flute-player [i.e., aulos player] to play him a tune and began to dance to it. Now it may well be that he danced to his own satisfaction; Cleisthenes, however, who was watching the performance, began to have serious doubts about the whole business. Presently, after a brief pause, Hippocleides sent for a table; the table was brought, and Hippocleides, climbing on to it, danced first some Laconian dances, next some Attic ones, and ended by standing on his head and beating time with his legs in the air. The Laconian and Attic dances were bad enough; but Cleisthenes, though he already loathed the thought of having a son-in-law who could behave so disgracefully in public, nevertheless restrained himself and managed to avoid an outburst; but when he saw Hippocleides beating time with his legs, he could bear it no longer. "Son of Tisander," he cried, "you have danced away your wife." "I could hardly care less," was the cheerful reply. [Hence the common saying, "It's all one to Hippocleides."][35]

Some of the most graceful works of Athenian vase painting portray symposia. Many of these scenes are painted on drinking cups, for which the favorite related themes, music and love, which have always gone well together, are appropriate. We moderns are often amazed at the deportment of these Athenian gentlemen, even allowing for artistic exaggeration. Though some, like Hippocleides, may go too far, it was obviously considered manly and right for a man to take pleasure in dancing and singing—and, after all, who could resist the god of wine? Many symposia spilled out into the street in a merry musical procession; often they ended at the house of a guest. Though public houses were known, such as the famous Corinthian taverns which inspired the wistful proverb, "Not every man may make the voyage to Corinth!" symposia were private parties held in private houses. Of course, they often managed to disturb the entire neighborhood. If we are to believe Aristophanes, the party broke up when the eldest guest abducted the girl aulos player. His play *The Wasps* includes an outrageous scene of this type.

Dionysian Music The divine counterpart to human revelry is the Dionysian orgy, celebrated by the *thiasos*, or band of dancing satyrs and maenads attendant on the god. Artistic representations often reflect human models—inebriated Athenian partygoers, and the human celebrants of Dionysian rites—for whom the orgy was a ritual. (A famous example of a mortal maenad is Olympias, the mother of Alexander the Great, who was said to have slept with a god at such an orgy, conferring divine parentage on Alexander.) At his revels Dionysus is sometimes spectator, sometimes participant. In late classical times, a more romantic age, he is often shown with his consort Ariadne. The wild women known as maenads, frenzied by music and wine, run barefoot over mountain and countryside, picking up snakes, and even tearing wild beasts apart with their bare hands. Almost tame by comparison are their companions, the horse-tailed, pig-eared satyrs, embodiments of bestial sexuality.

The shrill aulos appears gradually to have supplanted the lyre as the chief instrument of Dionysian music, its excitement heightened by a percussive rhythmic accompaniment of cymbals and tambourines. The effect may have been rather like that of the primitive oboe and drum festival music still played in rural Anatolia and, more rarely, in Greece.[36]

Actually the Greeks had many mystery religions which featured music and dance of a orgiastic character with the instrumentation favored by devotees of Dionysus. We cannot always be sure which are depicted in artistic representations, such as the dancing women with snakes on the vase illustrated in Figure 6.[37] (Note the aulos, tambourine, and cymbals.) I find these human "maenads" especially weird in their evident abandonment. One might wonder if music could be a sufficient stimulus to induce such a state of ectasy. Yet we have only to think of their counterparts—on a lower plane, perhaps, the Holy Rollers, or, on a higher, the "Whirling Dervishes" of Konya. The latter move to a "music of the spheres" almost Pythagorean in conception, and perhaps actually so in inspiration. The Anatolian goddess Cybele, mentioned earlier, whose rites were imported into Greece, is depicted on a Roman relief with the instruments which came to supplant aulos and kithara in her worship—tambourine or hand drum, cymbals, and the *tibia*, a late form of the aulos.[38] The vase painting with the dancing women, mentioned before, may actually show her followers. Both representations bring to mind the music associated with a particularly awesome and obscure female deity of the Underworld, Kotys, also hailing from Anatolia, described in this fragment of a play by Aeschylus:

Kotytto's ritual feast they keep.
One handles the chiselled wood that hums
Its droning music full and deep
To work on the soul till frenzy comes;
The brasses clash as a second sings;
Another howls to the twang of strings;
And the roar of a terrible bull-like note
Keeps time, from some invisible throat,
While tom-tom beats with a fearful sound
Like the voice of a thunderclap underground.[39]

The proliferation of Eastern mystery religions in late classical and Hellenistic times must have provided the Greeks with all kinds of exotic musical experiences. A sacrifice to Isis portrayed in a Roman wall painting shows massed choirs and priests in Egyptian garb, one shaking the sistrum.[40] We can scarcely imagine what weird sung liturgy they might be performing. The Egyptians, from very early times, had instruments comparable to the Greek, but they favored a much greater variety, including true flutes in addition to oboes, and many types of harp, also common in early Mesopotamia. Large varied instrumental ensembles are often portrayed in Egyptian tomb paintings. Many feature a long-necked lute, played with a plectrum. This instrument was known in Greece, at least by late classical times, but it is rarely represented there and must have been, like the harp, an exotic import. It is one, however, which fathers an important family of medieval western instruments, as well as some of the favorite folk instruments of modern Greece and the Aegean. A long-necked lute, as in Egypt, was the favorite instrument of ancient Anatolia, and still is to this day. And it may be well to note here that both the music and the musical instruments of Islam derive from the musical and philosophical legacy of ancient Greece. In Turkish and Persian miniatures one may see an oboe similar to the aulos, as well as Panpipes, tambourines, lutes, and even castanets that resemble instruments depicted on Athenian vases of the fifth century B.C.

The Audience Returning to the heyday of Greek music, we should consider briefly the effects that music of the higher sort had on the listening audience. One indication might be the common portrayal of men clutching their heads, evidently in ecstasies at the sound of the aulos, in depictions of symposia on Athenian vases. But perhaps a better testimony to musical appreciation is the rapt attitude of a spectator or judge listening to a kitharode at a festival competition, illustrated in Figure 3.[41] (Here it might be noted that Athenian audiences were enjoined to complete silence at concerts; they could not even applaud. That the rabble might have been inclined to do so is indicated by Plato's reference to policemen with sticks to keep the crowd quiet, even at the theater.) Another Athenian vase shows two ladies thrilling to the song of a female lyric poet, presumably in less formal surroundings.[42] Their expressions are especially dreamy, and it may be that listeners and performer are Muses, in which case the music is truly divine.

6

Orgiastic dance.
Athenian red-figured
krater. Ca. 445 B.C.
Ferrara. N. Alfieri and
P. E. Arias, *Spina*
(Florence, 1960), Pl. 35.

7   Orpheus and the Thracians. Athenian red-figured krater. Ca. 440 B.C.
National Museum, Berlin. Pfühl, *Malerei*, p. 217, Fig. 554.

In many instances the singer's appearance and personal reputation enhanced the appeal of his music. Archilochus, for example, famous for his drinking songs, describes himself as follows:

I am two things: a fighter who follows the Master of Battles,
and one who understands the gift of the Muses' love.[43]

His songs refer mostly to the military and amorous escapades which marked his checkered career and no doubt made him a favorite with the ladies.

To be both a handsome youth and an accomplished musician might be actually dangerous, as is well attested in mythology. Hyakinthos, Tithonos, and other legendary singers are often depicted, lyre in hand, resisting the advances of Olympians and their messengers. Surely, similarly gifted young Athenians had comparable difficulties! For more advanced performers greater dangers were in store. The god Apollo killed the human musician Linus for being his equal in singing—a truly classic example of professional jealousy. Worst of all was the dreadful end of the Apollonian bard Orpheus who opposed the spread of the Dionysiac cult in Thrace and especially its thrilling, crude orgiastic music. He met the horrid fate of all opponents of the god Dionysus, being torn limb from limb by the frenzied maenads.

But we remember Orpheus for his seductive effect upon his audiences. Even the wild Thracians were won over by the beauty of his music. In Orpheus we also see the embodiment of the ideal musician of classical Greece. In the vase painting illustrated in Figure 7,[44] he is portrayed, in contrast to his uncouth audience of Thracians, as an elegant young man with long curling locks and sideburns, completely enraptured by his own song. This type of charmer, also familiar to us from the famous statue of Hermes by Praxiteles, has been compared by a noted Greek scholar to the founder of rock-and-roll, Elvis Presley. Musical questions aside, a similarity in personal appeal and audience reaction is believable. Even the maenads who ripped poor Orpheus to pieces remind one of the deranged teenagers who claw at such idols as Elvis or the Beatles in the hope of a souvenir fragment of cloth or hair. But lest you get the impression that I regard the music of the latter as the goal of Greek tradition, I give you this caustic quote, from Aesop:

. . . in the animals' association with Orpheus all the rest showed only pleasure and admiration, never trying to imitate him. But some of the dogs, as you might expect of such a shameless and impudent species, turned their hand to music, went off by themselves to practice, changed to human appearance, and still pursue the art. This is your breed of lyre players. And that's why they can't entirely escape their own nature. They maintain something of the teaching of Orpheus, but for the most part their music shows the dog in them.[45]

This brief glimpse of ancient Greek musicians and musical life may leave you with many questions which can never be answered. Unless some undreamed-of treasury of early Greek musical texts is discovered, I doubt that the great musicians of Pericles' time will receive in ours their measure of due praise, comparable to that we so readily bestow on Greek architects and sculptors. But I hope that in reading Greek literature you will now hear some faint siren song in the background, even if it is largely a composition from your own imagination, and that you will feel a genuine pang of regret that we can never fully know and appreciate the musicians and composers of ancient Greece.

Tragedy is a peculiarly Greek phenomenon which had its origins in sixth century Athens. A man named Thespis, perhaps the leader of a dithyrambic chorus,[1] had the idea which resulted in giving the Greek hero a new medium of expression and a focus which he could not have attained through the traditional recitation of epic tales. Aristotle reports that "[at first] the chorus, while coming in, used to sing to the gods, and then Thespis invented a prologue and a set speech."[2] Instead of having a rhapsodist singing episodes from Homer or other cyclic poems, or a chorus chanting in unison, Thespis himself impersonated the hero and thus presented him face to face with the audience.

The impact of this direct approach, of seeing Dionysus or Achilles appear and speak in the first person, must have been great indeed. Plutarch tells a story about Solon's first encounter with Thespis and his performances which, although it may be apocryphal, exemplifies the reaction of conservatives throughout history before the mimetic art:

When Thespis and those around him began to develop tragedy, many were attracted by its newness, although it had not yet been moved into the sphere of competition [at the Great Dionysia festival]. Solon, who was by nature fond of hearing and learning, and still more in his old age gave himself to leisure and entertainment and even to drinking and music, went to see Thespis himself acting, as was the custom among the old poets. After the performance Solon addressed him and asked if he was not ashamed to tell such great lies in front of so many people. When Thespis answered that it was not terrible to say and do such things for entertainment, Solon struck the ground with his stick and said, "If we are so pleased with this sort of entertainment, we shall soon find it in our contracts also."[3]

Plutarch may have been leading up to the splendid story which follows, concerning the tyrant Peisistratus' own experiment with mimesis. In order to stage a return from exile, he arranged to be driven into town on a chariot with Athena herself at the reins, impersonated by a local maiden of goddesslike proportions. A man with such a flair for the theatrical would have been especially interested in Thespis' new idea, which had shown wide popular appeal. Thus, in the nexus of a tyrant's need to maintain popularity and the institution of a new festival to the god Dionysus, tragedy became the primary feature of the Great Dionysia, held every year in the early spring, and Thespis appropriately won the first victory about 534 B.C.[4]

Unhappily very little ancient evidence exists on which to base a description of Thespis' performances. We have only the titles of four of his plays, *Games of Pelias or Phorbas, Priests, Youths,* and *Pentheus,* and the titles and a few fragments from his immediate successors, Pratinas, Choerilus, and Phrynichus. Perhaps the best approach to early tragedy is to examine the plays of Aeschylus (ca. 513–ca. 456 B.C.), which are the first complete examples, and from them to extract some idea of the original forms.

The principal elements are the chorus and one actor. Until Aeschylus introduced a second actor some time before the *Persians* was produced in 472 B.C., the poet was his own single actor, probably taking the part of a mythological hero. According to Aristotle (quoted earlier) he entered to speak a prologue in which he would sketch perhaps the background of his story and give a résumé of events leading up to the moment chosen for the play.[5] The chorus in the person of citizens, followers or servants of the hero, or votaries of a god, would then enter singing a hymn to the gods. The first speech by the actor followed, probably arousing the chorus to some action or describing a further state of affairs to which the chorus could react. And so the short production proceeded with a series of set pieces separated by choral song. The focus of the play, at least as seen through later works, was that crucial moment in the life of the hero and his companions (the chorus) wherein he met his fate, often in suffering or death. It was his pathos, the tragic situation, which was always the core of Greek tragedy. Just as the hero is exceptional in his gifts and powers, so his suffering is beyond that of ordinary men and calls forth an appropriate response from the chorus which in the end finally mourns his downfall. Its role was not primarily narrative, however, as the chorus formed a link between the audience and hero, and through it every citizen could participate in the hero's fate.

But more than mere spectators of an event, the early chorus was itself closely involved in the tragic situation. In the *Persians* its members are the elders of state, personally affected by the king's defeat and loss of the army. The daughters of Oceanus in the *Prometheus Bound* so identify with Prometheus that they elect to share in his final punishment by Zeus. The Danaids are the protagonists in the *Suppliants,* and in the *Seven Against*

Thebes the women of Thebes stand to lose almost as much as Eteocles if their city is taken. The chorus of city elders in the *Agamemnon* plays a quasi mantic role in foreshadowing the disaster awaiting the king's return, and they are in a position to suffer greatly under his successor, Aegisthus. The chorus lends its name to each of the other two plays belonging to the *Oresteia* trilogy, the serving women inciting Electra and Orestes to their murder of Clytemnestra and Aegisthus in the *Libation Bearers*, and the Furies acting as the antagonists against which Orestes must struggle in the *Eumenides*.

For the time of Thespis, however, we must imagine that the elements of tragedy, the plot, language, meter, music, and dance, were still in an embryonic form. The interweaving of actor and chorus into a single and artistic whole awaited the master poets of the fifth century, Aeschylus, Sophocles, and Euripides.

After their deaths Aristophanes, the comic poet, was moved to write his masterpiece *The Frogs* (405 B.C.) about Dionysus' journey to the Underworld to bring one of them back to life, because in Athens they had no worthy successor. Revivals of their plays became a regular part of the Great Dionysia in the fourth century B.C. and so dominated the field that no complete work of any later tragic poet has survived. It is eloquent testimony to the decline of the tragic art that the actor thereafter took the poet's place as the most important figure in the theater. Although most of the illustrative material comes from the revivals of this later time, we will take the creative period of the fifth century as the foca point of our examination of actors and acting, their masks, costumes, and techniques.

Masks The impact of a classical play upon its audience cannot be fully appreciated without some understanding of the masks worn by actors and chorus. From the earliest days Thespis is said to have whitened his face with lead, and probably also the faces of his chorus,[6] perhaps with the intention of setting them clearly apart from the realm of ordinary mortals. He later improved on this by substituting plain linen masks, still apparently white, which even more effectively removed the players from the common world in terms of their appearance, as well as through the weight of their suffering. A report from the Roman poet Horace also credits Thespis with painting his face and the faces of his chorus with wine lees and with "driving his poems [tragedies] on wagons" (*Ars Poetica* 275–280). There was no softening, even

through a woman's grace, for the characters represented were at
first all male, and the actors themselves were always men until
the close of antiquity.

As with many other innovations in the theater, some contemporary, and others actually belonging to a later time, the first
colored masks and the first masks of a frightening character are
credited to Aeschylus.[7] Color would certainly have reduced the
ghostlike quality of the faces and would have given the designer
a much greater scope for characterization, as well as the possibility for gruesome representations of mythical monsters.

Descriptions contained in some of his plays corroborate this.
The daughters of Danaus who came to Argos as suppliants from
North Africa are characterized as having a complexion darkened
by the sun (*Suppliants* 71), and their father points out later
that he needs protection in the town, because nature gave him
a different appearance from that of the Argives, since the Nile
and the Inachus bear different races (496–498). Masks with dark
skin and possibly some Egyptian features would have been
made for them, while the hair would have been black, perhaps
curly. Scratches would have been painted on the masks of the
Libation Bearers, who describe their bloody faces in some detail,
"I come in haste out of the house to carry libations, hurt by
the hard stroke of hands. My cheek shows bright, ripped in the
bloody furrows of nails gashing the skin."[8] The masks of the
Furies gave the poet an opportunity for even greater effects
with the result that boys in the audience are reported to have
fainted and pregnant women to have miscarried.[9] The audience
was prepared for them by Orestes' vision at the end of the
Libation Bearers, where he sees them as Gorgons, entwined in
a thick mass of snakes, a hateful stream (of blood?) dripping
from their eyes (1048–1050). The Pythian priestess of Apollo
picks up the same strain at the opening of the *Eumenides*, which,
we may assume, followed almost immediately, and describes them
as black and utterly hideous. They snore with a repulsive breath,
and from their eyes drips a foul stream (48–54). In the end
Athena again brings up their frightful faces, but then for contrast
with the great good they have been persuaded to do for Athens
(990–991).

The Furies must have been a maskmaker's delight. The repeated mention of oozing eyes suggests some particular treatment
of eye sockets, perhaps enhanced with painted gore. The skin
would have been painted black, and the hair entwined with wrig-

gling snakes. Inasmuch as Aeschylus' plays alone were allowed
to be reproduced immediately following his death, new versions
of the Furies may have been created for each occasion. Tame
echoes of them are to be seen on some fourth-century B.C. vases
depicting scenes from the *Eumenides*, which, although they do
not live up to the horror of the poet's description, give an idea
of the snaky-haired creatures.[10]

Another mask which must have been outstanding is that of
Io who appears in Aeschylus' *Prometheus Bound*, after she was
turned into the form of a cow by a vengeful Hera. For reasons
of practicality the cow shape was probably conveyed only by
a special mask with horns, perhaps similar to the animal heads
worn by a comic chorus of horse-men shown on a black-figured
vase.[11]

Beautiful heroes and heroines could be distinguished by blond
hair as in the case of Phaedra, Iphigeneia, Helen, Hippolytus,
and Orestes, and short hair was used as a sign of mourning.[12]
Dionysus in Euripides' *Bacchai* (and perhaps also in the other
Dionysiac plays now lost) would have had a special male-female
mask to portray his unearthly, deadly beauty. The verbal picture
in the play is explicit: "A fellow with golden hair flowing in
scented ringlets, the flush of wine on his face and the charm of
Aphrodite in his eyes" (235–236).[13] The guard describes him at
his capture: "He didn't even turn pale, but kept the fresh color
you see in his face now, smiling . . ." (438–439), and Pentheus
continues. "Those long curls of yours show you are no wrestler—
cascading close over your cheeks, most seductively. Your complexion, too, shows a carefully-preserved whiteness" (455–458).
Little is left to the imagination, and we may expect that the
mask would have followed the poet's description.[14]

The earliest actual representation of a theatrical mask occurs
on a fragment of an *oenochoe* (pitcher) found in the Athenian
Agora, dated ca. 470 B.C.[15] The face (Figure 1), which is painted
with great care, portrays a young woman with her short hair
bound by a broad purple band over the forehead. That the flesh
is done in white paint is very likely indicative of her female
sex, which is often distinguished by white paint on earlier vases,
and the convention occurs again on the Pronomos vase which
will be discussed later. The mask covered the entire face and
included a wig of hair attached to the top and arranged at the
sides in a natural fashion, so that the actor's whole head was
covered. The face portion of the mask was apparently secured

to the head by a cord running under the wig, and it passed through three holes at the top for carrying purposes. The features are naturally rendered without distortion and exhibit the full chin apparent on sculpture of the period, as on the pediment statues from the temple of Zeus at Olympia. The lips are shown only slightly parted, and in one eyeball the trace of an iris would seem to be the vase painter's addition to the actual mask. In reality some opening in the eye sockets and perhaps a larger one for the mouth would have been necessary. The tendency of the vase painter to modify masks, and theater scenes in general, must always be borne in mind. The dual reality of the actor and the character he portrayed did not appeal to the fifth-century artist, but was more to the taste of his fourth-century followers. And even they, as we shall see, blended the character with the actor and often made little distinction between the representation of a play in the theater and its mythological counterpart.

With what play the figures on the Agora oenochoe can be associated is uncertain inasmuch as only the lower parts of two identically draped women, the sliver of a laced boot from a male actor, and a piece of drapery are preserved. Perhaps the *Seven Against Thebes* (produced in 467 B.C., when it won first prize) is a likely candidate because its female chorus could be identified with the two draped women, and Antigone, in mourning for her brothers, would be appropriate for the shorn hair of the girl's mask.[16]

The mask might have been manufactured as follows. A clay model of the face was formed and from it a mold taken. (Or in some cases, especially in the earlier phases when the poet was his own actor, the mold may have been taken directly from the actor's face.) Into the mold was "pressed a sheet of linen soaked in plaster. When the plaster hardened, the mold was removed and the mask sewn to a cap which fitted the actor's head. The wig was added and the face painted."[17] The large terracotta and marble masks preserved from antiquity were certainly never worn but served rather as decorative pieces.

Another important piece of fifth-century evidence for the theater is the Attic vase found near Ferrara, dated ca. 460–450 B.C. (Figure 2). The scene reveals a fully costumed and masked maenad doing a lively dance with gestures before a young man holding a mask.[18] The mask of the maenad, seen in profile, provides some details not visible in the full-front view of the Agora mask. Her lips are well parted, though not gaping, and the eye sockets are completely open. A narrow border of hair appears along the side of her face, apparently attached to the mask, while the rest of the head and hair is covered by a patterned snood (*sakkos*), from which a fringe of the actor's own hair escapes at the bottom. On this mask, then, the full wig was replaced by the snood for the back with hair only around the face, either painted on the mask or with false strands sewed to the linen. The edge of the mask is shown by a dark line following the hair and continuing down around the jaw bone and chin. The whole rendering of the mask is contrasted nicely with the face of the young man opposite, so that the artist left no doubt of his intention to show a maenad and a youth from the theater rather than merely mythological figures.

The other mask, held by the youth, is drawn front-face, but so carelessly that it adds little to our information on masks. It apparently represents a young man with curly long hair worn behind the ears, framing a heavy-chinned face. The lips appear closed, or almost so, and the eyes are shown with irises, which might, however, be large enough for the actor to see through if the mask was worn very close to his face. His association with a maenad very likely identifies him as Dionysus, although the painter hardly managed to convey beauty or charm.

A scene of a very different nature is presented on pieces of an Attic hydria (470–450 B.C.) found in Corinth, which are unfortunately very fragmentary.[19] A flute player sets the action in the theater. The central group (Figure 3) seems to be an oriental king rising out of a burning pyre from which oriental attendants draw back in fright and amazement. The king's face is not rendered so as to suggest a mask, although we may suppose that he is wearing one with a beard attached. The only possibility of identification with one of the extant plays is with the *Persians* (472 B.C.), but there Darius rises from his tomb, while here the king is on a burning pyre of wood. Apparently some lost play with an oriental setting inspired the vase painting.

A more satisfactory representation for our purpose is a dressing and rehearsal scene on a vase (Figure 4) of 450–430 B.C. now in the Boston Museum of Fine Arts.[20] An actor with his mask on the ground in front of him pulls on his boots, while his companion seems to be rehearsing his part fully costumed and masked. They are very similarly dressed and have corresponding masks of young women, shown in profile. The lips are open as if speaking, but the eyes appear to be filled in. The heavy hair of the

1

Theatrical mask on an Athenian
red-figured oinochoe. Ca. 470 B.C.
Lucy Talcott, "Kourimos Parthenos,"
Hesperia, Vol. 8 (1939), p. 269, Fig. 2.
Courtesy of the American School of
Classical Studies at Athens.

2   Theatrical masks on an Athenian red-figured krater. Ca. 460–450 B.C.
Ferrara. N. Alfieri and P. E. Arias, *Spina* (Florence, 1960), Pl. 66.

wig is clearly attached to the mask and bound up in the back with a fillet in a common feminine hairstyle. The mask on the ground even includes an earring on the right ear. The bareheaded actor has bound his hair with a band running over his forehead, perhaps to absorb some of the perspiration caused by the all-enveloping mask and wig. The two figures are undoubtedly members of a female chorus, but they lack any special characterization.

Near the end of our survey of theater scenes on vases falls the most famous and detailed exposition of masks and costumes, done in honor of the flute player Pronomos around 400 B.C. (Figure 5). The setting is an off-stage and mythologically enhanced gathering of a satyr chorus and three actors, accompanied by the poet, lyre player, and Pronomos himself, above whom rest Dionysos and Ariadne in a loving embrace upon a couch with footstool.[21] The masks for actors and chorus are especially carefully treated and have been obviously studied from all angles. Some are held by their strap at the top, others by inserting a hand to support them on the inside. The satyrs' reddish faces include pointed ears attached between shaggy hair and beard, and the mouths are open. The masks for the heroic king and Herakles are more elaborate with yellow-white skin, long hair and beards: Herakles' mask has his characteristic lionskin over the hair, while that of the king bears an oriental headdress. The actor representing the heroine is a more enigmatic figure from the fact that he (she) sits on the couch of Dionysus, is barefoot (actors generally wore soft boots), and, though maskless, is shown with the face of a woman rather than that of a male actor. The artist has merged his actors with the characters they personify, as can be seen also in the case of the bearded actors playing the king and Herakles. Surely actors did not wear beards under their masks. The satyrs, however, remain purely creatures of the theater, illustrating the manner in which ten Athenian gentlemen could be transformed into wild creatures of myth by donning the all-concealing mask and the hairy loincloth.

A vase at Würzburg (Figure 6) of about the same time and style is fragmentary, but does give us another example of actors and chorus, mixed with divine personages.[22] Here, too, the same blending of actor and character has taken place. The masks are very well done and are fitted with hair in kinky locks standing out from the face. They include ears and some fine lines at the roots of the hair, probably to indicate where the wig was stitched to the linen face. The features have a rather wild look emphasized

3   Theatrical scene on an Athenian vase from Corinth. Ca. 470–450 B.C.
J. Beazley, "Hydria Fragments in Corinth," *Hesperia*, Vol. 24 (1955),
Pl. 85. Courtesy of the American School of Classical Studies at Athens.

4

Dressing scene on an Athenian
red-figured pelike. Ca. 450–430 B.C.
A. Pickard-Cambridge, *The
Dramatic Festivals of Athens*,
2nd ed. rev. by John Gould and
D. M. Lewis (Clarendon Press,
1968), Fig. 34. Courtesy, Museum
of Fine Arts, Boston, Pierce Fund,
purchased of E. P. Warren.

by a mouth wider open than any seen so far and by the usual white paint for the flesh. The eyes have been painted in, as in other examples; open sockets were perhaps too inhuman for the painter's taste.

The final piece of evidence which falls within our scope is a marble relief from Peiraeus (ca. 400 B.C.), showing Dionysus on a couch visited by three figures in tragic dress carrying masks and tympana.[23] The first figure to the left was originally wearing his mask, but it has been cut away; the middle figure held the mask of an old man by the top; and the masked right-hand figure may be either a clean-shaven old man, a young woman, or the young Dionysus. In any case it is apparent that the mouths of the masks are gaping wide and the faces have taken on the unreal, distorted quality so typical of later Greek and Roman masks.

In all the masks from the fifth century that we have seen their outstanding quality is naturalness of features and expression. The eyes and mouth are not misshapen, the brows remain level and smooth, and the hair is arranged according to the character, short-cropped, long and curly, or tied in a smooth snood or fillet. The mask served merely to enhance the actor and to set him apart from the audience of ordinary citizens. It enabled him to switch from male to female parts smoothly and quickly, and to characterize women without incongruity. The features could also be made a little larger than life-size to make them visible from the upper rows of the great open-air theater on the Acropolis slope. The maskmaker (very likely the poet himself) evidently enjoyed considerable freedom in his characterizations, and only later did the types become grotesque and stereotyped, fixed into the numerous categories which are listed by Pollux in his encyclopaedia (late second century after Christ).

Another dimension for the mask has been proposed by Webster who suggests that the poet designed it to convey his conception of the character to the actor (when other than himself) and to the audience.[24] The actor Aesopus is reported to have "conformed his gestures and voice to the face of the mask," and in several paintings and reliefs a poet or actor is shown contemplating a mask.[25] A story told of both Sophocles and Menander relates that, "shortly before the production of a play, each of them was asked whether the play was ready and each replied that the plot was constructed and only the verses needed to be written," which the poet may have done with the masks before him as his *dramatis personae*. Aristotle (*Poetics* 1455a. 29) recommended that the

5   Drawing from the Pronomos Vase (satyr play). Athenian red-figured
           krater. Ca. 400 B.C. Naples. Margarete Bieber, *The History of the Greek
           and Roman Theater*, rev. ed. (Princeton, 1961), Fig. 32.

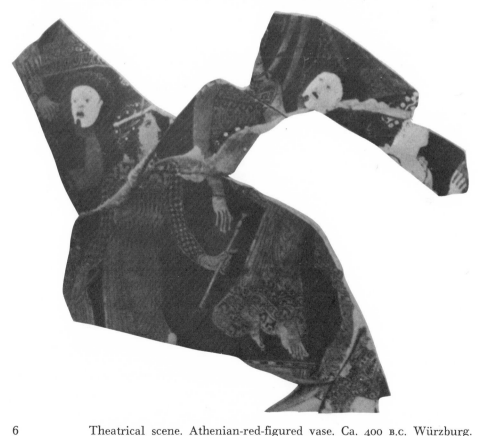

6   Theatrical scene. Athenian-red-figured vase. Ca. 400 B.C. Würzburg.
           Pickard–Cambridge, *Dramatic Festivals of Athens*, Fig. 50a.

poet should work out his speeches with actual gestures, and Aristophanes jests that Euripides naturally created lame characters, because he always wrote with his feet up (*Archarnians* 410); Agathon (a younger contemporary of Euripides) is wearing women's clothes, because he is writing a woman's part (*Thesmophoriazusae* 151); "A poet, sir, must needs adopt his ways to the high thoughts which animate his soul. And when he sings of women, he assumes a woman's garb and dons a woman's habits."[26] The scene in the *Archarnians* where Euripides gives out costumes and properties from his collection indicates that the poet possessed his own gear, which would also include the masks, although they are not specifically called for in the play. He very likely created new masks for new characters or new characterizations of old ones as he composed his plays from year to year, and the idea of the poet-actor may have persisted longer than the actual practice in the theater.

Costume   There is little evidence for the earliest costumes from the days of Thespis, although several vases from about the middle of the sixth century B.C. illustrate comic scenes. On one, men are shown dressed as maenads in short chitons and fawnskins; another represents men dancing in long women's clothing; and a most intriguing chorus is composed of three knights mounted piggyback on three men disguised as horses, accompanied by a flute player.[27]

Aeschylus again is credited with the major innovations in this field. The *Life* relates that "he ornamented the *skene* (scene-building) and he amazed the vision of the spectators with splendor, with paintings, with mechanical devices, with altars and tombs, with trumpets, phantoms, Furies (*Eumenides*), covering the actors with sleeves and honoring them with a trailing robe, and raising them up with larger boots." It is difficult to reconstruct just how much of this he actually did and what portion is the work of later innovators. He may have merely begun the use of these devices in some of his plays, with the exception of the elevated boots (*kothornoi*), which have no parallels until the late fourth century B.C. The costumes were then elaborated upon from century to century until they assumed the exaggerated forms of the Roman theater.[28] Aristophanes in the *Frogs* (1066ff.) makes Aeschylus say only that he gave his heroes nobler dress than other men to match their higher language; and he then berates Euripides for destroying all this by dressing his heroes in rags.

Even allowing for comic exaggeration, some change in costume between the two poets is evident.

Among his preserved plays, the *Persians* (472 B.C.), the *Suppliants* (ca. 467–463 B.C.), and the *Eumenides* (458 B.C.) gave Aeschylus an opportunity to experiment with exotic costume. The first is set at the Persian capital of Susa where a chorus of state councilors, the Queen Mother, Atossa, and Darius' ghost could have been attired with suitable pomp and splendor in heavy robes of Persian style. Indeed, when Atossa returns to invoke the dead Darius, she specifically states that she has come without her chariot and the elaborate ornaments (607–608) which had presumably accompanied her first entrance. The connotation of "Persian" as synonymous with wealth and luxury could have been put to good use for a theatrical spectacular, which would have included a train of brightly garbed attendants, chariots, banners, and richly decorated background hangings.[29] The daughters of Danaus who formed the chorus and are the protagonists of the *Suppliants* come from the no less exotic region of North Africa, close to Egypt. They are characterized as wearing foreign gowns (*barbaroi peploi*), closely wrapped in veils (235–236). When he first sees them the King of Argos speculates on their identity—are they women of Libya, Egypt, Cyprus, Aethiopia, or, he would have said, Amazons, except they lack the bow. The elaborately decorated costumes of the last are well-known from many vase paintings and the garb of the suppliant maidens may well have born some resemblance to them.[30] They were also provided with long girdles, or sashes, very likely crossed over the chest and around the waist, by which they threatened to hang themselves. Their father, Danaus, too would have worn foreign dress, as is clear from the passage mentioned above in connection with his mask, and the Egyptian herald would have been identified as such by his costume. Finally, the Furies in the *Eumenides* must have had garments appropriate to their hideous faces. They are merely called "black" in the play, and the rest is left to our imagination and the costumer's invention. Their change of character at the end is symbolized and emphasized by their being covered in handsome purple cloaks as they are led to their new home near the Acropolis.

For his other extant works Aeschylus needed no obviously non-Greek costumes except possibly for Io in *Prometheus Bound*. Her bovine head may have been accompanied by other animal attachments, such as a tail. Hephaestus and Hermes in the same play would have been identified by their traditional attributes; the abstract gods, Might and Force, could have had special dress expressive of their character. The chorus of Oceanids and their father, Oceanus, creatures of the sea, probably were robed like their mythological counterparts in contemporary art, the girls in flowing chitons and the father with a beard and cloak. Prometheus himself may have been nude. The story of the *Seven Against Thebes* (467 B.C.) was taken from heroic literature, as was that of the *Oresteia* trilogy (458 B.C.), and there is no reason to suppose that the human characters were costumed in other than highly ornamented Greek dress: armor for Eteocles, Agamemnon, and Aegisthus, long robes and mantle for Antigone, Ismene, and Clytemnestra, something dark and probably shabby for Electra and the Libation Bearers who are in mourning. The last actually mention their torn robes (27–29). Orestes and Pylades would have been dressed as travelers.[31]

The characters of Sophocles and Euripides are principally heroic figures who would have worn some version of Greek dress. Mourning was appropriate to Sophocles' Electra (191), and in Euripides' version she is so poorly dressed that she is taken for a slave (107–110, 185). Philoctetes and Oedipus at Colonus were also in tatters, as were Menelaus in Euripides' *Helen*, and the ill Orestes in his *Orestes*. A band of sailors comprises the chorus in the *Philoctetes* and *Ajax*. Aristophanes more than once twitted Euripides about his ragged, limping characters, but Euripides also employed special effects, as with his horrible Thanatos or figure of Death in the *Alkestis*, the elaborate peplos worn by Hermione in *Andromache* (147ff.) and the fine garments which Evadne dons before jumping onto her husband's funeral pyre in the *Suppliants* (1054–1055). Young Ion, too, as a servant of Apollo was well-dressed (326–327), but it would be difficult to see him in other than a short chiton and mantle.

We turn now to the representations of actors from the fifth century B.C., which we considered before in terms of their masks. The costumes that they wear are as natural as the masks in style and ornamentation, and not until the end of the century, on the Pronomos vase, do the long, elaborately decorated and sleeved gowns actually appear, though they are attributed to Aeschylus. The vase fragments from the Athenian Agora (see Figure 1), reveal the lower parts of two female figures wearing long, pleated gowns covered by a mantle with a stripe along the edge, and soft boots with turned-up toes. The third figure, perhaps male from his laced boot, is very fragmentary. Nothing on these figures distinguishes the actors from contemporary women. The same can be said for the young man on the vase from Ferrara (Figure 2) who wears a long, loose chiton with full sleeves to the elbow and a simple mantle clasped on one shoulder. He, too, seems to wear soft boots with turned-up toes, though they are hard to identify, being seen in front view. The maenad opposite him is dressed according to her role, in a long, loose chiton topped with a fawnskin. Her feet, however, are shod in the same boots as the man and they, together with her mask, place her in the theater, for the maenads of myth were usually barefoot. Whatever play of oriental subject is represented on the Corinth hydria fragments (Figure 3), the characters apparently wear traditional eastern costume and headgear, probably with boots. The fabric is ornamented with an over-all pattern of circles, and tunics are worn over a tight-fitting, long-underwear-type garment. The circle pattern is echoed on the dress of the flute player, which led Beazley to compare the common flute-player costume, as seen on many earlier and contemporary vases, to that of the oriental actors, and hence to see a relationship between theater costume and the earlier garb of flute players.[32] The two chorus members on the Boston vase (Figure 4) are unexceptionally dressed in the contemporary style, with chiton drawn up by a girdle, a mantle, and boots with turned-up toes, and must represent a play "in modern dress."

With the exception of those on the hydria from Corinth (Figure 3), exotic, heavily decorated robes with long sleeves appear in vase painting for the first time on the Pronomos (Figure 5) and Würzburg (Figure 6) vases of about 400 B.C. They are then repeated on a number of vases in the years following, many of which seem to have theatrical subjects.[33] The outstanding decoration of the robes consists of bands of embroidery, often with horse heads, chariots, and other animals running across the breast and hem. The long sleeves are ornamented with diamond patterns, waves, stripes, or dots, and a band of long, pointed rays running up the shirt is often seen. The robe is belted high under the breast and is usually accompanied by a mantle. Sleeves can be omitted for chorus members, as on the Würzburg fragments, and the skirt shortened for lesser characters, as on the Andromache vase. The same style of gown appears on the contemporary relief from Peiraeus, although whatever painted decoration may have been added to represent a patterned garment has vanished. This basic type of dress, once fixed, persisted into Roman times as standard stage costume. For the fifth century, however, the evidence from the vases and literature shows that, although elaborate robes may have been used on occasion, the poet could design his own costumes with considerable freedom and sometimes, at least, he chose contemporary dress.

The
Art of
Acting

Most elusive of all things about the ancient theater is the manner in which the actors and chorus performed their roles. We have been able to form some idea of their appearance from the descriptions in the plays and depictions on a few contemporary vases, but the fluid movements of a body and intonations of voice cannot be recaptured. Thus we must consider the requirements imposed on actors by production of the play in a large, open-air theater and by the possibilities and limitations of wearing a mask. Some information, too, is derived from the few representations of a chorus in action, and from anecdotes related by later writers.

The actor in such a large theater depended principally on his voice, together with gestures and body movements, to convey his character to the audience. Versatility was also important inasmuch as each actor played more than one role in a play, often changing from male to female, young to old, as the parts demanded. Aristotle stresses the actor's ability to characterize the "modes of speech" such as command, question, prayer, and threat as essential, including variation of tone when saying the same thing.[34] Clear enunciation was another important factor, for the actor was often required to speak lines heavily embroidered with imagery and, especially in the case of Aeschylus, with unusual words and metaphors. The story is told of Hegelochus, an actor of the fifth century B.C., that, when acting Euripides' Orestes, he gave the wrong pitch to one syllable thereby turning the line "from the waves once more I see the calm" (279) into "once more I see a cat coming out of the waves." He was laughed out of the theater (Scholiast on Euripides, *Orestes* 279). Being ridiculed by an Athenian audience could be a very unpleasant experience as evidenced by Demosthenes' comment that his rival Aeschines had endured a shower of fruit and stones at their hands (*On the Crown* 262).

Actors trained their voices with care, following a special diet and keeping in practice with exercises, probably in the manner of opera singers today. A comic actor at the end of the fifth century B.C., one Hermon, is reported to have missed his cue in the orchestra, because he was outside trying his voice (*Pollux* IV. 88).

A final story will illustrate the length to which an actor might go to achieve an effect. The famous tragedian Polus, when playing the title role in Sophocles' *Electra*, is said to have placed the ashes of his own dead son in the urn over which Electra grieves when she believes it to contain the remains of Orestes (Aulus Gellius *Attic Nights* VI. 5).

Gesture and bodily movement were the other important tools at the actor's disposal. Again as a consequence of the large, open theater, whatever the actor did had to be on a large scale: sweeping gestures, big movements, free use of the whole body to express emotion. With the mask presenting a fixed face to the audience, variations in mood had to be conveyed through tone and the gestures accompanying the words.[35] When some of the acts required of the characters were impossible, such as kissing and weeping, the poet provided a verbal description and gestures supplied the rest.[36] The importance of gesture is stressed by Aristotle when he exhorts the poet to work the gestures out when composing a speech, so that they will be in accordance with nature (*Poetics* XVII. 1455a. 29). That they could be overdone is illustrated by the nickname "monkey" given to one Kallippides (latter fifth century B.C.), who apparently carried his movement to extremes. The pattern of statuesque figures moving sedately around the orchestra and speaking grand lines in an immobile fashion does not seem to have been the case in the early period, although such a style may have become conventionalized in later times.

Both the fine maenad on the Ferrara vase (Figure 2) and the actor who is rehearsing on the Boston vase (Figure 4) demonstrate lively body movement and broad gestures. That they are probably both members of a chorus does not matter here, because the acting style of chorus and principal would have had much in common. The maenad bends her left knee and seems to pivot on her left foot, while swinging the right leg high and straightening the body as her arms fly out front and back. The chorus woman is slightly less free, but appears to be rehearsing a line as she raises high her right arm and extends a mantle in the left, all the while leaning forward to take a step. If the maenad on a vase in Berlin accompanied by a flute player can be considered to reflect a scene from the theater,[37] albeit her costume is more mythological than theatrical, her gestures, holding aloft the leg of a kid in one hand and a sword in the other, display great freedom and vigor. From the little we can see on the fragments from Corinth the oriental attendants also moved freely to convey their fright and astonishment.

Dancing is another kind of movement which played a large part in the early and classical productions but declined near the end of the fifth century B.C.[38] Phrynichus, one of Aeschylus' older contemporaries, along with Aeschylus himself, are credited with inventing many dances. Aristophanes even ends his play, the *Wasps*, with a dance contest wherein the old father, with steps first produced by Thespis, competes against a later tragic poet and his sons. His accompanying description indicates a lively dance of high kicks, twirling feet, clapping and spinning like a top. A fragment from another play of Aristophanes seems to refer to an Aeschylean chorus of Phrygians in his play of that name, now lost: "I remember seeing the Phrygians when they came in order to join with Priam in ransoming his dead son, how they often danced in many postures, now this way, now that" (frag. 678). An Attic vase of the mid-fifth century B.C., now in London, gives us some flavor of a tragic chorus in its variety of movements and graceful gestures.[39] A flute player accompanies the chorus of six figures dressed in contemporary female costume. A civilian figure, perhaps the trainer or sponsor (*choregos*), stands in their midst, thus identifying the scene as a rehearsal rather than a performance. Each member of the chorus seems to be demonstrating a different step with appropriate hand gestures. The motions are highly mimetic, and it is not hard to see various "shrinking" and "beckoning" movements as well as a "foretelling" attitude at the far right.

The poet-actor-director began, as we have seen, by giving a kind of one-man show with a chorus. As long as the actor could converse only with the corporate body of the chorus,[40] or give set speeches to the audience, his possibilities as a character were limited. When Aeschylus introduced a second actor (before 472 B.C.), he extended the scope of the action so that messages and reports could be brought in from off stage and a simple dialogue between actors ensued.[41] At first, the two actors had little contact and more often addressed the chorus than each other, but the possibilities for extended dramatization were so strong that soon a third actor was used by Sophocles. He, much more than Aeschylus, was interested in individual characterization which is the core of the actor's art. Sophocles early in his career withdrew from acting in his own plays, some say because his voice could not take the strain, and soon a group of professional actors was formed. By 449 B.C. a separate prize for acting was offered at the Great Dionysia, and at the end of the century the actors far overshadowed the chorus whose role had continually diminished in its relevance to the play. Indeed, in the fourth century B.C. the actors outstripped even the poets in importance, and the outstanding productions seem to have been revivals of classical plays.

When the final test came between Aeschylus and Euripides in their contest for supremacy in the *Frogs,* Dionysus says, "Whichever is likely to advise the city well, him I intend to take back."[42] Both poets propose solutions for the city's ills, since it had been agreed earlier that the poet's art is to make men better. It is in this didactic vein that Euripides is criticized for "training our youth in the art of sophisticated gabble. . . . Of what ills is Euripides not the cause?"[43] His characters and plots are accused of bringing out, not the noblest, but the basest in men, while Aeschylus argues that "a poet should seek to avoid the depiction of evil—should hide it, not drag into view its ugly and hideous features. For children have tutors to guide them aright; young manhood has poets for teachers. And so we must write of the fair and the good."[44] This dual role for tragedy, to inspire and instruct in nobility or baseness, to provide models of good or evil, to portray what is or what might be for the benefit of the state or to its harm was deeply felt by the Greeks. It is presaged in Solon's first encounter with Thespis and repeated again by Plato two centuries later in his *Laws:* "We also according to our ability are tragic poets, and our tragedy is the best and noblest; for our whole state is an imitation of the best and noblest life which we affirm to be indeed the very truth of tragedy."[45] But those poets who would portray anything less than the best, he carefully excluded.

Thus the power of a play is very strong. The characters live before the eyes of the spectators, moving them for good or ill, and they are given that life by the actor's art with the poet's words.

Notes

Chapter 1: Greek Building

1. Robert L. Scranton, "Greek Architectural Inscriptions as Documents," *Harvard Library Bulletin*, Vol. 14 (1960), pp. 159–182. For an extensive account of technical aspects of building, see Roland Martin, *Manuel d'Architecture Grecque* (Paris, 1965), Vol. I.
2. *Inscriptiones Graecae*, I², 24; M. N. Tod, *Greek Historical Inscriptions*, 2d ed. (Oxford, 1946), p. 78, No. 40. Here, as elsewhere, both for the inscriptions and for Plutarch we give our own translations, sometimes using different readings and restorations.
3. *I.G.*, I², 88.
4. For a discussion of this role, see J. A. Bundgaard, *Mnesicles* (Copenhagen, 1957).
5. *I.G.*, II–III², 1668; Bundgaard, pp. 117–131.
6. For the Erechtheum inscriptions in general see L. D. Caskey in J. M. Patton et al., *The Erechtheum* (Cambridge, Mass., 1927), chap. IV, pp. 277–422; also, H. R. Randall, "The Workmen of the Erechtheum," *American Journal of Archaeology*, Vol. 57 (1953), pp. 199–211. For this passage, *Erechtheum*, p. 331, frag. IX, lines 20ff. Caskey translates *ochetos* as "struts (?)" in one variant from our interpretation.
7. *I.G.*, II², 1666, lines 8ff. (with omissions).
8. *I.G.*, II², 1673, lines 64ff. See Fig. 5 in chap. 4.
9. A. Rehm, R. Harder, *Didyma*, II, "Die Inschriften" (Deutsches Archaeologisches Institut, Berlin, 1958), No. 41, lines 29ff.
10. For this, see G. P. Stevens, in Fowler and Wheeler, *Handbook of Greek Archaeology* (New York, 1909), pp. 96ff.
11. *I.G.*, VIII, 3073, lines 121ff. For illustration of the types of chisels mentioned, see Fig. 6 in chap. 4.
12. *Didyma* (note 9) No. 27, *obverse*, lines 7ff.
13. *I.G.*, VIII, 3073, lines 128ff.
14. *Erechtheum*, p. 331, frag. IX, lines 24ff.
15. *Erechtheum*, pp. 383f., frag. XIV; p. 391, frag. XVII, i, lines 35ff; p. 397, frag. XVII, ii, lines 46ff.
16. A. Trevor Hodge, *The Woodwork of Greek Roofs* (Cambridge, 1960).
17. *Erechtheum*, p. 331, frag. IX, lines 10ff.
18. *Erechtheum*, p. 339, frag. XI, ii, lines 21ff.
19. *Erechtheum*, p. 395, frag. XVII, ii, lines 1ff.
20. *Erechtheum*, p. 381, frag. XIII, i, lines 22ff.
21. *Erechtheum* p. 341, frag. XI, iii, lines 43ff.
22. *Erechtheum*, p. 383, frag. XIII, i, lines 43ff.
23. *Erechtheum*, p. 395, frag. XVII, ii, lines 34ff.
24. *Erechtheum*, p. 389, frag. XVII, i, lines 1ff.

Chapter 2: Roman Imperial Building

1. In his *Etruscan Cities and Rome* (London, 1967), pp. 78, 80–81, H. H. Scullard notes that the Romans themselves attributed the atrium and methods of founding cities to the Etruscans. The latter, while profoundly influenced by Hellenic and Hellenistic art forms, gave their work entirely original local characteristics (R. Bloch, *The Etruscans* [London, 1958], p. 164; *idem, The Origins of Rome* [London, 1960], pp. 107–108). D. S. Robertson, *A Handbook of Greek and Roman Architecture*, 2d ed. (Cambridge, 1959), p. 205, suggests that the later Greek styles penetrated central Italy in two waves: the first from South Italy and Sicily in the third century B.C., the second, from Greece, Asia Minor, Syria, and Egypt in the second and first centuries B.C.
2. Robertson (note 1), p. 194; Bloch, *Etruscans* (note 1), pp. 165–166. The Temple of the Capitoline Triad was such a shrine, Scullard (note 1), p. 252. Etruscan temples usually had triple cellas, although later Republican temples as, for example, the Temple of Hercules at Cori (Robertson, p. 209), often did not.

3. James Walter Graham, *Domestic Architecture in Classical Greece* (Baltimore, 1938), pp. 157ff., finds that open courts are common on many fourth-century B.C. sites in Greece, Olynthus in particular. On the House of the Surgeon, see A. Mau, *Pompeii, Its Life and Art*, tr. by F. W. Kelsey (New York, 1899), pp. 274–276.

4. F. E. Brown, *Roman Architecture* (New York, 1961), pp. 12–13, 22.

5. W. MacDonald, *The Architecture of the Roman Empire* (New Haven and London, 1965), I, pp. 3–4.

6. L. Crema, *L'architettura romana* (Turin, 1959), p. 15.

7. This chronological development applies only to Rome and Latium. Other sequences occur in Italy outside of Latium and in the provinces. For the names of the various wall facings, I am using the terminology of G. Lugli, *Tecnica edilizia romana* (Rome, 1957), I, pp. 48–49.

8. M. E. Blake, *Roman Construction in Italy from Tiberius through the Flavians* (Washington, 1959), pp. 10ff., 88ff.; MacDonald, (note 5) p. 19.

9. MacDonald, pp. 5–6; Brown (note 4), p. 83, pls. 30, 31 and E. Nash, *A Pictorial Dictionary of Ancient Rome* (London, 1962), II, pp. 238–240.

10. The most complete publication of the structure and its dependencies is by F. Fasolo and G. Gullini, *Il santuario della Fortuna Primigenia a Palestrina* (Rome, 1953).

11. MacDonald, pp. 10–12, points out that Augustus' regime encouraged trabeated Hellenistic architecture, and it was not until the reign of Nero that the vaulted style was officially patronized.

12. Cicero *De Divinatione* i. 87. A brief reference to this famous phrase occurs in Fasolo-Gullini, p. 4.

13. G. Giovannoni, *La tecnica della costruzione presso i romani* (Rome, n.d.), p. 12, n. 1. See also C. Daremberg and E. Saglio, "Architectus," *Dictionnaire des antiquités grecques et romaines* (Paris, 1873), I, pp. 374–382; MacDonald, p. 123; C. Promis, *Gli architetti e l'architettura presso i romani* (Turin, 1873).

14. Vitruvius *De Architectura* I. i. 3 and 11. Here and in the passages quoted from Vitruvius below I am using the translation of F. Granger, Loeb Classical Library (Harvard University Press, Cambridge, Mass., 1962).

15. M. S. Briggs, *The Architect in History* (Oxford, 1927), p. 32.

16. Vitruvius *De Architectura* vi. 6 (Preface).

17. Tacitus *Annales* xv. 42, mentions Severus and Celer. On the latter, see also MacDonald, p. 126, n. 12. Decrianus is called *architectus* in *Scriptores Historiae Augustae*, Hadrian xix. 12. The entire anecdote is translated by MacDonald, p. 130.

18. Dio Cassius lxiv. 4. On Apollodorus in general, see also R. Bianchi-Bandinelli, "Apollodoros di Damasco," *Enciclopedia dell'arte antica* (Rome, 1958), I, pp. 477–480; Briggs (note 15) p. 37; E. DeRuggiero, *Lo stato e le opere pubbliche in Roma antica* (Rome, 1925), p. 255; MacDonald, pp. 129–137.

19. Dio Cassius lxix. 3–5. The translation is that of E. Cary, *Dio's Roman History*, Loeb Classical Library (Harvard University Press, Cambridge, Mass., 1961), viii, pp. 431–433.

20. Dio Cassius lxix. 5; Vitruvius *De Architectura* i. 4; iiff.

21. R. Calza and M. F. Squarciapino, *Museo Ostiense* (Rome, 1962), p. 18, describe the base for a marble temple model (a votive offering?). Photographs of terra cotta models of *nymphaea* are given by N. Neuerburg in his *L'architettura delle fontane e dei ninfei nell' Italia antica* (Naples, 1965), pls. 3–10.

22. J. P. Waltzing, *Étude historique sur les corporations professionnelles chez les romains* (Louvain, 1895–1900), IV, pp. lff., lists these guilds. For the effects of the guilds on Roman architecture, see MacDonald, pp. 144–161.

23. On early imperial methods of building, see M. Choisy, *Le art de bâtir chez les romaines* (Paris, 1873). Dated in many ways, this work is still useful for its drawings. See also: Giovannoni (note 13), pp. 22ff.; *idem*, "Building and Engineering," *The Legacy of Ancient Rome*, C. Bailey, ed. (Oxford, 1951), pp. 429–474; Lugli (note 7), I, pp. 426–442 (the characteristics of early Imperial concrete); MacDonald (note 5), pp. 154–166; J. Packer, "Structure and Design in Ancient Ostia," *Technology and Culture*, Vol. 9 (1968), pp. 358–364.

24. As was the case in the Casa di Giove

e Ganimede at Ostia (I, iv, 2). The mezzanine floors of the south shops were supported by projecting moldings, while those of the inner rooms were sustained by travertine brackets. This peculiarity is described by J. Packer, "The Insulae of Imperial Ostia" (Ph.D. dissertation, University of California at Berkeley, 1964), pp. 369–371 and *passim*, pls. 7, 9, and is treated by G. Calza in "La preminenza dell' 'insula' nella edilizia romana," *Monumenti Antichi*, Vol. 23 (1915), pp. 595–597. In his "Gli scavi recenti nell' abitato di Ostia," *Monumenti Antichi*, Vol. 26 (1920), pp. 354ff., Calza gives a complete discussion of the Casa di Giove e Ganimede.

25. H. D. Mirick, "The Large Baths of Hadrian's Villa," *Memoirs of the American Academy in Rome*, Vol. ii (1933), pl. 8, shows a restored section of a roof of this nature. Such roofs were common in the baths and in such late vaulted structures as the Basilica of Constantine in Rome. Robertson (note 1), p. 267, Fig. 111, gives a restored section of the latter building.

26. DeRuggiero (note 18), pp. 78ff. lists in detail the edifices erected by successive emperors.

27. E. Baldwin Smith, *Architectural Symbolism of Imperial Rome and the Middle Ages* (Princeton, 1956), pp. 4–5.

28. E. G. Hardy, *Monumentum Ancyranum* (Oxford, 1923), pp. 91–101.

29. Tacitus *Annales* xv. 42; Suetonius *Nero* xxxi. 3.

30. Dio Cassius lxii. 16; Suetonius *Nero* xix.

31. Tacitus *Annales* xv. 38–41. My translations of Tacitus here and later, p. 45, are those of J. Jackson (Harvard and London: Loeb Classical Library, 1951); Suetonius *Nero* xxxviii.

32. J. Packer, "Housing and Population in Imperial Ostia and Rome," *Journal of Roman Studies*, Vol. 57 (1967), p. 81.

33. Suetonius *Nero* xxi; Tacitus *Annales* xv. 42.

34. MacDonald, p. 43; A. Boëthius, *The Golden House of Nero* (Ann Arbor, 1960), pp. 94–128, especially p. 105.

35. Suetonius *Vespasian* ix. The Colosseum was dedicated by Titus in A.D. 80 (*idem, Titus* vii. 3).

36. For photographs of these substructures see Nash (note 9), II, p. 473. They are described by G. Lugli, *I monumenti antichi di Roma e suburbio* (Rome, 1930–1938), I, pp. 217–221 and in R. Paribeni, *Optimus Princeps* (Messania, 1927), pp. 42–52.

37. For a complete list of other Trajanic projects in Rome, see R. Paribeni (note 36), II, pp. 23–64. The architecture of the Markets has been analyzed in detail by MacDonald, pp. 75–93. On the Emperor's harbor works, see Paribeni (note 36), pp. 109–113; G. Lugli and G. Filibeck, *Il porto di Roma imperiale e l'agro portuense* (Rome, 1935), pp. 31ff. and R. Meiggs *Roman Ostia* (Oxford, 1960), pp. 58–62.

38. For bibliographies and photographs of the Pantheon, see MacDonald, pp. 94–121 and Nash (note 9), II, pp. 170–175. B. d'Orgeval, *L'empereur Hadrien* (Paris, 1950), pp. 269–276, lists Hadrian's other public works.

39. Lugli (note 7), I, p. 440, describes the building materials used in Rome between A.D. 193 and 337. He points out (p. 615) that even when Aurelian and Probus partially resuscitated the brick industry in the late third century after Christ in order to supply bricks for the new city walls of Rome, old materials were still abundantly used. For a complete description of these late walls, see I. A. Richmond, *The City Wall of Imperial Rome* (Oxford, 1930).

40. G. Calza *et al.*, *Scavi di Ostia* (Rome, 1953–   ), I, pp. 233–288; hereafter cited as *SO*.

41. The remains of one such mansion have been exposed beneath the Scuola di Traiano (IV, v, 16). For a brief discussion of the building, see *SO*, I, p. 109; IV, p. 202. Another early imperial residence, the Domus di Apuleio (II, 5) is discussed by Meiggs (note 37), pp. 255–256, who suggests that it was probably never more than a modest dwelling. More pretentious was the Domus della Fortuna Annonaria (V, ii, 10) which remained in use until the late Empire when it was extensively remodeled. The best complete description of the latter structure is by G. Becatti, *Case ostiensi del tardo impero* (Rome, n.d.), pp. 23–25.

42. On the Insula del Graffito (III, ix, 21), see *SO*, IV, p. 123; on the Domus dei Dioscuri (III, ix, 1), see pp. 114–123 (a

brief description of the building and its mosaics) and Becatti (note 41), pp. 14–15.

43. The mosaics of the house are described in *SO*, IV, pp. 128–133. Brief descriptions occur in Calza, "Contributi alla storia della edilizia imperiale romana," *Palladio*, Vol. 5 (1941), pp. 6–8 and R. Calza and E. Nash, *Ostia* (Florence, 1959), pp. 117–123. Meiggs (note 37), p. 244, suggests that the owner of the house was wealthy. The paintings are classified by M. Borda, *La pittura romana* (Milan, 1958), p. 101, as a version of the Pompeian Fourth Style.

44. This plan is discussed by G. Calza (note 24), pp. 595–597. See also Meiggs (note 37), pp. 247–249 and Packer (note 24), I, pp. 118ff.

45. Packer (note 32), pp. 85–86. See also note 42.

46. This building is briefly treated by G. Girri, *La taberna nel quadro urbanistico e sociale di Ostia* (Rome, 1956), p. 27.

47. For the arrangements made to light Ostian buildings, see Calza (note 24), pp. 585–586; *idem*, "Le origini latine dell' abitazione moderna," *Architettura e arti decorative*, Vol. 3 (1923–1924), p. 13; Packer (note 24), I, pp. 49–59.

48. Pp. 43–44; Vitruvius ii. 9. 6; iv. 2. 1; MacDonald, p. 169, n. 4.

49. In his earlier excavations, Calza (note 24), pp. 578, 590, found few roof tiles and concluded, therefore, that most Ostian houses possessed flat terrace roofs, which could be used as sun decks (*solaria*). His later work, however, produced substantial evidence for tiled, pitched roofs. For these forms, see Meiggs (note 37), p. 241. An unused cache of tiles, stacked for storage, is shown in *SO*, I, pl. XIV, 4. Diagrams of timber and tile roofs, such as undoubtedly appeared in many Ostian buildings, are given in V. Spinazzola, *Pompei alla luce degli scavi nuovi* (Rome, 1953), I, pp. 35ff. and in A. Maiuri, *Ercolano, i nuovi scavi* (Rome, 1958), II, pl. 38.

50. A photograph of the structure—with its peeling plaster—is given by J. Packer, "Structure and Design in Ancient Ostia," *Technology and Culture*, Vol. 9 (1968), pl. 17.

51. According to Meiggs (note 37), p. 254, the travertine columns in the peristyle of the Domus della Fortuna Annonaria (note 41) were so finished. But, as in the case of the capitals of the engaged columns flanking the Porta Praenestina in Rome, many travertine capitals were probably never stuccoed. On the Porta Praenestina, see Blake (note 8), pp. 27–28 and Nash (note 9), II, pp. 225–228.

52. The most recent descriptions of the Villa are by H. Kähler, *Hadrian und seine Villa bei Tivoli* (Berlin, 1950) and S. Aurigemma, *Villa Adriana* (Rome, 1961). My account of the Villa is based upon these works and upon personal observation. All buildings mentioned in the following description appear on the general plan of the estate in Figure 4. The numbers of the structures cited in the text are shown on that plan.

53. Boëthius, (note 34), p. 165 and P. Grimal, *Les jardins romaines* (Paris, 1943), p. 468.

54. Aurigemma (note 52), pp. 24–25. H. Bloch, *I bolli laterizi* (Rome, 1938), pp. 182–183, has established these dates by careful examination of the brick stamps found in the ruins of the Villa.

55. The main baths have been described and conjecturally restored by Mirick (note 25), pp. 119–126. In the same issue of the *Memoirs*, W. L. Reichardt treats the adjacent complex of ceremonial buildings: "The Vestibule Group of Hadrian's Villa," pp. 127–132. The recent excavations and restorations of the Canopus have been published by S. Aurigemma, "Lavori nel Canopo di Villa Adriana, I," *Bollettino d'Arte*, Vol. 39 (1954), pp. 327–341; "II," Vol. 40 (1955), pp. 64–78; "III," Vol. 41 (1956), pp. 57–71.

56. On the Piazza d'Oro, see Aurigemma (note 52), pp. 154ff. and E. Hansen, "La Piazza d'Oro e la sua cupola," *Analecta romana Instituti Danici*, I, *Supplementum* (Copenhagen, 1960).

57. G. T. Rivora, "Di Adriano architetto e dei monumenti adrianei," *Rendiconti della Reale Accademia dei Lincei*, Series 5, Vol. 18 (1909), p. 174, suggests that the most brilliant architectural schemes of the Villa are due to Hadrian's direct influence. Rivora develops similar ideas in his *Roman Architecture*, tr. by G. McN. Rushforth (Oxford, 1925), pp. 118ff, where he characterizes Hadrian as the defender of native Roman architectural practices against such foreign interlopers as Apollodorus (p. 131).

58. A. Frova, *L'arte di Roma e del mondo romano* (Turin, 1961), p. 88; Crema (note 6), p. 466.

59. Sir Mortimer Wheeler, *Roman Art and Architecture* (London, 1964), p. 10.

60. Grimal (note 53), p. 472.

61. Boëthius (note 34), p. 106; Neuerburg (note 21), pp. 82–83, 91.

62. M. Cheilik, *Opus Albarium: A Chronology of Roman Stucco Decoration in Italy* (forthcoming in the *Memoirs of the American Academy in Rome*). I am deeply grateful to Professor Cheilik for allowing me to consult his manuscript prior to its publication.

63. In *SO*, IV, p. 248, Becatti stresses the fact that the business classes of Ostia, while well-to-do, did not demand fine examples of the mosaicist's art and were content to display the products of local workshops in their homes.

64. As for example the interesting series of late residences published by Becatti (note 41). For a complete description of one of the best preserved among these late mansions, see J. Packer, "The *Domus* of Cupid and Psyche in Ancient Ostia," *American Journal of Archaeology*, Vol. 71 (1967), pp. 123–131.

65. The absence of stucco in Ostian buildings may be due to accidents of preservation, however. Stucco fragments are to be seen in the Terme del Faro (IV. ii. 1), the Casa di Diana (I. iii. 3, 4), and the Horrea Epagathiana (I. viii. 3). On the Terme, see R. Calza and E. Nash (note 43), pp. 77–78; on the Casa di Diana, G. Calza, "La casa detta di Diana," *Notizie degli Scavi*, 5th series, Vol. 14 (1917), pp. 324ff.; on the Horrea Epagathiana, Calza (note 43), pp. 19–20.

Chapter 3: Bronze Working

1. *Corinthian bronze*. The term must have more than one meaning. For detailed analysis of the literature, see Humfry Payne, *Necrocorinthia* (Oxford, 1931), pp. 348ff.; for scientific study with explanation of certain uses of the term, see Earle R. Caley, "The Corroded Bronze of Corinth," *Proceedings of the American Philosophical Society*, Vol. 84 (1941), pp. 689–761.

2. For the older literature on alloying and casting technique, see my *Catalogue of Classical Bronze Sculpture in the Walters Art Gallery* (1949), introduction, with notes. See also: A. Steinberg, *Master Bronzes of the Classical World*, exhibition catalogue, Fogg Art Museum and others (Mainz, 1967), pp. 9–15; D. Haynes, *Mitteilungen des Deutschen Archäologischen Instituts (Röm. Abt.)*, Vol. 67 (1960), pp. 45–47; R. J. Forbes, *A History of Technology* (Oxford, 1956), II, pp. 41ff.; D. Haynes, *Archäologische Anzeiger* (1962), cols. 803–807 (piecing in wax casting); B. S. Ridgway, "The Bronze Apollo from Piombino in the Louvre," *Antike Plastik*, Vol. 7 (Berlin, 1967), pp. 68–70; *idem*, "A Lady from the Sea," *American Journal of Archaeology*, Vol. 71 (1967), pp. 329–334; E. R. Caley, *Analysis of Ancient Metals* (New York, 1964), pp. 81ff., with bibliography and tables; "Orichalcum and Related Ancient Alloys," *Numismatic Notes and Monographs*, Vol. 151 (1964); "Composition of Ancient Greek Bronze Coins," *Memoirs of the American Philosophical Society*, Vol. 11 (1939). For an attempt to estimate the price of the bronze in a statue, A. De Ridder, *Rev. Arch.*, 5th series, Vol. 2 (1915), pt. 2, pp. 97–113. For evidence of the casting of the Alkamenes group in Athens, see D. B. Thompson, "The Garden of Hephaistos," *Hesperia*, Vol. 6 (1937), p. 399, Fig. 2 (at B) and W. B. Dinsmoor, "Observations on the Hephaisteion," *Hesperia*, Sup. 5 (1941), pp. 109f. On these and other casting pits and fragments of molds from the Athenian Agora see H. A. Thompson, *American Journal of Archaeology*, Vol. 42 (1938), p. 123; for photographs and drawings of material from the Athenian Agora, with some discussion: *Hesperia*, Vol. 6 (1937), pp. 342ff., Figs. 7–8 and pp. 82f., Fig. 43 and *Agora Guide*, 2d ed. (1962), pp. 60, 155–157, Fig. 28; also *Hesperia*, Vol. 26 (1957), p. 100, pl. 28; *Hesperia*, Vol. 17 (1948), pp. 170–172, Fig. 7, pl. 48, 1 and Vol. 20 (1951), p. 269, p. 136, Fig. 1 (in House O). Dates of all these: 6th, 5th, 4th, 2nd centuries B.C. A huge casting pit south of the Acropolis, discovered in the 1870's, was recognized and re-excavated in the 1960's; *American Journal of Archaeology*, Vol. 69 (1965), p. 353.

3. On equestrian monuments as token of royalty or the equivalent, see H. v. Roques de Maumont, *Antike Reiterstandbilder*

(Berlin, 1958) and a forthcoming article by Ruth I. Hicks. On equestrian and other large bronze statues in late antiquity, my article "ERZ" in T. Klauser, *Reallexikon für Antike und Christentum* (Stuttgart, 1966), VI, cols. 457ff.

4. T. L. Shear, "The Sculpture," *Hesperia*, Vol. 2 (1933), pp. 519–527; D. B. Thompson, "The Golden Nikai Reconsidered," *Hesperia*, Vol. 13 (1944), pp. 173–209; H. A. Thompson, "A Golden Nike from the Athenian Agora," *Athenian Studies*, *Harvard Studies in Classical Philology*, *Supplement* (Cambridge, 1940), I, pp. 183–210; M. Farnsworth and I. Simmons, "A Unique Cement from Athens," *Hesperia*, Vol. 29 (1960), pp. 118–122.

5. On the use and mounting of statuettes, see my *Catalogue* (note 2), pp. xxiii–iv, with notes 70–73; H. G. Niemeyer, *Promachos* (Waldsassen, 1960) (early dedications in Athens); Ch. Karusos, *Charites*, ed. K. Schauenburg (Bonn, 1957), pp. 33–37 (archaic Laconian); *Studi Etruschi* Vol. 14 (1940), pl. IX (Etruscan male figure, mounting hooks exactly like our Fig. 4); K. A. Neugebauer, Staatliche Mus. zu Berlin, *Katalog der statuarischen Bronzen* (Berlin, 1951), II, p. 15, considers the mounting of the spinner, 5th century B.C., by lead in a truncated cone of bronze, to be a remounting, perhaps modern, utilizing a vase fragment: see his pls. 9–10. Yet the mounting is startlingly like that of the statuette from the sieve cover of the Vix krater, in which case the final attachment to the cover was by solder; see *Monuments Piot*, Vol. 48, Fasc. 1 (1954) pp. 19f., pl. XVI; the statuette without the conical base, pls. XVII–XVIII.

6. K. A. Neugebauer, *Antike Bronzestatuetten* (Berlin, 1921), pp. 42f.

7. D. Mustilli, "Botteghe di scultori, marmorarii, bronzieri e caelatores in Pompei," *Pompeiana, Biblioteca della parola del passato*, 4 (Napoli, 1950), pp. 206–229. Wages paid to bronzeworkers are not known before the Edict of Diocletian, for which see T. Frank, *An Economic Survey of Ancient Rome* (Baltimore, 1940), V, pp. 341f.

Chapter 4: Stone Carving: Sculpture

1. The most recent discussion of this problem is by R. M. Cook, "Origins of Greek Sculpture," *The Journal of Hellenic Studies*, Vol. 87 (1967), pp. 24–32, who advocates a purely internal and local development. A more extensive treatment of the same point of view, though with less emphasis on the relationship with Egypt, is to be found in E. Homann-Wedeking, *Die Anfänge der griechischen Grossplastik* (Berlin, 1950). For an opposite position see R. Carpenter, *Greek Sculpture* (Chicago, 1960), pp. 5–17.

2. To Cook's bibliography on this point should be added R. Anthes' paper, "Affinity and Difference between Egyptian and Greek Sculpture and Thought in the Seventh and Sixth Centuries B.C.," *Proceedings of the American Philosophical Society*, Vol. 107 (1963), pp. 60–81, and B. S. Ridgway, "Greek Kouroi and Egyptian Methods," *American Journal of Archaeology*, Vol. 70 (1966), pp. 68–70, with further references. *See also* F. Schachermeyr, *Die frühe Klassik der Griechen* (Stuttgart, 1966), pp. 184–186 and E. Iversen, "Diodorus' Account of the Egyptian Canon," *Journal of Egyptian Archaeology*, Vol. 54 (1968), pp. 215–218.

3. See Homann-Wedeking (note 1), pp. 54–56, for the base and the inscription. More recent bibliography is mentioned in an article attributing a *kouros* to the Euthykartides' base: G. Bakalakis, "Notes cycladiques," *Bulletin de Correspondance Hellénique*, Vol. 88 (1964), pp. 539–553.

4. There are several good books on the technique of ancient stone carving; the most recent is by Sheila Adam, *The Technique of Greek Sculpture in the Archaic and Classical Periods*, British School of Archaeology at Athens, Supplementary Volume No. 3 (London, 1966). Of fundamental importance are also C. Blümel, *Griechische Bildhauer an der Arbeit*, tr. by L. Holland as *Greek Sculptors at Work* (London, 1955), and S. Casson, *The Technique of Early Greek Sculpture* (Oxford, 1933). Some interesting technical comments can also be found in Carpenter (note 1), *passim* and especially chap. 2; and G. M. A. Richter, *Ancient Italy* (Ann Arbor, 1955), especially chap. 3 and Appendixes 1 and 2. By the same author see also *The Sculpture and Sculptors of the Greeks* (New Haven, 1950), pt. I, sec. 9. Important information,

though primarily focused on architecture, can be found in A. K. Orlandos, *Ta Ylika Domis ton Archaion Hellinon* (Athens, 1955-1960), and in R. Martin, *Manuel d'Architecture Grecque* (Paris, 1965), I. Some interesting technical details are illustrated in H. J. Etienne, *The Chisel in Greek Sculpture* (Leiden, 1968), but the text should be read with caution. See also pp. 13-18.

5. See Adam (note 4), pp. 42-44 and Fig. 5; Martin (note 4), pp. 147-148 and n. 8, where he comments on the similarity between Greek practices and Egyptian methods in granite quarries.

6. This important point is made by Adam (note 4), pp. 7-8, who sees in it further evidence for the existence of a common canon.

7. Adam (note 4), p. 8. For an unfinished statue of Roman date see J. Wiseman, "An Unfinished Colossus on Mt. Pendeli," *American Journal of Archaeology*, Vol. 72 (1968), pp. 75-76.

8. See especially Carpenter (note 1), pp. 37-40. For the fluting of columns see W. B. Dinsmoor, *The Architecture of Ancient Greece* (London, 1950), pp. 175-176 and Fig. 65. See also p. 29, Fig. 13.

9. See Adam (note 4), pp. 8-10, who attributes the paucity of preserved tools to "corrosion and lack of interest on the part of the excavators."

10. On the date of the invention, see Adam (note 4), p. 19. On the diffusion abroad, see C. Nylander, "The Toothed Chisel in Pasargadae: Further Notes on Old Persian Stonecutting," *American Journal of Archaeology*, Vol. 70 (1966), pp. 373-376, especially n. 27 with previous bibliography.

11. Cf. Adam (note 4), p. 66, with references.

12. The resulting opaque effect is comparable to that apparent on a block of ice, when it has been hit by a heavy object without actual chipping or breaking of the surface. A comparable technique is that of burin "tapping" on a special kind of Italian dark marble called Bardiglio, where the image is created in light color by graduated taps of the instrument onto the surface, which, however, remains entirely smooth.

13. Adam (note 4), p. 39. For an expression of the opposite point of view see, e.g.,

R. Lullies and M. Hirmer, *Greek Sculpture*, 2d ed. (New York, 1960), p. 49; also Blümel (note 4), p. 26.

14. Adam (note 4), p. 39.

15. For Archaic examples of inserted heads see, e.g., C. Blümel, *Archaisch griechischen Skulpturen* (Berlin, 1963), no. 50, Figs. 139-140; no. 54, Figs. 148-151. On attachments in general see Adam (note 4), pp. 80-82; on metal additions to marble statues cf. also B. S. Ridgway, "Stone and Metal in Greek Sculpture," *Archaeology*, Vol. 19 (1966), pp. 31-42.

16. On the general subject of painting on ancient sculpture see P. Reuterswärd, *Studien zur Polychromie der Plastik: Griechenland und Rom* (Stockholm, 1960). The Archaic palette was mostly limited to four basic colors: red, blue-green, black, and brown, but a few shades were also possible. Red was at times used as sizing for gold, and yellow was certainly known. In late classical and early Hellenistic times a tendency began toward light and airy polychromy, and a more varied palette was also used: witness the Alexander sarcophagus in Istanbul with its violet, purple, and pink tones.

17. On *ganosis* see Reuterswärd (note 16), pp. 71-74, who would date the inception of the practice ca. 500 B.C. Richter, *Sculpture and Sculptors* (note 4), pp. 153-156, stresses that literary sources refer to this technique more for its preserving qualities than for aesthetic merits.

18. Akroliths (statues with appendages of stone on a body of different, cheaper material, usually wood covered with cloth) have not yet been extensively studied. For an account of research in progress see C. W. Carpenter, "Akrolithic Sculpture," *American Journal of Archaeology*, Vol. 72 (1968), pp. 162-163.

19. As pointed out by A. J. B. Wace, *An Approach to Greek Sculpture* (Cambridge, 1935), pp. 14-15.

20. For a more recent discussion, superbly illustrated, see B. Ashmole and N. Yalouris, *Olympia, The Sculptures of the Temple of Zeus* (London, 1967).

21. See, e.g., East Pediment L (Ashmole & Yalouris [note 20], Figs. 58-61); West Pediment Q (Fig. 90); and perhaps a few others. Some of this evidence has already been pointed out by Blümel (note 4), pp. 51-53, and Wace (note 19),

p. 36; cf. also Ashmole and Yalouris (note 20), p. 20. But the inferences drawn from the evidence do not seem to have found wide acceptance among other scholars. The problem is increased by the fact that no traces of such "points" would be preserved on a thoroughly finished piece of sculpture; only on pedimental statuary, not to be observed at close quarters, are such traces likely to survive. That the practice of taking measurements from a plumb line may have survived also in Roman times is perhaps attested by traces of lead fastening for a plumb point on the base of the Lansdowne Herakles, in the J. Paul Getty Museum, Malibu, California. See S. Howard, *The Lansdowne Herakles*, J. Paul Getty Museum Publication No. 1, 1966, p. 8, Fig. 10 and p. 16, Fig. 22 (the dark round spot near the left foot), p. 9, Fig. 13 (on the base, within the cavity of the lion skin).

22. RISD Inv. No. 55.027; listed as MS 7 in a forthcoming catalogue of the ancient collection in that museum (classical marbles discussed by B. S. Ridgway). I am indebted to the museum authorities for kind permission to anticipate here some of the conclusions which shall appear in my section of the catalogue.

23. On the pointing technique and its modern application see most recently G. M. A. Richter, *The Portraits of the Greeks* (London, 1965) I, pp. 24–27, Figs. V–VII and no. 26 at p. 115, Fig. 527; by the same author see also "An Unfinished Portrait of Sokrates," *Studi in onore di Luisa Banti*, ed. R. Bianchi Bandinelli (Rome, 1965), pp. 389–391. For an example of a classical head copied in antiquity see E. Harrison, "New Sculpture from the Athenian Agora, 1959," *Hesperia*, Vol. 29 (1960), pp. 369–370, pl. 81 a-b. On the question whether statues could be duplicated fairly closely even in classical times see F. Brommer, "Vorhellenistische Kopien und Wiederholungen von Statuen," *Studies presented to David M. Robinson*, ed. G. Mylonas (St. Louis, 1951), I, pp. 674–682, and his bibliography.

24. See J. J. Pollitt, *The Art of Greece 1400–31 B.C., Sources & Documents in the History of Art Series* (New York, 1965), p. 151 and ns. 80 and 82. See also Carpenter (note 1), pp. 232–236.

25. Richter, *Ancient Italy* (note 4), pp. 112–116 and especially p. 113, n. 1.

26. See, e.g., Richter, *Ancient Italy* (note 4), p. 38, for several examples in the Metropolitan Museum in New York. The whole question of exact versus approximate copying, of adaptations and elaborations of famous monuments in the first century B.C., and of the so-called classicizing current, has not yet been treated extensively and remains highly controversial.

27. See Plutarch, *Perikles*, chap. 2; Lucian, *Somnium* 6–9, and comments by Pollitt (note 24), p. 226.

28. Cf. M. Bieber, *The Sculpture of the Hellenistic Age*, 2d ed. (New York, 1961), p. 31. An idea of the distribution of work in the building of an important temple can be obtained through the lucid account by A. Burford, "The Builders of the Parthenon," *Parthenos and Parthenon*, Supplement to Vol. 10 of *Greece and Rome* (1963), pp. 23–34, which includes comments on the sculptors.

29. See pp. 32–34.

Chapter 5: Pottery Manufacture

1. Gisela M. A. Richter and Marjorie J. Milne, *Shapes and Names of Athenian Vases* (New York, 1935).

2. Joseph Veach Noble, *The Techniques of Painted Attic Pottery* (New York, 1965). The subjects treated in this chapter on pottery manufacture are presented in an expanded form in this book.

3. Herbert Hoffmann, "Two Deer Heads from Apulia," *American Journal of Archaeology*, Vol. 64 (1960), pp. 276–278, pls. 77–78.

4. Martin Robertson, *Greek Painting* (Geneva, 1959). Paolo Enrico Arias, *A History of 1000 Years of Greek Vase Painting* (New York, 1961). Both of these books illustrate the development of vase decoration.

5. Marie Farnsworth, "Draw Pieces as Aids to Correct Firing," *American Journal of Archaeology*, Vol. 64 (1960), pp. 72–75, pl. 16. R. M. Cook, "The 'Double Stoking Tunnel' of Greek Kilns," *The Annual of the British School of Archaeology at Athens*, Vol. 56 (1961), pp. 64–67, pl. 7, gives a list of more than fifty ancient Greek kilns. Other kilns, including recent finds in

Russia, are given by Juliusz Ziomecki, "Die keramischen Techniken im antiken Griechenland," *Raggi: Zeitschrift für Kuntsgeschichte und Archäologie*, Heft 1/2, 1964, pp. 27ff., 93.

6. J. D. Beazley, "Potter and Painter in Ancient Athens," *Proceedings of the British Academy*, Vol. 30 (1946), pp. 87–125.

7. See pp. 206–211.

Chapter 6: Farming

1. All translations and paraphrases from the ancient sources were prepared especially for the present study.

2. For lists of earlier writers see Varro *De Re Rustica* (*RR* 1. 1. 7–11), who names fifty; Columella *De Re Rustica* (*RR* 1. 1. 7–14), who adds later authorities; and Pliny's *Natural History*, both at *HN* 18. 22–23 and in his general list of sources for *Book* 18. See also M. Rostovtzeff, *The Social and Economic History of the Roman Empire* (cited as "Rostovtzeff, *Empire*"), 2d ed. rev. by P. M. Fraser (Oxford, 1957), I, pp. 314–315; and Rostovtzeff, *The Social and Economic History of the Hellenistic World* (cited as "Rostovtzeff, *Hellenistic World*"), (Oxford, 1941), II, pp. 1194–1195.

3. Pliny *HN* 18. 22–23. The Greek translation by Cassius Dionysius (Varro *RR* 1. 1. 10; Columella *RR* 1. 1. 10) naturally made Mago's materials accessible to the Greek world in turn.

4. Cf. R. M. Haywood, "Roman Africa," *An Economic Survey of Ancient Rome*, Tenney Frank, ed. (Baltimore, 1933–1940), IV, p. 5.

5. Observe Varro's humor in this miscellaneous category. As he would explain (*RR* 2. 8), mules, being sterile hybrids from asses and horses, cannot be raised from their own kind. He would, of course, expect dogs and herdsmen to breed.

6. *Agr.* 7. 2. 2–4. See K. D. White, *Agricultural Implements of the Roman World* (Cambridge, 1967), pp. 157–173 with plates, and see pp. 165–167.

7. E.g., Vegetius *Mulomed*, 1. 56. 5 (on the height of hayracks for horses) and Servius on *Geo.* 1. 164 (on the *traha* as a drag without wheels).

8. The ancient authors cited in this paper can generally be found in English trans-

lation (except for Palladius and the *Geoponica*) in the *Loeb Classical Library*, published by the Harvard University Press. Much additional information can be gleaned from the following modern studies and accounts devoted to agricultural topics or containing major sections devoted to them: G. E. F. Chilver, *Cisalpine Gaul* (Oxford, 1941); Tenney Frank, "Rome and Italy of the Empire," *An Economic Survey of Ancient Rome*, Tenney Frank, ed. (Baltimore, 1933–1940), V; Haywood (note 4); W. E. Heitland, *Agricola* (Cambridge, 1921); Naum Jasny, *The Wheats of Classical Antiquity* (Baltimore, 1944); E. M. Jope, "Agricultural Implements," *A History of Technology*, Charles Singer, ed. (Oxford, 1954–1958), II; H. Michell, *The Economics of Ancient Greece*, 2d ed. (Cambridge, 1957); C. Parain, "The Evolution of Agricultural Technique," and C. E. Stevens, "Agriculture and Rural Life in the Later Roman Empire," *The Cambridge Economic History of Europe*, 2d ed., Vol. I, M. M. Postan, ed. (Cambridge, 1966); Rostovtzeff, *Empire*; Rostovtzeff, *Hellenistic World*; Ellen C. Semple, *The Geography of the Mediterranean Region* (New York, 1931); J. Toutain, *The Economic Life of the Ancient World*, tr. by M. R. Dobie (London, 1930); and White (note 6). But see also notes 33 and 34.

9. The following statements are based upon the Latin version by Terence, which seems to have been relatively true to its Greek original. See T. B. L. Webster, *Studies in Menander* (Manchester, 1960), p. 83.

10. Dionysius of Halicarnassus (*Ant. Rom.* 10. 8) says he lived a life of toil, working his farm with the help of a few slaves. Livy portrays him working with his own hands as later generations came to picture their hardy forebears. See Heitland (note 8), pp. 135–138, but also R. M. Ogilvie, *A Commentary on Livy, Books 1–5* (Oxford, 1965), p. 441.

11. Cf. H. Jordan, *M. Catonis Praeter Librum De Re Rustica Quae Extant* (Leipzig, 1860), p. 43.

12. *Epist.* 1. 14, from which the complaints below have been paraphrased. Cf. Seneca's recognition of the realities of a transfer from town to country (*De Ira*

3. 29. 1–2) and Columella's warning about such an action (*RR* 1. 8. 1–2).

13. *RR* 1. 17. 3. Cf. R. S. Cotterill, *The Old South* (Glendale, Calif., Arthur H. Clark Co., 1939), p. 263, on the antebellum Southern demand for day laborers in dangerous tasks "in which the farmer or planter did not wish to risk the life of a slave. If an Irishman died it merely increased the Kingdom of Heaven; if a slave were killed there was $1,500 gone."

14. Note that *opera* (Columella *RR* 2. 4. 8–11, but also Varro *RR* 1. 18. 6) can denote either a "man-day" or a "workman" in various contexts (cf. Cato *Agr.* 2.2). With Columella *RR* 2. 12. 8–9, cf. K. D. White, "The Productivity of Labor in Roman Agriculture," *Antiquity*, 39 (1965), pp. 102–103, 106–107.

15. E.g., Cato (*Agr.* 39) and Vergil (*G.* 1. 259–267).

16. For legal limitations see also Varro (*RR* 1. 2. 9).

17. Details here are translated or paraphrased from Petronius *Satyricon* 37. 8; 53. 2; and 48. 2–3.

18. Cf. Rostovtzeff, *Empire*, Vol. I, p. 99.

19. *Epist.* 1. 14. 1. See Heitland (note 8), pp. 215–216, and Rostovtzeff, *Empire*, I, pp. 59–61.

20. See Frank (note 8) pp. 172–173; and Rostovtzeff, *Empire*, I, pp. 61–64 (with plans and plates), and II, pp. 551–553, n. 26 (a list of thirty-six villas).

21. Cf. Frank (note 8), pp. 173–175. The inscriptions are *CIL*, XI. 1147 and IX. 1455.

22. *S. H. A. Aurel.* 10.2 Cf. also Rostovtzeff, *Empire*, II, pp. 629–630, nn. 22–23 for evidence about large estates in Sicily and Sardinia.

23. Varro (*RR* 1. 7. 1; 1. 16. 1–6), Pliny (*HN* 17. 36; 18. 26–31). Pliny offers the apparently proverbial suggestion that persons buying land should observe "water, road, and neighbor."

24. Cato (*Agr.* 4), Pliny (*HN* 18. 31), and Palladius (*Agr.* 1. 6. 1) all subscribe to this idea, but the nature of Columella's audience dictates greater stress upon it (*RR* 1. 1.18–2.2). Columella alleges that overseas estates become virtual "inheritances" to their slaves. Cf. G. Steiner, "Columella and Martial on Living in the Country," *The Classical Journal*, Vol. 50 (1954), especially pp. 85–86.

25. For other details cf. *RR* 1. 13. 1–7; also 57. 1–3, and Vitruvius, *De Arch.* 6. 6. 1–7.

26. *Arbustum*, here translated "grove," normally denotes a vineyard (with vines wedded to trees) or else an orchard. In Cato (*Agr.* 1. 7 and 7. 1) it seems to be a "woodlot" or "grove," but the context in Cicero scarcely settles which meaning he had in mind.

27. Compiled chiefly from Frank (note 8), pp. 139–168, but with frequent attention to the Latin agricultural writers.

28. Columella, *RR* 6. Pref. 1, and 2. 10. 1–35.

29. See Frank (note 8), pp. 160–162, who cites many of the appropriate passages from Columella and Pliny.

30. Cf. Parain (note 8), p. 147.

31. Cf. Varro *RR* 2. 7. 15, for pack animals; Parain (note 8), p. 144 for horse collars; Strabo *Geog.* 5. 1. 12 for Cisalpine hogs; and Varro *RR* 2. 4. 3 for household swine. Columella (*RR* 7. 9. 2) notes that bakeries commonly kept white pigs (as Plautus *Capt.* 807–808 makes clear) to eat surplus bran.

32. See Horace *Sat.* 2. 8. 88 for goose liver fattened on figs; Suetonius *Vitellius* 13. 2, for peacock brains; and Columella *RR* 8. 1–15, for general instructions.

33. See Varro *RR* 1. 43; Columella *RR* 5. 12. 1–5 and *Arb.* 28. 1–4; Pliny *HN* 13. 130–134, etc.; John Sargeaunt, *The Trees, Shrubs, and Plants of Vergil* (Oxford, 1920), p. 40; Elfriede Abbe, *The Plants of Vergil's Georgics* (Ithaca, N. Y., Cornell University Press, 1965), pp. 116–118; and A. Ernout, *Pline L'Ancien: Histoire Naturelle, Livre XIII* (Paris, 1956), p. 111, par. 130, n. 1. See also Vergil *Ecl.* 1. 78; 2. 64; 9. 31; 10. 30; and *G.* 2. 431 and 3. 394.

34. Sargeaunt (note 33), and Abbe (note 33), the latter with many useful woodcuts, are valuable in connections with many other plants. For wheats (which present a complex set of problems) see Jasny (note 8), but also L. A. Moritz, *Grain-Mills and Flour in Classical Antiquity* (Oxford, 1958). For certain vegetables, see, for example, the articles by A. C. Andrews in *Isis* 33 (lovage) and 39 (orach), *Classical Journal* 43 (rue), *Classical Philology* 44 (carrot, celery, and parsley) and 53 (parsnip). For general remarks on ancient food and drink, see

R. J. Forbes, "Food and Drink," *A History of Technology*, Charles Singer, ed. (Oxford, 1954–1958), II, especially pp. 118–146.

35. Hesiod (*WD* 410–413): "Don't postpone work until tomorrow or the next day; the lazy workman does not fill his granary. . . . The procrastinator wrestles ever with ruin."

36. The synodic month, which brings sun, moon, and earth back to the same apparent relative positions, being about twenty-nine and a half days, produces too few days in twelve months and too many in thirteen.

37. Farming operations may be performed in relation to folk beliefs about the moon, but not to make them right with the solar year. See Eugene Tavenner, "The Roman Farmer and the Moon," *Transactions of the American Philological Association*, Vol. 49 (1919), pp. 67–82. But see also E. R. Leach, "Primitive Time-Reckoning," *A History of Technology*, Charles Singer, ed. (Oxford, 1954), I, 118–120 for primitive methods for correcting the lunar cycle to match the solar year.

38. Hesiod (*WD* 504–563) says the month of Lenaion offers the worst winter weather during which the oxen will be kept on limited rations, but for this the precise dates of the months in any one year (normally late January to February) would be unimportant. Cato uses the civil calendar only in phrasing legal contracts (*Agr.* 146–150) since the dates would be valid in the civil courts.

39. Stevens (note 8), p. 97. With this entire discussion of techniques and equipment, see Stevens (pp. 92–124), Parain (note 8), pp. 125–179, and Semple (note 8), especially pp. 376–405.

40. Cf. Homer *Il.* 18. 542; *Od.* 5. 127; Hesiod *Theog.*, 971, and Pliny *HN* 18. 181. Pliny the Younger *Epist.* 5. 6. 10, also refers to the nine plowings in Etruria.

41. See *White* (note 6), pp. 123–145 with plates and appendices, but especially pp. 125–126 and 139–140.

42. See White (note 6), pp. 20–24, and Stevens (note 8), p. 97.

43. Cato *Agr.* 45, 46, 48; Columella *Arb.* 1. 3. and Pliny *HN* 15. 3.

44. Columella *RR.* 5. 9. 12–13 and Stevens (note 8), p. 101.

45. Stevens (note 8), p. 101, and Parain (note 8), p. 131.

46. Varro *RR* 1. 8. 5. In modern Italy a man must obviously at times climb a ladder to reach the tops of the vines.

47. Semple (note 8), especially pp. 397–399.

48. White (note 6), pp. 157–173. A reconstruction, made prior to the identification in the reliefs, may be seen among reapers in the Smithsonian Institution. Parain (note 8), pp. 133–136, suggests that the scientific agriculture of the classical period had paved the way for later progress.

49. For a more extended examination of the evidence touched upon here, see K. D. White, "Wheat Farming in Roman Times," *Antiquity*, Vol. 37 (1963), pp. 207–212.

50. Cf. Wilhelmina F. Jashemski, "Excavations in the 'Foro Boario' at Pompeii," *American Journal of Archaeology*, Vol. 72 (1968), pp. 69–73 and the subjoined plates. For a smaller yard near an inn, see Jashemski, "The *Caupona* of Euxinus at Pompeii," *Archaeology*, Vol. 20 (1967), pp. 36–44.

51. Varro *RR* 1. 2. 7, quoting from Cato's *Origines*; cf. Jordan (note 11), p. 10.

52. Cf. Jashemski, "Foro Boario" (note 50), p. 73.

53. CIL 8. 11824. For other comment upon this inscription and for related matters, cf. Haywood (note 8), p. 71; Rostovtzeff, *Empire*, I, p. 331; Toutain (note 8), pp. 279–280; and G. Steiner, "The Fortunate Farmer: Life on the Small Farm in Ancient Italy," *The Classical Journal*, Vol. 51 (1955), pp. 65–66.

54. Doubtless the Harvester has had his spiritual descendants in every age. This author's own father did custom threshing in northeastern Illinois during the closing decades of the nineteenth century and in the early 1900's, using the proceeds, like the Harvester, to buy himself a house and farm. But see also Gene Logsdon, "A Thousand Farmers Call us Neighbor," *Farm Journal*, Vol. 92, No. 7 (1968), pp. 24–25 and 32, for excerpts from a diary of a contemporary custom harvester. In answer to the question (p. 25) why a man drives "a combine from Texas to Canada with the sun burning holes in the skin" (cf. the Harvester's *bis senas messes rabido sub sole totondi*), he asserts that money is but a partial ex-

planation. Rather, the work is indeed a way of life, for (p. 32) "once you are a combiner you never seem quite at home any place else. On a summer evening in a wheat field it's good to be alive."

Chapter 7: Sailing

1. I have used the following abbreviations:

AM = L. Casson, *The Ancient Mariners* (New York, 1959).

AS = C. Torr, *Ancient Ships* (Cambridge, 1894; reprinted 1964).

GOS = J. Morrison and R. Williams, *Greek Oared Ships* (Cambridge, 1968).

IH = L. Casson, *Illustrated History of Ships and Boats* (New York, 1964).

RIN = C. Starr, *The Roman Imperial Navy* (Ithaca, 1941; repr. Cambridge, 1960).

TAPA = *Transactions of the American Philological Association*

2. For sailing conditions in the Mediterranean, see the introductions in the United States Navy Hydrographic Office's *Sailing Directions for the Mediterranean*, i–v (U.S.N., H.O. Publications, Nos. 151–154).

3. The *locus classicus* for the sailing season is Vegetius *Re Mil.* 4. 39. Additional references from Latin authors in E. de Saint-Denis, "Mare clausum," *Revue des études latines*, Vol. 25 (1947), pp. 196–214.

4. *Placidi pellacia ponti*, Lucretius 2. 559.

5. On ancient rafts and coracles, see J. Hornell, *Water Transport* (Cambridge, 1946), pp. 20–34, 46–51, 101–108.

6. Clearest examples are the two boats found at Dahshur; see G. Reisner, *Models of Ships and Boats* (Cairo: *Catalogue général des antiquités égyptiennes du Musée du Caire*, Institut français d'archéologie orientale 1913), nos. 4925, 4926 (XII Dynasty).

7. L. Casson, "Sewn Boats," *Classical Review*, Vol. 13 (1963), pp. 257–259.

8. E.g., *AM*, pl. 1a (3500 or 3400 B.C.).

9. For the earliest certain examples of sails, see *IH*, ills. 14–15 (late Gerzean).

10. On Egyptian craft, particularly of the Old Kingdom, see C. Boreux, *Études de nautique égyptienne* (Cairo: *Mémoires de l'Institut français d'archéologie orientale*), Vol. 50 (1925).

11. Cf. Hornell (note 5), pp. 213–225.

12. S. Marinatos, "La marine créto-mycénienne," *Bulletin de correspondance hellénique*, Vol. 57 (1933), pp. 170–235 (much important new material has appeared since).

13. Cf. H. Nelson, "The Naval Battle Pictured at Medinet Habu," *Journal of Near Eastern Studies*, Vol. 2 (1943), pp. 40–55.

14. Thucydides (1. 10. 4) took the fifty-oared ship to be the minimum size in the Achaean fleet. On Greek galleys of the preclassical period, see *GOS*, chaps. 1–6.

15. The much argued question of the oarage of the trireme, save for some details, has now been settled; see *GOS*, chaps. 7–12, especially 7 and 11, where all the evidence, both literary and archaeological, for galleys of the fifth and fourth centuries B.C. is given.

16. L. Casson, "The Emergency Rig of Ancient Warships," *TAPA*, Vol. 98 (1967), pp. 43–48.

17. See W. Kolbe in *Athenische Mitteilungen*, Vol. 26 (1901), pp. 386–397.

18. *RIN*, p. 53.

19. The frequently cited view of W. W. Tarn (summarized in his *Hellenistic Military and Naval Developments* [Cambridge, 1930], pp. 122–138), which makes all the supergalleys, even the very biggest, single-banked, is untenable. Tarn put ten men to the oar in his key reconstructions, taking it for granted that this was the practice of later ages. Such a number is not only unheard of in later ages, but does not at all square with the ancient evidence we have. For the views given above, see R. C. Anderson, *Oared Fighting Ships* (London, 1962), chap. 3.

20. For the importance of the man at the head of the loom, see P. Pantera, *L'armata navale* (Rome, 1614), p. 133. Pantera was an officer in the Papal navy. For the stroke used with long sweeps, see *IH*, ill. 92.

21. A possible clue to the oarage of the monster "twenties," "thirties," and "forties" lies in Athenaeus' mention that the last was "double-prowed and double-sterned" (5. 204a), i.e., was what we call a catamaran, a vessel made up of two hulls yoked together (cf., e.g., *IH*,

ill. 264). If we assume that *both* sides of each hull were fitted with oars, arrangements can be worked out that make sense. For example, the "forty" could have had three banks with eight-man sweeps in the uppermost, seven-man sweeps in the next, and five-man sweeps in the lowest; this would make each hull a "twenty," and the two together a "forty." The "thirty," conformably, would easily work out as a twin-hulled version of a "fifteen," and the "twenties" as twin-hulled versions of "tens." See L. Casson, "The Super-Galleys of the Hellenistic Age," *Mariner's Mirror*, Vol. 55 (1969), pp. 185–193.

22. A graffito of a Roman "four" (it is titled "*tetreris*") of probably Augustan date shows a hull so shallow it could accommodate only one, just possibly two, banks of oars; see M. Guarducci, "Alba Fucens—Graffiti nell'antico tempio sul colle di S. Pietro," *Atti della Accademia Nazionale dei Lincei, Notizie degli scavi di antichità* (1953), pp. 117–125, esp. 119–120.

23. On Greek navies see *GOS*, chap. 11 and *AM*, pp. 153–156; on the Roman, *RIN*, chap. 4.

24. See Polyaenus 3. 11. 7; Polybius 1. 21. 1.

25. L. Casson, "Galley Slaves," *TAPA*, Vol. 97 (1966), pp. 35–44.

26. *AM*, pp. 125 and 255.

27. A. Hunt and C. Edgar, *Select Papyri* (London, Loeb Classical Library, 1932), I, No. 112.

28. E.g., *AM*, pls. 1c, 6a.

29. Except perhaps the Chinese lugsail, which uses a somewhat similar principle; see *IH*, pp. 176–177.

30. On sailing speeds, see L. Casson, "Speed under Sail of Ancient Ships," *TAPA*, Vol. 82 (1951), pp. 136–148.

31. E.g., *AM*, pl. 5c; cf. *AS*, p. 94, n. 202.

32. On the efficiency of steering oars, see O. Crumlin-Pedersen, "Two Danish Side Rudders," *Mariner's Mirror*, Vol. 52 (1966), pp. 251–261, especially 256–258. He reports on the remarkable performance of a modern replica of a Viking ship steered by a nearly exact replica of a Viking steering oar. Those who, like Lefebvre des Noettes (*La révolution du gouvernail*, Paris, 1935), have based sweeping conclusions on the assumption that the steering oar was a primitive apparatus, could not have been more wrong.

33. Often overlooked by ancient artists but distinctly noticeable in, e.g., *IH*, ill. 61.

34. For the literary and epigraphical evidence on size see L. Casson, "The Size of Ancient Merchant Ships," *Studi in onore di Aristide Calderini e Roberto Paribeni* (Milan, 1956), I, pp. 231–238. For the evidence from wrecks see the reports published by J. du Plat Taylor in *Marine Archaeology* (London, 1965). On tonnage measurements and stowage see H. Wallinga, "The Unit of Capacity for Ancient Ships," *Mnemosyne*, Vol. 17 (1964), pp. 1–40.

35. On ancient shipbuilding, see L. Casson, "Ancient Shipbuilding," *TAPA*, Vol. 94 (1963), pp. 28–33; "Odysseus' Boat," *American Journal of Philology*, Vol. 85 (1964), pp. 61–64; "New Light on Ancient Rigging and Boatbuilding," *The American Neptune*, Vol. 24 (1964), pp. 81–94. See also the reports on wrecks mentioned in note 34 and F. Dumas, *Épaves antiques* (Paris, 1964), which includes an exemplary report, with comprehensive photographic coverage, on the so-called Chrétienne A wreck. *AS* gives the literary evidence for shipbuilding. The definitive work on ancient Mesopotamian boats, A. Salomen's *Die Wasserfahrzeuge in Babylonien* (Studia Orientalia viii. 4, Helsinki, 1939), assumes (pp. 83–88) that these were built on a pre-erected skeleton. This is wrong; see L. Casson, "The River Boats of Mesopotamia," *Mariner's Mirror*, Vol. 53 (1967), pp. 286–288, 302.

36. Theophrastus *Hist. Plant.* 5. 7. 4. The term *kollesis* in this passage, usually translated "gluing," should be translated "joining" (i.e., by means of mortices or the like). In traditional boat-building planks are never glued.

37. Dumas (note 35), pp. 154–156.

38. On ship's paint, see *AS*, 34–37.

39. See *AS*, 31–33, and the reports mentioned in note 34.

40. Information kindly supplied by Prof. F. van Doorninck, Jr., from his detailed report, to be published shortly, on the Yassi Ada Byzantine wreck. For a reconstruction, based on all the available evidence, see *National Geographic*, September 1968, pp. 418–419.

41. The literary evidence is given in *AS*.
42. P. Gargallo, "Anchors of Antiquity," *Archaeology*, Vol. 14 (1961), pp. 31–35; cf. G. Kapitän in *Archaeology*, Vol. 21 (1968), p. 63.
43. The Mahdia wreck; see A. Merlin in *Mélanges Cagnat* (Paris, 1912), pp. 392–393.
44. C. Moschetti, *Gubernare navem*, Quaderni di Studi Senesi 16 (Milan, 1966), pp. 13–100.
45. For the *proreus* see Xenophon, *Oeconomicus* 8. 14. For the *toicharchos* see Artemidorus 1. 35, 2. 23; he was the superior of the *perineos* who, as Philostratus shows (*Vita Ap*. 6. 12), was a kind of cargo clerk.
46. Casson, "Galley Slaves" (note 25), p. 35, n. 1.
47. Much relevant information is in *AS*, Appendix.
48. L. Casson, "The Sails of the Ancient Mariner," *Archaeology*, Vol. 7 (1954), pp. 214–219; "Studies in Ancient Sails and Rigging," *Essays in Honor of C. Bradford Welles* (New Haven, 1966), pp. 43–58.
49. The basic work on Greek harbors is K. Lehmann-Hartleben, *Die antiken Hafenanlagen des Mittelmeeres*, Klio, Beiheft 14 (Leipzig, 1923).
50. R. Meiggs, *Roman Ostia* (Oxford, 1960), pp. 149–171; O. Testaguzza, "The Port of Rome," *Archaeology*, Vol. 17 (1964), pp. 173–179.
51. L. Casson, "Harbor and River Boats of Ancient Rome," *Journal of Roman Studies*, Vol. 55 (1965), pp. 31–39.

Chapter 8: Trading

1. For general studies of Greek economic organization, including trade, see: F. M. Heichelheim, *An Ancient Economic History from the Palaeolithic Age to the Migration of the Germanic, Slavic, and Arabic Nations*, rev. English ed., tr. by Mrs. Joyce Stevens (Leyden, 1964), II (with copious bibliography); Gustave Glotz, *Ancient Greece at Work*, tr. by M. R. Dobie (New York, 1926); Humfrey Michell, *The Economics of Ancient Greece*, 2d ed. (Cambridge, 1958); J. Hasebroek, *Trade and Politics in Ancient Greece*, tr. by L. M. Fraser and D. C.

MacGregor (London, 1933). For recent discussion of the controversial question of the political aspect of Greek trade, see: M. I. Finley, "Classical Greece" (comment by Cl. Mosse) and Édouard Will, "La Grèce Archaique" (comment by Carl Roebuck), *Deuxième Conférence Internationale d'Histoire Économique, Aix-en-Provence, 1962* (Paris, 1965), I.
2. This and the other translations and paraphrases from ancient sources are my own.
3. J. M. Cook, "Old Smyrna, 1948–1951," *The Annual of the British School of Archaeology at Athens*, Vols. 53–54 (1958–1959), pp. 1–34.
4. J. M. Cook, *The Greeks in Ionia and the East* (London, 1962), p. 70, Fig. 19.
5. For general studies of Greek colonization, see: A. Gwynne, "The Character of Greek Colonization," *The Journal of Hellenic Studies*, Vol. 38 (1918), pp. 88–123; A. J. Graham, *Colony and Mother City in Ancient Greece* (New York, 1964). For the West: T. J. Dunbabin, *The Western Greeks* (Oxford, 1948); for the East: Carl Roebuck, *Ionian Trade and Colonization*, Archaeological Institute of America, Monograph Series, Vol. IX (New York, 1959). For recent bibliography and discussion of problems, É. Will (note 1), pp. 43–58.
6. See note 4.
7. For difficulties involved in the use of pottery as evidence of trade, see: R. M. Cook, "Bedeutung der bemaltem Keramik für den griechischen Handel," *Jahrbuch des deutschen archaeologischen Instituts*, Vol. 74 (1959), pp. 114ff.; G. Vallet and F. Villard, "Céramique et histoire grecque," *Revue Historique*, Vol. 225 (1961), pp. 295ff.
8. See pp. 118–120.
9. New York, Metropolitan Museum of Art, No. 56.171.13 (formerly Hearst SSW 9938). D. A. Amyx, "An Amphora with a Price-Inscription in the Hearst Collection at San Simeon," *University of California Publications in Classical Archaeology*, Vol. I, 8, 1941, pp. 179–198; "The Attic Stelai, Part III," *Hesperia*, Vol. 27 (1958), pp. 300–302.
10. This suggestion is very conjectural. It is made by projecting what little we know of the cost of living in the fifth century B.C., when there is enough evi-

dence for a reasonable guess, backward into the sixth century, when there is not. The standard daily wage in the late fifth century, known from the building inscription of the Erechtheum (pp. 26–28) was one drachma. It is estimated that the cost of food was about one obol (one-sixth of a drachma) per day (Henry Immerwahr, "An Athenian Wineshop," *Transactions and Proceedings of the American Philological Association*, Vol. 79 (1948), p. 148); W. K. Pritchett ("The Attic Stelai," *Hesperia*, Vol. 25 [1958], pp. 196–198) estimates that from a salary of 300 drachmas per year 45 drachmas would have been spent for food. It is usually assumed (Schulten, *Pauly-Wissowa—Kroll's Real-Encyclopädie der classischen Altertumswissenschaft*, Vol. XV², Col. 2081) that the price ratio between the early sixth century and the late fifth century was 1:3 (Pritchett [this note] p. 198, n. 170 has some doubts). Thus, if food cost one-third obol per day when the vase was made, the price of the vase represents a value of six days' food—two days' full salary. Good vases were also very expensive in relation to the daily wage in the fifth century B.C. For example, a good-quality red-figured amphora cost 4–4½ obols, and about 475–450 B.C., a fine, large, red-figured hydria cost 12–18 obols (Amyx [note 9], p. 277). To purchase the latter, then, would have required two or three days' wages.

11. This aryballos was a dedication at the Temple of Apollo at Corinth (Mary C. and Carl A. Roebuck, "A Prize Aryballos," *Hesperia*, Vol. 24 [1955], pp. 158–163); most recently, Leslie Threatte, "An Interpretation of a Sixth-Century Corinthian Dipinto," *Glotta*, Vol. 45 (1967), pp. 186–194. The alabastrons: Saul S. Weinberg, "A Cross-Section of Corinthian Antiquities," *Hesperia*, 17 (1948), pl. LXXIX (D 14, 15).

12. Mary T. Campbell, "A Well of the Black-Figured Period at Corinth," *Hesperia*, Vol. 7 (1938), p. 606, Fig. 29.

13. Roebuck (note 5), pp. 39–40.

14. Roebuck (note 5), pp. 94–101.

15. M. Finkelstein, "Emporos, Naukleros and Kapelos," *Classical Philology*, Vol. 30 (1935), pp. 320ff.; G. M. Calhoun, *The Business Life of Ancient Athens* (Chicago, 1926).

16. C. M. Kraay, "Hoards, Small Change and the Origin of Coinage," *The Journal of Hellenic Studies*, Vol. 84 (1964), pp. 76–91.

17. R. M. Cook, "Speculations on the Origins of Coinage," *Historia*, Vol. 7 (1958), p. 257.

18. E. S. G. Robinson, "The Coins from the Ephesian Artemision Reconsidered," *The Journal of Hellenic Studies*, Vol. 71 (1951), pp. 156ff.; "The Date of the Earliest Coins," *Numismatic Chronicle*, Vol. 16 (1956), pp. 1ff.; Édouard Will (note 1), pp. 78–84.

19. Herodotus 3. 57–58; Roebuck (note 5), pp. 90–91.

20. S. Noe, "A Bibliography of Greek Coin Hoards," *Numismatic Notes and Monographs*, Vol. 78 (1937), Nos. 143, 323, 362, 722, 888, 1178; Dressel and Regling, "Zwei Ägyptische Funde altgriechischen Silbermünzen," *Zeitschrift für Numismatik*, Vol. 37 (1927), pp. 1–138. See also C. H. V. Sutherland, "Corn and Coin," *American Journal of Philology*, Vol. 64 (1945), pp. 129–147.

21. See pp. 167–168.

22. Carl Roebuck, "The Economic Development of Ionia," *Classical Philology*, Vol. 48 (1953), pp. 13–14.

23. M. N. Tod, *A Selection of Greek Historical Inscriptions*, 2d ed. (Oxford, 1946), I, No. 23.

24. Carl Roebuck, "The Grain Trade Between Greece and Egypt," *Classical Philology*, Vol. 45 (1950), pp. 236–247.

25. Oscar Broneer, "Excavation at Isthmia, 1954," *Hesperia*, Vol. 24 (1955), p. 135.

26. F. Chamoux, *Cyrène sous la Monarchie des Battiades* (Paris, 1953), pp. 246–263.

27. Chamoux, *Cyrène*, pp. 258–263.

28. Herodotus 2. 135. Rhodopis' freedom was purchased by Charaxos, Sappho's brother.

29. Carl Roebuck, "The Organization of Naukratis," *Classical Philology*, Vol. 46 (1951), pp. 212–220.

30. C. L. Woolley, "Al Mina-Sueidia," *The Journal of Hellenic Studies*, Vol. 58 (1938), pp. 1–30 and p. 14, Fig. 3.

31. C. F. A. Schaeffer, "Une Trouvaille de monnaies archaiques grecques à Ras-Shamra," *Mélanges syriens offert à R. Dussaud*, Vol. 30 (1950), pp. 461–487; W. Schwabacher, "Geldumlauf und Munzprägung im Syrien im vi. und v. Jahrhundert V. Chr.," *Skrifter utgivna av*

Svenska Institut i Rom, Vol. 15 (1950), pp. 142–143.

32. R. Wycherley, *How the Greeks Built Cities,* 2d ed. (London, 1962), pp. 50–86 and pl. V.

33. For a general study of trade in the Hellenistic Period see: M. I. Rostovtzeff, *Social and Economic History of the Hellenistic World,* 3 vols. (Oxford, 1941); in the Roman Empire: Rostovtzeff, *Social and Economic History of the Roman Empire,* 2d rev. ed., 2 vols. (Oxford, 1957); also, Eric K. Warmington, *The Commerce Between the Roman Empire and India* (Cambridge, 1928); M. P. Charlesworth, *Trade-Routes and Commerce of the Roman Empire,* 2d rev. ed. (Cambridge, 1925); Sir Mortimer Wheeler, *Rome Beyond the Imperial Frontiers* (London, Pelican Book, 1954).

Chapter 9: Musicians and Music

1. One of the best, yet most concise, discussions of ancient Greek music is that of I. T. Henderson, "Ancient Greek Music," *The New Oxford History of Music,* ed. Egan Wéllesz (London, 1966), pp. 336–403. Henderson discusses critically the major sources for Greek musical history, theory, and notation, and provides a basic bibliography. Other especially useful general works are: Max Wegner, *Das Musikleben der Griechen* (Berlin, 1949); Theodore Reinach, *La Musique grecque* (Paris, 1926); Curt Sachs, *The Rise of Music in the Ancient World* (New York, 1943). There is no book, unfortunately, which gathers together all the archaeological evidence for Greek instruments and music.

2. The best collection of such representations is that of Max Wegner, "Griechenland," *Musikgeschichte in Bildern,* eds. Heinrich Besseler and Max Schneider (Leipzig, 1963), II. A musicological commentary is provided for each illustration. Others may be found in such books on Greek vase painting as: P. E. Arias and Max Hirmer, *A History of Greek Vase Painting* (London, 1962), and Ernst Pfühl, *Malerei und Zeichnung der Griechen* (Munich, 1923).

3. After Wegner (note 2), p. 47, Fig. 22.

4. Illustrated in Ekrem Akurgal, *Die Kunst Anatoliens* (Berlin, 1961), Figs. 55–59. (The figure of Cybele is now restored holding a pomegranate, instead of her breasts.)

5. Illustrated in *Archaeology,* Vol. 13 (1960), cover and p. 56.

6. For recorded examples of this type of music, with a scholarly commentary, see J. A. Notopoulos, *Modern Greek Heroic Oral Poetry* (Ethnic Folkways Library Album FE 4468, 1959).

7. For a recent study of the relationship between Greek music and poetry, see Heinrich Koller, *Musik und Dichtung im alten Griechenland* (Bern 1963).

8. On the relationships between Greek musical theory, philosophy, and Greek thought in general, see E. A. Lippman, *Musical Thought in Ancient Greece* (New York, 1964) and W. D. Anderson, *Ethos and Education in Greek Music* (Cambridge, Mass., 1966).

9. On *harmoniae,* modes and scales, see especially I. T. Henderson (note 1), pp. 344–363 and R. P. Winnington-Ingram, *Mode in Ancient Greek Music* (Cambridge, 1936).

10. A good example is a traditional song from Epirus, the *Pogonissios,* featuring parallel fourths and fifths. It is recorded by D. Startou, *Panegyris: Greek Island and Mountain Songs* (Esoteric Records Album ES-531, 1954), Side 1, Band 5.

11. Iamblichus *De Vita Pythagorica* Liber XXV. 112 in Kathleen Schlesinger, *The Greek Aulos* (London, 1939), pp. 117–118. This book comprises the most complete study of the aulos and contains additional information on Greek music and other instruments. However, musicologists have criticized it in respect to musical theory.

12. Tr. by Richmond Lattimore, in *Greek Lyrics* (Chicago, 1955), no. 2, p. 25.

13. For a recent discussion, see R. R. Holloway, "Music at the Panathenaic Festival," *Archaeology,* Vol. 19 (1966), pp. 112–119.

14. Illustrated in Wegner (note 2), p. 71, Fig. 42.

15. After Pfühl (note 2), p. 122, Figs. 393–394.

16. See p. 251.

17. Illustrated in Wegner (note 2), p. 65, Fig. 36.

18. After Wegner, p. 65, Fig. 37.

19. For example, the vase illustrated in Wegner, p. 63, Fig. 35.
20. Henderson (note 1), p. 336.
21. After Pfühl (note 2), p. 63, Fig. 468.
22. Discussed in Henderson (note 1), pp. 363–376. The First Delphic Hymn and Epitaph of Seikilos are recorded in *The History of Music in Sound:* Vol. I: *Ancient and Oriental Music* (RCA Victor Album LM-6057), Side 4, Bands 2 and 3, with transcriptions and notes by Egan Wéllesz (Oxford University Press).
23. *Idyll* XV. 99; tr. by Jack Lindsay, *The Oxford Book of Greek Verse in Translation*, ed. T. F. Higham and C. M. Bowra (Oxford, 1950), No. 502, p. 567. Henceforth referred to as *Oxford Book*.
24. Illustrated in Wegner (note 2), p. 83, Fig. 52.
25. Lucilius, tr. by Humbert Wolfe, in *Oxford Book* (note 23), No. 606, p. 637.
26. Tr. by C. M. Bowra, *Oxford Book* (note 23), No. 98, p. 182.
27. The *Serra* is recorded by D. Stratou (note 10). Side 1, Band 5; also in *Folk and Traditional Music of Turkey* (Ethnic Folkways Library Album P. 404, 1953), Side 2, Band 4, henceforth referred to as *Music of Turkey*. The *Sousta, Pentozales*, and *Hassapiko* are recorded by D. Stratou in *Panegyris: Greek Folk Songs and Dances* (Esoteric Records Album ES-527, 1954), Side 2, Bands 4, 5; Side 1, Band 1.
28. A fine recording of a modern Greek shepherd's pipe is to be found in *Songs and Dances of Greece* (Philips Record Album PCC 213), No. 11, Side 2, Band 5. (Henceforth referred to as *Dances of Greece.*)
29. Illustrated in Pierre Demargne, *The Birth of Greek Art* (New York, 1964), pp. 171–172, Fig. 233.
30. For a modern Greek text, see C. A. Trypanis, *Mediaeval and Modern Greek Poetry* (Oxford, 1951), No. 107, pp. 107–108 and G. A Megas, *Greek Calendar Customs* (Athens, 1958), pp. 82–84, with a translation of the ancient text by J. M. Edmonds.
31. For further information, see G. A. Megas (note 30).
32. Good recordings of the *Tsakonikos* and a *Syrtos* may be found in *Dances of Greece* (note 28), Side 2, Bands 3, 1.
33. Illustrated in Megas (note 30), pl. XVII.
34. Tr. by Edna M. Hooker, *History of Music in Sound* (pamphlet) p. 35.
35. Herodotus 6. 129.2–4; tr. by Aubrey de Sélincourt, *Herodotus, The Histories* (Edinburgh, 1962), p. 407.
36. A typical selection is recorded in *Music of Turkey* (note 27), Side 2, Band 6.
37. After N. D. Alfieri and P. E. Arias, *Spina* (Florence, 1960), pl. 35.
38. Illustrated in Georg Fleischhauer, "*Etrurien und Röm,*" *Musikgeschichte in Bildern*, eds. Henrich Besseler and Max Schneider (Leipzig, 1964), II, 5, p. 85, Fig. 47.
39. *Oxford Book* (note 23), No, 258, p. 286.
40. Illustrated in Fleischhauer (note 38), p. 91, Fig. 50.
41. After Wegner (note 2), p. 115, Figs. 73–74.
42. Illustrated in G. M. A. Richter, *Red-Figured Athenian Vases in the Metropolitan Museum of Art* (New Haven, 1936), II, pl. III, Fig. 110.
43. Tr. by Richmond Lattimore (note 12) No. 1, p. 1.
44. After Pfühl (note 2) p. 217, Fig. 554.
45. *Fables*, 448; tr. by Lloyd W. Daly, *Aesop Without Morals* (New York, 1961), p. 240.

Chapter 10: Actors and Acting

1. Choruses of fifty men and boys were trained to sing the dithyramb, a poetic composition sacred to Dionysus. Its creation as a literary genre may be traced to Arion who lived in Corinth under the tyrant Periander (ca. 625–585 B.C.). See: A. Pickard-Cambridge, *Dithyramb, Tragedy, and Comedy*, 2d ed., rev. by T. B. L. Webster (Oxford, 1962), pp. 9ff. (hereafter referred to as P-C, *Dithyramb*). Aristotle names the leader of the dithyramb as responsible for the development of tragedy, and it has often been argued that the beginning was a short dialogue between the chorus leader and the chorus. See P-C, *Dithyramb*, pp. 89ff. for a full discussion and bibliography.
2. Themistius (*Orat.* XXVI. 316d) preserves the quotation, probably from a lost work of Aristotle, *On Poets.* See: P-C *Dithyramb* (note 1), pp. 70, 78–79; A. Pickard-Cambridge, *The Dramatic Fes-*

tivals of Athens, 2d. ed., rev. by J. Gould and D. Lewis (Oxford, 1968), pp. 130–131 (hereafter referred to as P-C, *Festivals*); G. Else, *The Origin and Early Form of Greek Tragedy*, Vol. XX, *Martin Classical Lectures* (Cambridge, Mass., 1967), pp. 53ff. There is no agreement among scholars on most matters concerning the origin of tragedy and its early form. The various arguments are collected by P-C, *Dithyramb*, pp. 6off. Else has recently presented a new interpretation which emphasizes the role of the actor over that of the chorus. He advances the theory that Thespis invented both the dramatic speeches of the hero and the tragic chorus, instead of adding the role of actor to an already existing choral presentation. Although this seems to satisfy many questions, it does not take into sufficient account the marked predominance of chorus over actor in the early plays of Aeschylus which are preserved. Many plays of Aeschylus and other early poets, only the titles of which are extant, are named after the chorus; for example, *Priests* and *Youths* of Thespis, *Egyptians*, *Danaids*, and *Phoenician Women* of Phrynichus, an earlier contemporary of Aeschylus, and the *Persians*, *Suppliants*, *Women of Aetna*, *Bacchantes*, *The Edonians*, *Women of Crete*, *Thracian Women*, *Libation Bearers*, and *Eumenides* of Aeschylus.

3. Plutarch *Life of Solon* 29. 4. If this story is historical, its date would fall in the later years of Solon's life, ca. 560 B.C. (P-C, *Dithyramb* [note 1], p. 77). Although Thespis may have tried out his new idea for some time before 534 B.C. (note 4), twenty-six years seems excessive.

4. The date is given in an inscription from Paros, called the *Marmor Parium*, dated about 260 B.C.: "From when Thespis the poet first acted, who produced a play in the city [Athens], and the prize was a goat, years 270 (?), when . . . naios, the earlier, was archon at Athens." See also the Suda lexicon (Suidae *Lexicon*, ed. by Ada Adler [Leipzig, 1928–1938]), under Thespis "He produced in" the 61st Olympiad (536/5–533/2 B.C.), and P-C, *Dithyramb* (note 1), p. 71, n. 14.

5. Else discusses early tragedy at length (note 2), pp. 51ff.; his ideas are the basis for this description.

6. Cf. Suda (note 4), under Thespis, where a second step is mentioned, in which Thespis hung flowers over his face, but for what effect it is hard to imagine. P-C, *Festivals* (note 2), pp. 190ff. contains a recent discussion of masks; see also M. Bieber, *The History of the Greek and Roman Theater*, 2d. ed. rev. (Princeton, 1961), pp. 22ff. and T. B. L. Webster, *Greek Theater Production* (London, 1956), pp. 35ff. (hereafter referred to as Webster, *GTP*).

7. Suda (note 4), see under Aeschylus.

8. Aeschylus, *The Libation Bearers*, tr. by R. Lattimore in *The Complete Greek Tragedies*, ed. by D. Greene and R. Lattimore (Chicago, 1959), pp. 21–25. All other translations quoted here are taken from this edition.

9. A late *Life of Aeschylus* was prefixed to an edition of his works, but it is not reliable in some details.

10. Cf. Bieber (note 6), Figs. 96–97; A. Pickard-Cambridge, *The Theater of Dionysos in Athens* (Oxford, 1946), Fig. 11. The last, a vase from Ruvo, shows them with black skin.

11. Bieber (note 6), Fig. 126; P-C, *Dithyramb* (note 1) Fig. 23. The faces of the men are also clearly visible, for the horse head and neck was worn on top and on back of the head rather than completely covering it.

12. See P-C, *Festivals* (note 2), p. 192.

13. Euripides, *The Bacchae*, tr. by P. Vellacott (Baltimore, Md., 1954).

14. E. Pfuhl, *Masterpieces of Greek Drawing and Painting*, tr. by J. Beazley (New York, 1955), Figs. 20, 57, 105. A similar guise can be seen on vases from the sixth century on. Cf. Bieber (note 6), Figs. 19, 21, 80. Webster, *GTP* (note 6), p. 42 notes an Apulian vase (No. 129 in his catalogue) with a mask which closely fits the description; it is illustrated in Bieber (note 6), Fig. 72.

15. It was originally published by L. Talcott, "Kourimos Parthenos," *Hesperia*, Vol. 8 (1939), pp. 267ff., Fig. 2, with a full description, and it is reproduced in P-C, *Festivals* (note 2), Fig. 32.

16. So Talcott (note 15), but see T. B. L. Webster, "Greek Dramatic Monuments from the Athenian Agora and Pnyx," *Hesperia*, Vol. 29 (1960), p. 255; *idem*, "Monuments Illustrating Tragedy and

Satyr Play," *Bulletin of the Institute of Classical Studies*, Supplement 14 (London, 1962), A 9, pp. 44, 46 (hereafter referred to as Webster, *Monuments*). Webster feels a Dionysiac subject is more likely, and considers the women as maenads, the man as Pentheus or Lykourgos.

17. Talcott (note 15), p. 272, n. 22, quoting K. G. Kachler in *Der Antike*, Vol. 15 (1939), pp. 89–93.

18. P-C, *Festivals* (note 2), pp. 181ff., Fig. 33; Webster, *Monuments* (note 16), AV 10, p. 46, pl. 1.

19. J. Beazley, "Hydria Fragments in Corinth," *Hesperia*, Vol. 24 (1955), pp. 305ff., pl. 85. Cf. P-C, *Festivals* (note 6), pp. 182f., Fig. 36; Webster, *Monuments* (note 16), AV 13, p. 44.

20. Cf. Bieber (note 6), p. 26, Fig. 90; P-C, *Festivals* (note 2), p. 182, Fig. 34.

21. The vase has been much discussed. Cf. Bieber (note 6), pp. 10–11, n. 26; P-C, *Festivals* (note 2), pp. 186–187, Fig. 49; Webster, *GTP* (note 6), pp. 40–41; *idem, Monuments* (note 16), AV 25, pp. 47–48. Beazley (note 19), pp. 313–314 notes that Bulle has established the original as being a votive picture dedicated by Pronomos to Dionysus. In terms of the actors' masks and costumes there appears to have been little difference between tragedy and satyr drama, for the latter parodied the former by making the tragic hero the butt of its satire; cf. Pollux IV. 42. The satyr play was produced as the fourth work of the poet following his three tragedies, and it was usually written by him. The practice slowly declined during the fifth century.

22. Bieber (note 6), pp. 11–12, Figs. 34, 35; P-C, *Festivals* (note 2), pp. 187–188, Figs. 50 a–c. It was first published by H. Bulle, "Weihebild eines tragischen Dichters," *Corolla Curtius* (Stuttgart, 1937), pp. 151–160, pls. 47–54. Cf. Webster, *GTP* (note 6), pp. 40–41; *idem, Monuments* (note 16), AV 27, p. 48.

23. Bieber (note 6), p. 32, n. 66, Fig. 113 a–b; P-C, *Festivals* (note 2), p. 188, n. 1, Fig. 51; Webster, *GTP* (note 6), p. 41; *idem, Monuments* (note 16), AS 1, pp. 32–33.

24. T. B. L. Webster, "The Poet and the Mask," *Classical Drama and Its Influence*, ed. by M. Anderson (London, 1965), pp. 5ff. The quotations which follow are taken from this article.

25. Bieber (note 6), Figs. 201, 300 a–b, 306 a–b, 316–17.

26. *Thesmophoriazusae*, tr. by B. Rogers in *The Complete Plays of Aristophanes*, ed. by M. Hadas (New York, 1962).

27. P-C, *Dithyramb* (note 1), Nos. 20, 21, 23, pls. VI a–b, VII.

28. Cf. Bieber (note 6), pp. 22–28. She takes the account in the *Life* almost literally. P-C, *Festivals* (note 2), pp. 197ff. is more cautious.

29. A. Alföldi, "Gewaltherrscher und Theaterkönig," *Late Classical and Medieval Studies in Honor of A. M. Friend* (Princeton, 1955), pp. 15–55 argues that the style for tragic costume was set by Aeschylus' Persian king. O. Broneer, "The Tent of Xerxes and the Greek Theater," *University of California Publications in Classical Archaeology*, Vol. I, No. 12 (1944), pp. 305–312, suggests that the tent of the Persian king captured at Salamis was used as the *skene* and scenic backdrop in the early theater.

30. Cf. Pfühl (note 14), no. 47 (end of the sixth century B.C.), where they wear "long underwear" completely covering their bodies; in no. 71 (ca. 460 B.C.) a short chiton is added; cf. also nos. 75 and 76. Cf. D. von Bothmer, *Amazons in Greek Art* (Oxford, 1957).

31. Cf. L. Séchan, *Études sur la tragédie grecque dans ses rapports avec la céramique*, (Paris, 1926). The vases confirm this.

32. Beazley (note 19), pp. 310ff. Cf. P-C, *Festivals* (note 2), Figs. 35, 42, 63 and pp. 199ff.

33. Bieber (note 6), chap. II; P-C, *Festivals* (note 2), pp. 198ff., Figs. 60 a–b. It is most interesting that Theseus on the François vase (ca. 570 B.C..) wears just such a robe while playing the lyre and leading a mixed chorus. The horses and chariots there are arranged in bands; the only difference is in the shorter sleeves, cf. Bieber, Fig. 14.

34. *Poetics* XIX. 1456b. 10. Cf. P-C, *Festivals* (note 2), pp. 167ff. for a full discussion.

35. Cf. Bieber (note 6), pp. 80–82 and n. 5 for a bibliography on acting; P-C, *Festivals* (note 2), pp. 156ff.

36. The Oceanids weep for Prometheus; Electra weeps for Orestes, Antigone for her father, Admetus, Medusa, Kreousa, and many others all cry more than once in a play. Changes of expression presented rather greater problems, as for the Furies, who became friendly at the end of the *Eumenides*, and for Sophocles' Electra who cannot show the joy she feels. Cf. P-C, *Festivals* (note 2), pp. 171ff.

37. Beazley (note 19), p. 312f., pl. 87; P-C, *Festivals* (note 2), p. 182, Fig. 35.

38. P-C, *Festivals*, pp. 246ff.

39. Beazley (note 19), p. 316, pl. 88a; Webster, *Monuments* (note 16), AV 17, p. 45.

-40. A. Dale, "Chorus in the Action of Greek Tragedy," *Classical Drama and Its Influence*, ed. by M. Anderson (London, 1965), pp. 17ff., discusses the formal limitations of the chorus in dialogue and speeches.

41. Else (note 2), pp. 86ff.

42. *Frogs*, tr. by R. Webb in *The Complete Plays of Aristophanes*, ed. by M. Hadas (New York, 1962), p. 412. The following quotations from the *Frogs* are from this translation and edition.

43. *Ibid.*, pp. 43–44.

44. *Ibid.*, p. 43.

45. Plato, *The Laws*, tr. by B. Jowett in *The Dialogues of Plato*, 2 vols. (New York, 1937), VII. 817.

Index

A

Acting, 266–269
Actor, 251, 252, 255, 256, 258, 260, 262, 264–269
Aeschylus, 236, 245, 251–252, 253, 254, 262, 266, 268, 269
  Agamemnon, 252
  Eumenides, 252, 253, 254, 262, 263
  Libation Bearers, 252, 253, 264
  Persians, 251, 256, 263
  Prometheus Bound, 251, 254, 263
  Seven Against Thebes, 252, 255, 264
  Suppliants, 252, 253, 263
Aesop, 248–249
Agora, 222
Agriculture, calendar of, 161–162
  nature of, 151
  sources of information on, 148–151
  techniques of, 162–167, 168
Agronomists, 148–151, 170
Al Mina (Syria), 206, 210, 221–222
Alabastron, 210
Amphora, 118, 208–210
Anathyrosis, 20, 22
Apollo, 228, 232, 248
Apollo Didymaios Temple 14, 16, 24
Apollodorus of Damascus, 41
Archilochus, 248
Architects, Greek, 2, 3, 5–10, 12, 13, 28, 34
  Roman, 40–42
Aristophanes, 236, 244, 252, 262, 264, 268
  Acharnians, 262
  Frogs, 236, 252, 262, 269
  Thesmophoriazusae, 262
  Wasps, 244, 268
Aristotle, 250, 251, 260, 266, 267
Arms and armor, 92, 94
Arsenal in Peiraeus, 7–9
Aryballos, 210
Athena, 5, 68, 72, 232, 250
Athena Nike Temple, 5
Athens, 2–5, 14, 26, 30, 70, 71, 112, 122, 132, 134, 183, 202–203, 208, 214, 216
Audience, for music, 234, 236, 246, 248–249

Audience, for theater, 250, 251, 252, 260, 266, 269
Augustus, 44
Aulos 228, 231, 232, 233, 234, 237, 240, 241, 245
Aurichalcum, 61

B

Barbitos, 232
Barbotine Ware, 140
Basilicas, 36
Black-figure style (in pottery), 132
Brass, 61
Brickwork, Roman, 37, 43, 50
Bronze, composition of, 61
  Corinthian, 64
Bronze Age, 60, 228
Bronzes, armor, 92, 94
  chariot groups, 70
  colossal, 68, 70–71
  copying of, 69–70
  equestrian groups, 70–71
  excavation of, 67–69
  furniture, 88, 90, 92
  gilded, 71–72
  mirrors, 88
  statuettes, 72–80
  tripods, 90
  vessels, 80–88
Bronzeworking, casting, 65–66, 69, 72, 74, 75–76, 82, 83, 108, 112
  finishing, 66, 76
  hammering, 65, 72, 81, 82
  repoussé, 81
Building, authorization of, 3–5
  commissions on, 3, 13
  concepts of, 2–3, 36–37, 57–58
  Etruscan, 36
  Roman Republican, 36–38

C

Carving. *See* Stone, Wood
Cato the Censor, 149, 152, 154, 156, 157
Chios, 214, 219
Chorus, 234, 236, 250–252, 262, 268, 269

DF
78
M84   The Muses at work